Clean Tech, Clean Profits

Using effective innovation and sustainable business practices to win in the new low-carbon economy

Consultant editor: Adam Jolly

LONDON PHILADELPHIA NEW DELHI

This book has been endorsed by the Institute of Directors.

The endorsement is given to selected Kogan Page books which the IoD recognizes as being of specific interest to its members and providing them with up-to-date, informative and practical resources for creating business success. Kogan Page books endorsed by the IoD represent the most authoritative guidance available on a wide range of subjects including management, finance, marketing, training and HR.

The views expressed in this book are those of the author and are not necessarily the same as those of the Institute of Directors.

Publisher's note

Every possible effort has been made to ensure that the information contained in this book is accurate at the time of going to press, and the publishers and authors cannot accept responsibility for any errors or omissions, however caused. No responsibility for loss or damage occasioned to any person acting, or refraining from action, as a result of the material in this publication can be accepted by the editor, the publisher or any of the authors.

First published in Great Britain and the United States in 2010 by Kogan Page Limited

120 Pentonville Road
London N1 9JN
United Kingdom
www.koganpage.com

525 South 4th Street, #241
Philadelphia PA 19147
USA

4737/23 Ansari Road
Daryaganj
New Delhi 110002
India

ISBN 978 0 7494 6117 1
E-ISBN 978 0 7494 6118 8

British Library Cataloguing-in-Publication Data

A CIP record for this book is available from the British Library.

Library of Congress Cataloging-in-Publication Data

Jolly, Adam.
Clean tech clean profits : using effective innovation and sustainable business practices to win in the new low-carbon economy / Adam Jolly.
p. cm.
ISBN 978-0-7494-6117-1 -- ISBN 978-0-7494-6118-8 (ebk) 1. Business enterprises--Environmental aspects. 2. Strategic planning--Environmental aspects. 3. Technological innovations--Environmental aspects. 4. Sustainability. 5. Greenhouse gas mitigation--Economic aspects. 6. Carbon dioxide mitigation--Economic aspects. I. Title.
HD30.255.J65 2010
658.4'083--dc22

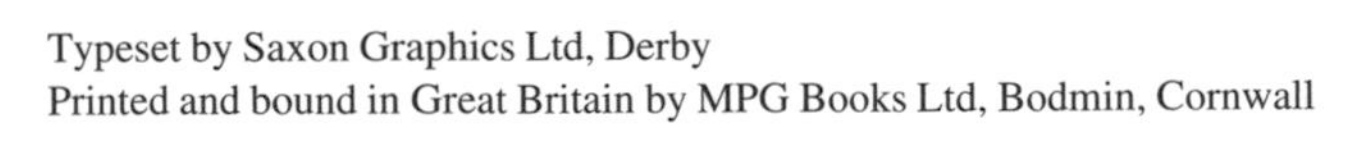
Typeset by Saxon Graphics Ltd, Derby
Printed and bound in Great Britain by MPG Books Ltd, Bodmin, Cornwall

Contents

Foreword *xiii*
Miles Templeman, Director General IoD

PART 1 The size of the challenge **1**

1.1 Global problems, technology challenges and innovation opportunities 3
David Bott, Technology Strategy Board
The role of markets 4; We must innovate 6

1.2 Zero Carbon Britain 7
Paul Allen, Alternative Technology
Climate security 7; Energy security 8; Economic security 9; Joining the dots on energy 10; A Zero Carbon Britain 11

1.3 The race for the green economy 13
Cameron Hepburn, Vivid Economics
Climate change policies are creating business opportunities 13; Domestic policies matter 13; The growth in clean tech may be as fast as that in personal computing 14; Simple arithmetic indicates the scale of the transition is significant 14; The investment flow that would be triggered would be even larger, and is expected to reach around US$1 trillion per annum by 2030 14; Global clean energy investment is already at around US$150 billion per annum 14; The race is on 15; The United Kingdom has made a solid start 15; There are opportunities in the United Kingdom, and UK firms are reasonably well positioned to take market share globally 15; Success will require company agility and a solid understanding of policy developments 15; Notes 16

1.4 Renewable power generation 18
Sam Cheung, McLellan
Introduction 18; Government regulations and incentives 19; Renewable technologies 19; A brighter future? 21; Notes 22

1.5 New housing and transport solutions 23
David Bott, Technology Strategy Board.
Housing 23; Personal transport 25

PART 2 Making a return 27

2.1 Clean tech as an investment class 29
Rob Wylie, WHEB Ventures
Clean tech as an investment theme 29; Opportunities abound or not? 32; How to succeed? 33

2.2 Funding clean tech 34
Simon Bond, Bath Ventures Innovation Centre, University of Bath
Clean tech: another biotech or ICT? 34; The role of regulation 35; Three sub-sectors 36; And possibly a fourth 36; Clean tech lessons – it's the 3Rs 37

2.3 Oceans of potential 39
Tony Lewis, Raymond Alcorn and Mark Healy, Hydraulics and Maritime Research Centre at University College Cork
Potentially enormous resource meets growing drivers 39; Technical and non-technical challenges thus far 40; Getting to commercialization and generating returns 41; Dawning of an industry 42; Notes 43

2.4 Gold rush or money pit? 46
Brian Kennelly, EarthEnergy
Dawn of a new era? 48; Easy as 1, 2, 3… 48; Don't all rush at once 50

2.5 Clean energy in the emerging economies 51
Kate Levick, Carbon Disclosure Project
Companies in BASIC countries are leading the way on investment in clean energy 51; What drives companies to invest in clean energy? 52; What is the role of policy as a driver for corporate investment? 53; Future developments 54; Note 54

PART 3 How the market works **55**

3.1 The policy framework 57
Roger Salomone, EEF
Skills 58; Tax 59; Facilitating industrial development 60; Innovation support 61; Public procurement 62; Planning 62; Conclusion 62

3.2 Sustainable investing 64
Penny Shepherd, CUKSIF
Plentiful rewards 64; So who is investing? 65; Introducing opportunities 65; Note 68

3.3 Carbon capital and technology transfer 69
Paul Kelly, Chief Executive Officer at EcoSecurities
What constitutes technology transfer? 70; The Clean Development Mechanism 70; Amatitlán: a CDM and technology transfer success story 70; Success of the CDM 71; What next for climate change and the private sector? 72

3.4 Intellectual property for clean tech 74
Nick Sutcliffe, Mewburn
Intellectual property protects innovation 74; Intellectual property is a business asset 75; Patents protect technical innovations 76; Any technical innovation may be patentable 76; Strategies for intellectual property 76; Management of intellectual property 77; Other people's intellectual property 77; Recycling old intellectual property 78

PART 4 Clean energy **81**

4.1 Wind power 83
Nick Medic, RenewableUK
The potential of wind 83; The challenges ahead: skills and supply chain 84; Finance 84; Planning 85; Grid 85; Big task – big benefits 86

4.2 Marine 88
John Griffiths, JWG Consulting
Resources 88; State of technology 89; Key developers and important companies 89; Market size and prospects 90; Economics 90; Opportunity 91

4.3 Solar 93
Barry Marsh, Solar Technologies, part of British Gas
Solar photovoltaic 93; Solar heating 94; Conclusion 95; Notes 95

4.4 Nuclear power 97
Roane Knowles-Rapson, National Nuclear Laboratory
A new generation of reactors 98; A new generation of acceptance and support 99; A new generation of skills 101; Conclusion 102; Notes 102

4.5 Energy from waste 104
Andrew Williams, M+W
Combustion 105; Gasification 105; Pyrolysis 106; Investment and the Renewables Obligation 107; Notes 107

4.6 Biomass 110
Mike Bradley, Wolfson Centre for Bulk Solids Handling Technology, University of Greenwich
What is it about biomass? 111; Examples of common handling problems with biomass 111; Why the problems? 112; Choosing the right solutions 112; Feedstock variability 112; Know your enemy 113; Note 114

4.7 Microgeneration 115
Barry Marsh, Solar Technologies, part of British Gas
Heat pumps 117; Micro-CHP 117; Conclusion 118; Notes 118

PART 5 Low-impact buildings 119

5.1 Construction resource efficiency 121
Katherine Adams, BRE
What is the issue? 121; How can resources be managed more efficiently? 122; The importance of measurement 123; What does the future hold? 123

5.2 Zero carbon development 124
Sarah Youren, Sarah Youren Planning Solicitors
What does zero carbon actually mean? 124; What will the new rules apply to? 125; How do you achieve zero carbon development? 127; Rising to the challenge 128; Notes 128

5.3 Domestic refurbishment 129
Richard Hartless, BRE
Barriers to meeting the challenge 130; Business opportunities to address barriers 130; Note 132

Profile: The University of Edinburgh – a living laboratory 134
David Somervell, University of Edinburgh
Sustainability focus 135; Three energy centres 136; Note 138

PART 6 Transport 139

6.1 The shift to low carbon vehicles 141
Greg Archer, Low Carbon Vehicle Partnership
Geopolitical drivers of future vehicles 141; There are regulatory pressures for more efficient cars 142; Customer preferences are changing 142; The efficiency of petrol and diesel vehicles can be doubled – at a cost 143; Electric cars 143; Alternative fuels 144; Opportunities and challenges 145

6.2 Electric vehicles 147
Huw W Hampson-Jones, OXIS Energy
Electricity versus oil, the early years 147; Enter new compounds 147; Battery technology for electric vehicles: its changes, potential and economics 148

6.3 Aviation fuel 152
Douglas Blackwell, Bio Partners
Cap and trade 153; Food or fuel? 153; Carbon in chains 154; Sustainable for everyone – community development 154; The scale of the need 155

PART 7 Land and water use 157

7.1 Water technology 159
Ian Bernard, British Water
The water industry 160; Water technology investments 161; Water technology 161; Clean technologies 161

7.2 Wood technology 164
Mats Johnson, SweTree Technologies
Some examples 165

PART 8 Carbon removal **167**

8.1 Geo-engineering 169
Colin Brown and Tim Fox, Institution of Mechanical Engineers
Technologies 170; Moving forward 171; Conclusions 172; Note 172

8.2 Carbon capture and storage 173
Judith Shapiro, Carbon Capture and Storage Association
What is CCS? 174; Challenges and positive steps 174; Conclusion 176; Note 176

8.3 Low carbon purchasing 177
Nick Cottam and James Cadman, ERM

PART 9 Creating solutions **181**

9.1 Shifting to a smart, sustainable age 183
Molly Webb, The Climate Group

9.2 Building on experience 188
Gerwyn Williams, J P Kenny
UK companies begin with an advantage 188; But the renewables and oil and gas sectors should work together 189
We have started but more can be done 191

9.3 Finding energy solutions 192
Chris Harrison, Low Carbon Innovation Centre University of East Anglia
Biomass 193; Small-scale wind turbines 193; Domestic energy 194; Note 195

Profile: A new radioactive waste regime for the United Kingdom 197
Dick Raaz, LLW Repository Limited

Profile: MATRIX: The Northern Ireland Science Industry Panel – facilitating business leadership to exploit technology and R&D for economic growth 201
Bernard McKeown, MATRIX, DETI Northern Ireland
Introduction: Northern Ireland and the global knowledge economy 201; MATRIX vision: industry leadership 201; Structuring an Industry-led Innovation Community 202; Government support – the Innovation Gateway 203; MATRIX – thought leadership 204; Conclusion 206

PART 10 Clean commercialization **207**

10.1 The business model 209
Julian Wheatland, Hatton International
The golden rule 209; Approaching the business 210; Guide to the four business model elements 211; Conclusion 213

10.2 Proof of market 214
Peter White, YTKO.
It's innovation, yes, but is it needed? 215; Shouting about innovation still doesn't get sales 215; Proof of market and value propositions 215; All of this is common sense 216

10.3 Clean tech start-ups 218
Lesley Anne Rubenstein, LAR Consultancy
Questions to ask yourself 218; Carbon Trust incubators 219; At the 'coalface' 222; Thoughts from overseas 223; In short 224; Note 224

10.4 Value in green technology patents 226
Neil Forsyth, EIP
Patent office encouragement of green technology 229; What does the future hold? 229; Notes 229

Index *231*

Index of advertisers *241*

Foreword

The squeeze on carbon is beginning in earnest. By a combination of innovation and regulation, the script for how the economy operates is about to be totally re-written. By 2020, we will have made a start in running our homes, workplaces and vehicles in smarter ways. By 2050, we should have re-configured how we generate power, conserve water and manage waste.

But talk of an 80 per cent cut in carbon emissions remains an extraordinarily ambitious goal, particularly if you include the new economic powers like China and India. If we are to have any chance of achieving it, the market for clean technology has to start working more efficiently.

The gap between where we are now and where we would like to be remains enormous. If we are to bridge it, we will rely on a whole series of innovations, a massive re-allocation of capital and ultimately the creation of new industries.

Ideas for switching to a low-carbon world are bound to take a number of forms. They could be breakthroughs or a combination of existing techniques. They might be a flash of insight or a response to pressure from regulators and consumers. They might be an engineering design or a software programme. They could have global applications or be a quick fix. What is certain is that questions will be asked in all spheres of economic activity.

For business, the challenge is to find a way of commercializing these ideas. Their scale is often too small and sales are uncertain. They remain expensive compared to carbon alternatives and returns are hard to project in the absence of a firm price for carbon. But the overall potential of this shift is enormous, as evidenced by the amount of private capital and public funds looking for a clean technology in which to invest.

This book is designed as a practical guide for entrepreneurs, innovators, directors and investors on how to bring clean technologies to market. Drawing on wide range of expertise and experience in strategy, technology, engineering, intellectual property, construction and finance, our contributors discuss how enterprises can best position themselves for the growth in clean technology that is waiting to happen. The IoD is grateful to them all for sharing their knowledge and experience so freely.

Miles Templeman, Director General IoD

Part 1

The size of the challenge

1.1

Global problems, technology challenges and innovation opportunities

***David Bott**, Director of Innovation Programmes at the Technology Strategy Board, discusses the ways in which technologies and markets are likely to evolve.*

The threat of climate change caused by human activity over the last 100 or so years has become a convenient, if important, hook on which to hang much of the current 'green' activity. But the truth is that we would need to be addressing sustainability issues in terms of supply, even if we didn't need to address them because of their likely consequences for the climate. We have become a truly rapacious society, consuming at pace many resources that once seemed infinite but are now understood to be worryingly finite. The debate over the past 30 years as to whether and when oil would run out is just one example.

A quick scan of the UK's economic and societal growth over the last century gives an insight into the scale and ubiquity of these changes. From 1900 to 2000, the population of the UK rose from 38 million to 61 million – an increase of about 60 per cent. In that same time, the number of houses rose from around 7.5 million to 25 million – an increase of over 200 per cent. During the same time the number of cars in the country went from around 15,000 to over 30 million – at which point simple percentage increases become inadequate to describe the change. There are many other statistics that can be used to quantify the dramatic changes over this time frame and the consequent impact on our resources.

It is not that we set out to use up these basic resources; it is more that our vision of the future did not include such limits. As we have come to understand the limits, we have begun to adjust our behaviour to take account of them. In many cases, governments have moved to regulate activities that lead to this overuse of limited resources. These regulations affect markets – and companies have learnt to respond to these changes in the market and develop new products and services that address them.

The government policy of cutting greenhouse gas emissions by 80 per cent by 2050 (from 1990 levels) underpins many of the regulatory and market changes. But that does not mean that we should, or could, achieve 80 per cent reductions across all the causes of such emissions. For example, the Committee for Climate Change in its 2009 report suggests that cars should be fully decarbonized, because the technology is more easily and economically implemented than in other forms of transport. Our targets in specific areas need to be a mixture of what is desirable and what is achievable.

The systems we have developed that produce greenhouse gas emissions are complex, and the solutions we need to reduce them will necessarily be multifaceted. One of the challenges we face, given the urgency of the need to change, is how to make decisions about the right way to get to a solution as quickly and efficiently as possible. Most of our current systems have been developed over a long time, in an evolutionary rather than revolutionary manner, and according to criteria and priorities markedly different from those we now face.

The role of markets

Because of the economic structure of our society, an absolutely central aspect of the problem is that of markets. What will constitute the market for the changes that will be needed? At the moment, much is driven by government policy, but that may not be enough on its own in future. Can the true power of the market be unleashed in a way that will bring the results we need?

There are early adopters, such as those who bought the early hybrid cars, but we need to be careful not to let early sales encourage us down what might be developmental backwaters, where the development pathway runs out of steam before the solution has made enough of a contribution to the demanding targets we have set ourselves as a society.

We have to take account of what the consumers who buy these products are already used to. For example, the worries that people are expressing about the range of electric cars are a reflection of the different infrastructures behind the refuelling of the different options we now have available. The system of petrol stations across the country has taken about 100 years to build up, the distribution is in line with usage patterns and the resupply of these stations is now so accepted that we don't often think of the dangers of transporting a liquid that can cause such harm once ignited, in tankers each containing around 9,000 gallons. With electric cars, there is no similar network of public refuelling points, and the time taken to recharge a battery is significantly longer than the time needed to fill a car fuel tank with 50 or so litres of liquid fuel. On the question of range, despite the fact that most cars travel less than 50 miles in a day and that is already well within the range of battery-powered cars, there is a perception among potential low carbon car buyers that this is not yet good enough.

As well as trying to understand how the markets (in truth the people that they comprise) work, and the rate of change they will accept or drive, there is the cost of the change. We are lucky with cars, in that their typical lifetime means that we will probably have three or four new generations of cars between now and 2050. That gives the market a chance to adjust its expectations and evolve. What is needed is confidence in what the future might hold. This is probably best done by showing people what it might look like. The early market penetration of hybrid and electric cars is allowing the classic 'early adopters' to try out the new technologies and feed back to the manufacturers what works and what doesn't. In this way, the manufacturers can gain confidence that their new products and services will find larger markets, and the speed of change can accelerate. What is needed is a sure start to the process and openness on both sides to make sure we end up with the cars we want, with the performance that both the users and the rest of society can afford.

There is a different challenge with housing. The characteristic lifetime of a house, and the rate of new build, means that most of us will have to adapt our current living space rather than move to a new one. This means that we might have to undergo disruption – changing the fabric and control systems of a house is not a small job – and that we have to consider the payback time of the investment. The cost of retrofitting an existing house will come down markedly over the next few years, but the payback period will still possibly remain longer than the average tenancy. This means that the current system for financing (a personal mortgage) might not be the right one for the future. This is a good example of a market driver requiring both new technology and a new business model. What is needed is a fairly quick development of the retrofit technologies to be significantly cheaper than they are today. This is a classic scaling problem – to retrofit one house will cost X, but to retrofit a million will cost very much less per house. What is needed is the rapid development and evaluation of the required technologies and systems. Looking at the UK, there are over 20 million houses we need to retrofit and we only have 40 years to do it – but the range of houses means that there will not be a single way of doing things. Although the market characteristics are different the message is the same – we need to get started as soon as possible to make sure we hit a target that is 40 years away.

In other areas market barriers to change are more complex. Take energy generation and supply, where the scale and complexity of the system, and the cost and timescale of developing new infrastructure, make transformational change difficult to contemplate and plan. In the UK, the Energy Technologies Institute is looking at every aspect of the energy system and its complex interdependencies to see where the opportunities for change are, and then working alongside the Technology Strategy Board and the Carbon Trust to stimulate innovations and improvements, according to each organization's strengths.

The biggest opportunities of the coming years will lie in finding the market-changing solutions – but no less important are the many areas where incremental solutions can start to make a difference immediately.

There are gains to be made, and business to be done, at every level. One example, developed with the help of the Technology Strategy Board, is a fuel-cell-based combined heat and power unit from UK company Ceres Power. The unit replaces a conventional boiler, and each household adopting this technology could reduce CO_2 emissions by up to 2.5 tonnes per year and save 25 per cent of energy use. The company has won a contract from British Gas to supply thousands of units over the coming years.

We must innovate

None of this is particularly easy. Innovation takes vision, ideas, time, resources, partners and collaborators. But in the UK we have a world-leading research base, a strong entrepreneurial spirit and a support structure for innovation that is probably better now than at any time in recent years, with national bodies such as the Technology Strategy Board complemented by a host of regional and sectoral initiatives.

So the advice for business is: engage with the innovation agenda. Work to understand where technologies and markets are going. Keep an eye on policy. Join networks and seek collaborators who can help you to see things in new ways, or to spot and access opportunities that you might not be able to alone. Seek to demonstrate viability. Learn from others, whether about funding sources, supply chains or approaches to product development. And be part of shaping the clean technology products and markets of tomorrow.

David Bott is Director of Innovation Programmes at the Technology Strategy Board. He can be reached at david.bott@tsb.gov.uk. For more information on the work of the Technology Strategy Board please visit www.innovateuk.org.

1.2

Zero Carbon Britain

*The challenges of the next two decades cannot be met with a 20th-century mindset. **Paul Allen** at the Centre for Alternative Technology discusses the new rules on which the economy is going to run.*

The most important aspect of transition away from fossil fuels dependency is to integrate the three key drivers of the necessity for change. Although increasingly familiar individually, these drivers are usually considered in isolation, with experts working in silos, so consequently their respective solutions are rarely considered in unison. In Britain, just like everywhere else that has been industrialized for a long time, the well-being of individuals and communities is underpinned by:

1. *climate security* – our hospitable, reliable climate;
2. *energy security* – access to abundant, cheap fossil fuels;
3. *economic security* – stable economic and monetary systems.

Given their importance it is vital that we understand how they relate to each other. All three are now in crisis, and left unchecked they will compound and synergize. In our report, *Zero Carbon Britain 2030*, we took a look at the science behind our most recent understanding of these key challenges.

Climate security

Since the Industrial Revolution, global atmospheric concentration of carbon dioxide has increased from 260 parts per million to around 380 parts per million. So far we have raised the average global temperature by 0.8°C. Even if we were able to stick at

380 parts per million, we are locked into another two or three decades of warming, which will take us up to around 1.5°C.

Below a 2°C rise on average global temperature we know the earth's natural 'carbon sinks' work to buffer us from the worst effects of our fossil fuel emissions, slowing climate change by helping sink around half of the carbon dioxide we release back into the earth.

Over recent years, clear and robust evidence has emerged that a global temperature rise above 2°C has a high likelihood of triggering an array of much larger climate feedbacks, which will run beyond control and unleash climate chaos. Allowing this to happen on an Earth supporting 6 to 9 billion inhabitants would unleash widespread economic collapse, massive agricultural losses, international water shortages, dangerous rises in sea levels, food famines and widespread ecological degradation, and would create tens of millions of environmental refugees – basically a global catastrophe that would dwarf recent hurricanes or floods and last for tens of thousands of years.

Long-industrialized countries are responsible for the majority of the problem and possess infrastructure and wealth achieved through burning fossil fuel over the past 150 years. Historical responsibility for climate change rests overwhelmingly on the long-industrialized world, but it is the rest of the world that will be hit hardest by the consequences. The long-industrialized world, which has already spent so much of the global carbon budget, should therefore set the pace to help foster a global agreement. All of these facts suggest that a programme to avoid a 2°C rise must aim for zero emissions as quickly as is possible.

However, even a 2°C rise cannot be considered 'safe'. It would still mean we have made the Earth warmer than it has been for millions of years. An alliance of the most vulnerable (small island states and least developed countries) has called for the maximum to be 1.5°C. So 2°C must be considered as the very maximum absolute upper limit for an acceptable level of risk, and it is imperative that this target at least is not exceeded.

There is no time to delay. In light of the most recent evidence, the UK must aim for as close to a 100 per cent cut as possible, as fast as possible. The Zero Carbon Britain 2030 scenario explores how this could be achieved in just two decades.

Energy security

Climate security is not the only reason we should embark on a transition away from fossil fuels. Our unstoppable oil economies are now being halted by the immovable facts of geology. For the first time in our history, just as demand is exploding across the globe, humanity will soon no longer be able to increase fossil fuel production year on year. No one is talking about oil 'running out', but rather the realization that, despite accelerating demand, global rates of production must inevitably plateau and go into decline, with what remains being dirtier, considerably more expensive and harder to extract.

Of the 98 oil-producing nations in the world, 64 are thought to have passed their geologically imposed production peak and, of those, 60 are now in terminal production decline. Britain has now joined those in decline.

In 2005 the UK again became a net energy importer, as shown in Figure 1.2.1. The principal reason for this is the decline in North Sea oil and gas production. Britain has been producing gas from the North Sea since 1967 and oil since 1975. The basin is now 'mature' (UK Oil & Gas 2009). The UK's North Sea oil production reached its peak in 1999; UK gas production peaked in 2000, and is now declining at 2 per cent per annum. If the UK continues to rely on gas, it will increasingly have to import it from Norway, the Netherlands, the former Soviet Union and Algeria.

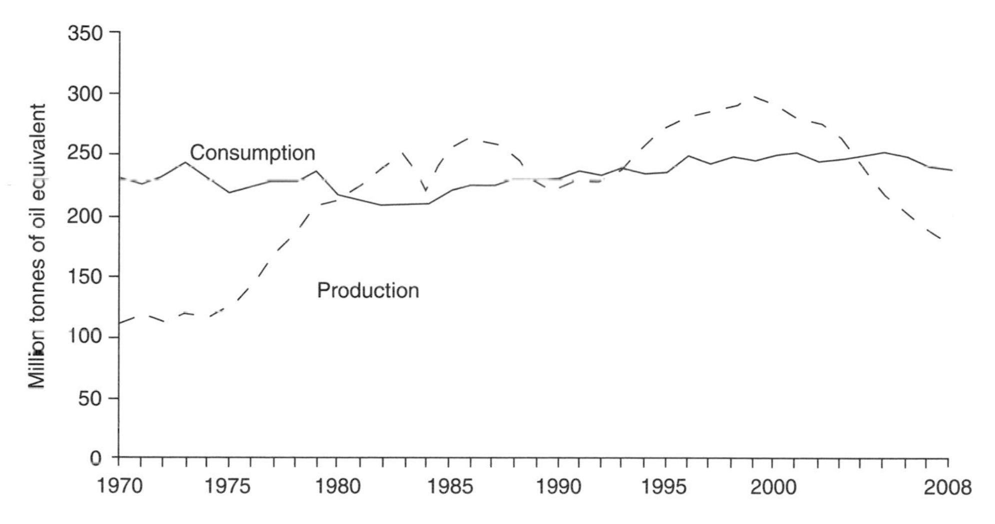

Figure 1.2.1 UK energy production and consumption 1970 to 2008

If the UK can find or borrow the money, importing energy from overseas can for now substitute for failing domestic production. But, owing to global geological constraints, this cannot offer a reliable long-term solution. There are other short-term energy security options, such as a return to coal, which would of course accelerate climate change. Coal, therefore, is not an environmentally sustainable option and may quickly become uneconomic if carbon pricing is deployed.

Our longer-term energy security is dependent on our development of alternative sustainable sources. These sources can be powered up to meet the drivers of both climate and energy security.

Economic security

The rules that determine the next two decades will be very different from those that determined the previous two. From the late 1970s the North Sea oil and gas reserves enabled the UK to be a net energy exporter, making a significant contribution to the UK's balance of payments. It has been estimated that replacing North Sea extraction with imports would add £45 billion to the trade deficit, based on a rough estimate of 100 billion cubic metres of gas at 2p/kWh, 680 million barrels of oil at $60 per barrel and an exchange rate of $1.75 to the pound. In addition, the Exchequer raised nearly £13 billion in tax from the offshore oil and gas industry in 2008.

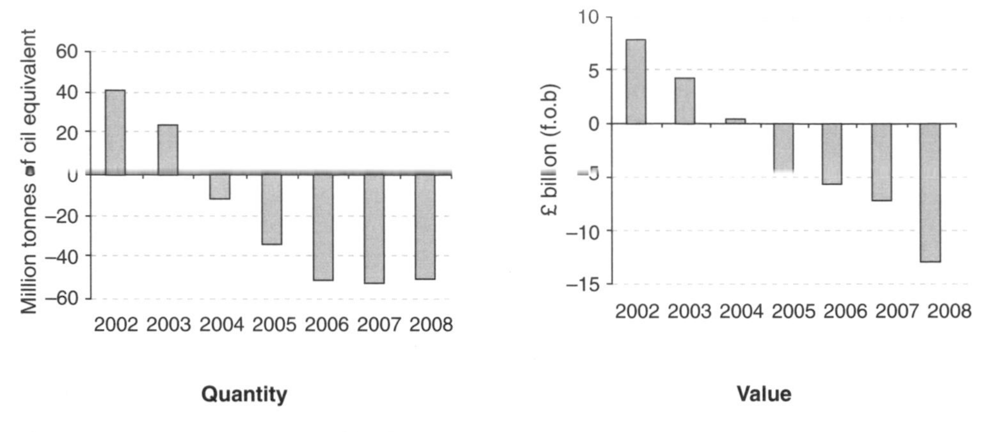

Figure 1.2.2 Net exports of fuel 2002 to 2008

Joining the dots on energy

So what does this all tell us? Well, on numerous fronts, the consequences of the past 150 years of rapid industrialization are all simultaneously coming home to roost. Many of us still haven't really grasped the serious nature of our predicament. Even senior experts, scientists, NGOs and political leaders fail to appreciate that the most recent evidence on both climate and energy security reveals a situation more urgent than had been expected, even by those who have been following it closely for decades.

A clear and widening gulf has now emerged between our current targets and the rapid transition away from fossil fuels dependence that our most recent science tells us is urgently required. The urgent challenges of the 21st century cannot be solved with a 20th-century mindset; they require a smart, conscious and integrated approach.

Once we join the dots and look for the bigger picture, we find that a great many of the solutions to climate security are the same as the solutions to energy and economic security. This requires an immediate and fundamental overhaul of the way we use energy to deliver our well-being, and a massive new programme to harvest our indigenous renewable energy sources.

Never in our history has it been so vitally important to grasp a closing window of opportunity. The credit crunch has shown us the consequences of not reacting ahead of events. If we ignore the warnings and wait until the climate/energy/economic crunch is really upon us before becoming serious about scaling up the solutions, in the ensuing chaos and dislocation we may struggle to muster the resources required.

A Zero Carbon Britain

If the problems are left unchecked they will compound and synergize, but if we act in time the solutions will also synergize, but in a positive way. To foster debate around such a transition, the Centre for Alternative Technology has developed the Zero Carbon Britain 2030 strategy to show how we can integrate our detailed knowledge and experience from the built environment, transport, the energy industry and agriculture into a national framework offering a common, coherent vision linking government, industry and citizens – endorsing, supporting and connecting actions across all sectors of society.

By taking the right actions now, we stay ahead of events – through rethinking our attitudes and taking an uncompromising new approach to energy we find we can deliver well-being with a lot less energy, and we can extract the energy we do need from our indigenous renewable energy sources.

The built environment, for example, can play a significant role in reducing the UK's greenhouse gas emissions through measuring and reducing emissions in construction and maintenance as well as regulation to enforce the reduction of emissions from both new buildings and the existing stock. Putting a price signal on carbon will further encourage businesses and individuals to upgrade their buildings, and creative business models such as 'energy service companies' plus improved design and refurbishment standards can play a vital role. Through careful selection of building materials a national campaign can enable the building stock to lock away carbon, helping to reduce atmospheric levels of CO_2.

Rather than residing at the leaky end of a peaking pipeline of polluting fossil fuel imports, Britain can head its own indigenous energy-lean renewable supply chain. Every field, forest, island, river, coastline, barn or building holds the potential to be a power station, with different technologies appropriate to every scale or region.

By their very nature these renewable reserves will not peak. In fact, as the technology matures and becomes economic in a wider range of applications, the available reserve actually increases.

This transition is the cornerstone of a new economic approach that will move society on from doing the things that got us into so much trouble in the first place. By learning the hard economic lessons of the past few decades we can refocus the ingenuity of the finance sector on the actual challenges at hand.

Investment in such an economic stimulus would not only create a vast carbon army of reskilled workers, and inject money into the economy at ground level, but also deliver very tangible returns to repay the taxpayer, or pension fund, from the price of the energy saved or generated. Through this approach, we not only tackle climate and energy security, but also get the nation back to work, within a stable economy, by our indigenous renewable energy sources, and head off an escalating balance-of-payments crisis as North Sea exports tail off and the price of imported energy goes through the roof.

A zero carbon transition will, of course, entail a challenging period in our history, requiring bold decision making and an urgent sense of common purpose, more akin to that which pertained during the Second World War than in any period since. There is little to be gained, however, by comparing the way we live today with a zero carbon future, because life as we know it now must inevitably change whether we prepare for it or not. A more useful comparison is between a future where we have been proactive and acted ahead of events and a future where we have let events overtake us.

Britain can stay ahead of events through creating a new kind of economy: stable in the long term, locally resilient but still active in a global context, rich in quality jobs, with a strong sense of purpose and reliant on indigenous, inexhaustible energy. But the window of opportunity is closing – now is the time to act. Such a rapid decarbonization will be the biggest undertaking we have made in generations, so it will require a great many to commit to the challenge, but in doing so we will find a sense of collective purpose that we have been craving for a very long time.

Paul Allen, BEng (Hons), FRSA holds an honours degree in electronic and electrical engineering from Liverpool University. As External Relations Director at the Centre for Alternative Technology, he heads the Zero Carbon Britain strategy programme, liaising directly with key policy makers in government, business, the public sector and the devolved assemblies to disseminate the findings of the programme's evidence-based scenario work. The full report is available free to download at www.zerocarbonbritain.com. Contact Paul Allen (tel: 01654 705958; e-mail: paul.allen@cat.org.uk; websites: www.cat.org.uk, www.zerocarbonbritain.com).

1.3

The race for the green economy

*Climate policies are now being put in place round the world, and clean tech could take off as quickly as personal computing once did, says **Dr Cameron Hepburn** at Vivid Economics.*

Climate change policies are creating business opportunities

Many countries have already set ambitious targets for reducing carbon emissions and for increasing renewable energy generation and energy efficiency. The United Kingdom and other European Union member states were among the early movers, but others are implementing a large number of green policies. In 2009, China invested more money than any other country in overall clean energy finance and investment, and is now second in the world only to the United States in total renewable energy capacity, at over 50 GW.[1] In the United States, Republican Senator Graham has said that 'every day we delay trying to find a price for carbon is a day that China uses to dominate the green economy'.

Domestic policies matter

The Copenhagen Accord was agreed (and indeed drafted) by a coalition of heads of state of key countries – China, India, Brazil, South Africa and the United States – and subsequently signed up to by the EU, Japan, Australia and over 100 other countries. The Accord is widely seen as a failure, because it does not have the full force of international law and because it is highly unlikely to limit increases in global mean temperature to below 2°C. However, it has served an important coordinating function for the passage of domestic policies; there have been over 500 major new policy announcements globally since July 2008.[2] Further climate policies are inevitable over the next few years, with corresponding new mechanisms and institutions. In combination with technological advances, these new domestic polices will underpin emerging opportunities in unconventional gas, renewables, electric vehicles, smart grids, smart appliances, energy efficiency and energy storage.

The growth in clean tech may be as fast as that in personal computing

In 2008 the European Union announced a target to source 20 per cent of its energy needs from renewables by 2020. The planned increase in renewable energy is equivalent to the total energy consumption of the United Kingdom today. These targets imply a compound annual growth rate in the renewable energy market in the UK of about 30 per cent to 2020.[3] For comparison, at the height of the late 1990s technology boom, global sales of personal computers experienced compound annual volume growth rates of 15–20 per cent.

Simple arithmetic indicates the scale of the transition is significant

By 2050, many climate scientists and economists argue that global emissions should be reduced by 60 per cent from current levels of 50 $GtCO_2$/year, to around 20 $GtCO_2$/year, a reduction of 30 $GtCO_2$/year. If the unit cost of reducing emissions is between US$10 and US$100/tCO_2, this would equate to a total annual cost of between US$300 billion/year and US$3,000 billion/year. This is greater than the current annual value of global sales of wheat or steel, and about 0.5–5 per cent of current (not contemporaneous) world GDP.

The investment flow that would be triggered would be even larger, and is expected to reach around US$1 trillion per annum by 2030

The total investment requirement will be many multiples higher than the incremental unit cost. Indeed, the International Energy Agency estimates that the total investment required to avoid dangerous climate change will be more than US$1 trillion per annum by 2030. The numbers are large, but note that US$1 trillion would represent less than 6 per cent of global investment in 2030. In 2007, energy subsidies were US$300 billion per annum.

Global clean energy investment is already at around US$150 billion per annum

The annual value of global clean energy investments has more than quadrupled in the past five years, rising to around US$150 billion in 2009. Investment in the renewable energy sector is expected to expand to US$600 billion a year (£360 billion) by 2020.[4]

The race is on

Christine Lagarde, the French finance minister, has been blunt: 'It's a race and whoever wins that race will dominate economic development.' Many low carbon technologies will be competing in a global marketplace, and a great deal of the research and development spending will occur outside the UK, potentially supported by other governments. The UK might develop a leadership position in one or several low-carbon technologies or, alternatively, wait for these technologies to be developed abroad and then import the resulting equipment. The only certainty is that surprises will occur, as we have seen in recent months with the breakthroughs in shale and unconventional gas, suggesting that reductions in emissions may be cheaper than expected.

The United Kingdom has made a solid start

The UK was recently ranked third in an analysis of the low carbon competitiveness of the G20 nations.[5] UK exports are the least carbon-intensive of any of the G20 countries, and the UK was second only to the United States in attracting venture capital and private equity (VC/PE) investment in low carbon technologies,[6] although both the United States and the UK were overtaken by China in terms of overall clean energy finance and investment in 2009.[7] Already by 2007, VC/PE investment in renewable energy and energy efficiency technologies in the UK was $1.9 billion (£1.1 billion), 41 per cent of the EU total and more than double that of any other European country.

There are opportunities in the United Kingdom, and UK firms are reasonably well positioned to take market share globally

Policy in the United Kingdom contemplates a rapid increase in investment in offshore wind. Wave power, gas, electric vehicles and smart grids look likely to have significant potential. The UK has become the global hub for 'carbon finance', with many of the leading emission reduction project developers listed on AIM, or based in London. The UK has a market share of over 20 per cent of CDM projects, more than any other developed country, and more than double that of the next largest country (Switzerland). International opportunities for UK firms may be scaled up by the emergence of multilateral 'public finance mechanisms' and 'advance market commitments'.[8]

Success will require company agility and a solid understanding of policy developments

Firms can contribute to the transition to a low carbon economy by creating new technologies and business models. Smart businesses will work with government, and will be more likely to create profits in the course of so doing. Business also has a role in assisting government in the design and function of the policy instruments and mechanisms that are deployed to incentivize behaviour. Moreover, given the rapid pace of change, and the unpredictability of the climate policy rollercoaster, corporate agility would appear to be a *sine qua non* of succeeding during a low carbon transition.

Notes

[1] Pew Charitable Trusts (2010) Who's winning the clean energy race? Growth, competition and opportunity in the world's largest economies, *G20 Clean Energy Factbook*, Pew Charitable Trusts, Philadelphia, PA.

[2] Deutsche Bank Climate Change Advisors (2010) *The Green Economy: The race is on*, March, Deutsche Bank Climate Change Advisors, New York.

[3] Vivid Economics (2008) The race to capture the carbon pound: The UK's place in the global market for low-carbon innovation, Report for Shell Springboard, October.

[4] UNEP and NEF (2008) Global Trends in Sustainable Energy Investment 2008: Analysis of trends and issues in the financing of renewable energy and energy efficiency, Report for the United Nations Environment Programme, UNEP and NEF, Geneva.

[5] Vivid Economics (2009) G20 low-carbon competitiveness, Report for the Climate Institute and E3G, September.

[6] Vivid Economics (2008) The race to capture the carbon pound: The UK's place in the global market for low-carbon innovation, Report for Shell Springboard, October.

[7] Pew Charitable Trusts (2010) Who's winning the clean energy race? Growth, competition and opportunity in the world's largest economies, *G20 Clean Energy Factbook*, Pew Charitable Trusts, Philadelphia, PA.

[8] Vivid Economics (2009) Catalysing low-carbon growth in developing countries: Public finance mechanisms to scale up private sector investment in climate solutions, Report for UNEP and Partners, October.

Vivid Economics was established in 2006. It achieves lasting beneficial impacts for society and for clients by putting economics to good use. It provides clear vision, client-focused communication and robust analysis based on sound economic frameworks and evidence. Dr Cameron Hepburn is an expert in market economics, commercial strategy, and environmental economics and ethics. He has over a decade's experience working on environmental and climate change issues, with particular interests in the theory and implementation of emissions trading, the economics and ethics of cost–benefit analysis, and the economics of apparently irrational individual behaviour. He currently holds research fellowships at Oxford University (New College and the Smith School of Enterprise and the Environment) and at the London School of Economics (Grantham Research Institute). He is a member of the UK Defra Academic Panel and the Ofgem Environmental Economists Panel, an Associate Editor of the Oxford Review of Economic Policy, and a co-founder and director of Climate Bridge Ltd. Contact Cameron Hepburn (e-mail: cameron.hepburn@vivideconomics.com; website: www.vivideconomics.com).

Renewable power generation

Dr Sam Cheung at McLellan reviews Britain's progress towards generating 15 per cent of its power from renewables by 2020.

This chapter outlines the UK government strategy on renewable energy from now to 2020 and presents the regulations and incentives in place to encourage uptake. It also discusses the potential of major technologies available for power, heat and transport applications. If the implementation is done diligently, the UK has a good chance of achieving its target of 15 per cent from renewables by 2020 and is also well placed to be a global leader in renewable energy.

Introduction

The threat of global warming, together with international agreements like the Kyoto Protocol[1] on sustainable development, has led to significant interest in the potential of using renewable energy as a source of power. Amongst relevant declarations, the UK government made a commitment to ensure that 10 per cent of energy production would be from renewable sources by 2010 and would progressively increase to 15 per cent by 2020.[2] This is an extremely challenging target. A concerted effort is therefore required from industry, the general public and the government to achieve these targets. However, the UK cannot act alone to tackle climate change, and international collaborations are required. As demonstrated in the recent COP15 Copenhagen Conference,[3] getting an international agreement is never easy. Since the Kyoto agreement will expire in 2012, time is against the international community on a new agreement.

According to the government, meeting our renewable energy targets is not just about tackling climate change and securing our future energy supplies. Achieving our targets could provide £100 billion of investment opportunities and create up to half a million new jobs in the renewable energy sector by 2020. Therefore, it could be a win–win situation for the UK if the strategy is implemented diligently.

This chapter will mainly concentrate on issues relating to renewable power generation. Moreover, it will briefly discuss renewable energy in heat and transport applications. We first consider the measures implemented by the government to encourage the renewable energy sector.

Government regulations and incentives

The UK government renewable energy policy is based on guidance from the EU Renewable Energy Directive.[4] Central to the UK policy is the Renewables Obligation Order[5] for power generation, which requires electricity suppliers to source a certain proportion of their electricity from accredited renewables, such as biomass, wind, tidal, landfill gas and so on.

Another mechanism is the Climate Change Levy (CCL), which is a tax on energy used by businesses. Electricity produced from designated renewables is exempt from CCL.

Apart from these, the UK also operates the EU Emission Trading Scheme (ETS) for carbon trading, which covers power sector and energy-intensive industrial sectors.

Feed-in tariffs (FiTs)[6] are financial support measures recently introduced by the government to increase the uptake of small-scale renewable generation (less than 5MWe). The mechanism provides renewable generators with a 20-year grace period (25 years for solar photovoltaic).

To meet the 15 per cent renewables target by 2020, heat generated from renewables must also be considered. At present, only about 1 per cent of the total heat demand in the UK comes from renewables; this needs to rise to 12 per cent by 2020. On 1 February 2010, the government published a consultation on the Renewable Heat Incentive (RHI)[7] scheme, which it aims to introduce in April 2011.

On the transport front, the government has established a goal that 5 per cent of the total transport fuel must be from renewables (eg biodiesel) by 2010 under the Renewable Transport Fuels Obligation (RTFO).[8] The target is set at 10 per cent for 2020.

The next section discusses the technologies available for power generation, heat and transport.

Renewable technologies

On the technology front, a wide range of renewable technologies is available for exploitation. However, the potential of some is much greater than that of others. Also, the degree of maturity is variable between different technologies. A brief review of the major technologies is given below.

Figure 1.4.1 represents the contribution of various renewable resources for the UK.

The UK has approximately a third of the total wind energy potential in Europe. However, the development of wind energy in the UK has been slow until recently. Planning restrictions have hampered the development of onshore wind in the past. The

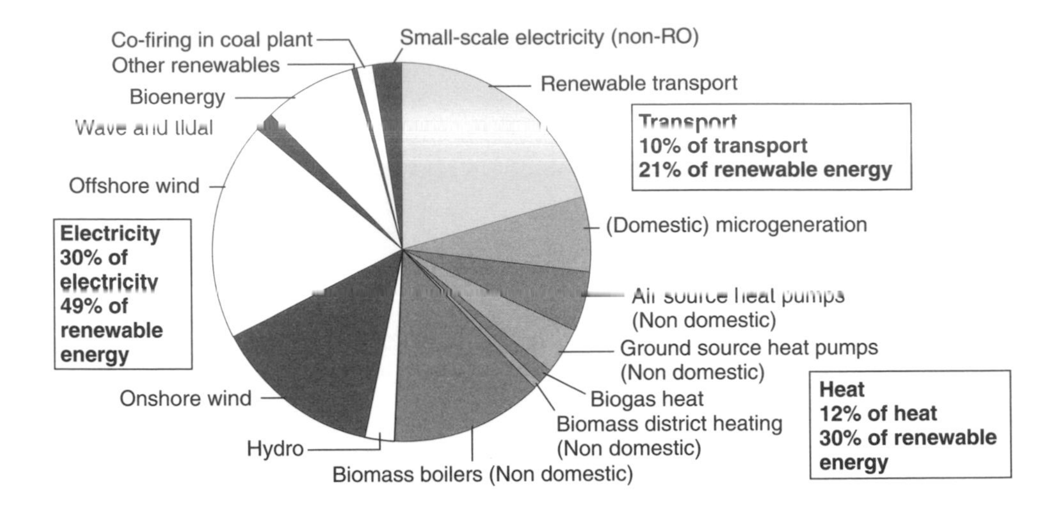

Source: The UK Renewable Energy Strategy, July 2009,
http://www.decc.gov.uk/en/content/cms/what_we_do/uk_supply/energy_mix/renewable/res/res.aspx.

Figure 1.4.1 Illustrative mix of technologies in 2020

situation is unlikely to change significantly in the near term. On the other hand, offshore wind has taken a giant leap forward recently, mainly owing to government incentives in offering 1.5 Renewables Obligation Certificates (ROCs) for each MWh generated. As a consequence, an additional 32GWe (Round 3 – installation will probably begin in 2014) of wind-generated electricity will be fed into the UK grid, on top of 8GWe from previous rounds. The total amount of wind power should provide about 30 per cent of the total UK power demand by 2020. However, upgrading and strengthening the UK's electricity grid will be necessary. A note of caution is that wind does not blow all the time. It is important to have an energy mix so that we do not solely rely on wind to meet our renewable needs.

Owing to its unique location, the UK also has significant wave and tidal energy potentials (2GWe). Both technologies are receiving a great deal of attention. Past UK offshore oil and gas experience can be transferred to wave and tidal energy development. Regions of particular importance are the coast north of Scotland, the Irish Sea, the Severn Estuary and the coast off Cornwall. The UK also has the world's leading testing and demonstration facilities in the New and Renewable Energy Centre (NaREC), the European Marine Energy Centre (EMEC) in Orkney and the proposed Wave Hub off Cornwall.

Landfill gas has long been a major contributor of renewables in the UK. Currently, the UK has a generation potential of approximately 500MWe. However, owing to the EU Landfill Directive,[9] the amount of waste going into landfills will reduce, as will the number of landfill sites. In the longer term, the contribution from landfill gas is likely to remain stable. At present, generating electricity using the gas is inefficient (only 30 per cent efficiency). Studies are currently under way to mix the gas with biogas from anaerobic digesters and feed the mixed gas (a potential of 2.5GW) into the national gas grid so that it can partly meet residential gas demand for heating and cooking.

The UK has significant biomass energy potential. Recent estimates show that energy crops alone can provide approximately 3GW (both heat and power) of renewable energy. Food and wood waste can contribute another 5GW. With the proposed introduction of RHI, the adoption of biomass for combined heat and power (CHP) generation is envisaged to take off in a big way soon to meet the 12 per cent renewable heat target.

Other renewable technologies such as air/ground source heat pump, fuel cell and micro-CHP will make useful contributions to the renewables target. Again, they are expensive technologies (three to four times more) compared with conventional technologies. Therefore, government incentives or subsidies are needed for wider adoption.

Another important renewable resource is biofuel. Two principal biofuels are currently in commercial production: bioethanol from fermenting agricultural crops such as sugar beet, sugar cane or wheat; and biodiesel produced from oily crops such as rapeseed and soya or by processing oily waste such as used cooking oil or animal fats. Biodiesel can be used in conventional diesel engines for heat and power generation. It can also blend in with diesel in varying proportions to form transport fuel. The supply of biofuels in the UK is driven by the RTFO. There is a global market for the sourcing and supply of biofuels, and the majority of feedstocks used in the UK are sourced from abroad. To encourage local supply, the government should encourage better use of crop waste.

An area worthy of consideration is the use of renewable resources in electric vehicles. Although the government recognizes electric vehicles as an important means to reduce emissions, little is done to encourage companies to invest in the infrastructure of charge points and to improve the operating range of these vehicles. The rail industry can also play a useful role in adopting renewables by purchasing more green electricity and using biodiesel to power diesel locomotives. Through the Department for Transport, the government has required rail companies to make new high-speed trains as fuel efficient as possible and flexible enough to adapt to future change in power sources. For example, if fuel cells or biofuels become sustainable and cost-effective then these could replace, or be utilized in, the train's diesel engine.

A brighter future?

As discussed earlier, the UK has a diverse portfolio of renewable technologies. However, the main focus is on wind energy. The UK should learn from past mistakes such as the 'dash for gas' by not over-relying on a particular resource. Wind is an intermittent resource, and contingency arrangements must be in place to meet the shortfall. Therefore, the country should have a diverse but also balanced portfolio of energy supply. For example, nuclear energy and fossil fuels must be included as part of the energy mix to meet base load demands.

Is the government doing enough to help? The answer is maybe, but more could be done. The government deserves credit in setting up initiatives to adopt renewable energy for a large number of public sector buildings and to require all public sector buildings to be zero carbon by 2018. On the downside, industry is accusing it of not doing enough. For example, the UK's largest biomass user, Drax Power,[10] has recently decided to suspend co-firing, as the company complains of insufficient long-term subsidy given to biomass to make it competitive with coal. This certainly does not send out the right signal to industry for higher biomass uptake.

Is the future bright for the UK? Overall, the UK has a good chance of achieving its renewables targets in 2020 and possibly beyond. It is also well placed to be a global leader in the so-called 'Green Revolution', especially in wind and tidal energy. The government must continue to support investments and provide further incentives so that UK businesses can create more employment and wealth.

Notes

[1] Kyoto Protocol, http://unfccc.int/kyoto_protocol/items/2830.php.
[2] *The Renewable Energy Strategy*, July 2009, http://www.decc.gov.uk/en/content/cms/what_we_do/uk_supply/energy_mix/renewable/res/res.aspx.
[3] United Nations Framework Convention on Climate Change, http://unfccc.int/2860.php.
[4] Directive 2009/28/EC of the European Parliament and of the Council of 23 April 2009 on the promotion of the use of energy from renewable sources and amending and subsequently repealing Directives 2001/77/EC and 2003/30/EC.
[5] The Renewables Obligation Order 2009, http://www.opsi.gov.uk/si/si2009/uksi_20090785_en_1.
[6] Feed-in tariffs: Government's response to the summer 2009 consultation, February 2010.
[7] Renewable Heat Incentive (RHI), http://www.decc.gov.uk/en/content/cms/what_we_do/uk_supply/energy_mix/renewable/policy/renewable_heat/incentive/incentive.aspx.
[8] Renewable Transport Fuels Obligation, http://www.renewablefuelsagency.gov.uk/aboutthertfo.
[9] Council Directive 99/31/EC, http://ec.europa.eu/environment/waste/landfill_index.htm.
[10] Drax power plant suspends plan to replace coal with greener fuel, *The Times*, 19 February 2010.

McLellan and Partners Ltd have a long association with the applications of renewable energy in many industrial sectors. They have carried out numerous projects on biomass, wind, combined heat and power, landfill gas, waste to energy, biodiesel and other renewables. They are also experienced in transmission, distribution and grid connection issues and are well placed to assist industry to exploit renewable resources. For further details contact Sam Cheung, McLellan and Partners Ltd, Sheer House, West Byfleet, Surrey KT14 6NL, UK (tel: +44 (0)1932 343271; e-mail: sam.cheung@mclellan.co.uk; website: www.mclellan.co.uk).

1.5

New housing and transport solutions

*Reaching the carbon reduction targets we have set ourselves as a society will not be possible without new solutions. This represents a huge opportunity for innovation in many areas, including buildings and transport, says **David Bott**, Director of Innovation Programmes, the Technology Strategy Board.*

Two of the major sources of greenhouse gas emissions in the UK are caused by what we now regard as everyday life. Our houses produce about 30 per cent of our emissions and our use of personal transport adds almost another 20 per cent.

Housing

The increases in these sources have been dramatic. Over the last century we have doubled the number of houses compared to the number of people, while the ratio of cars to people has increased by over 1,000. But even these numbers do not capture the true impact of the changes. Our houses are more comfortable – but they use more energy to achieve that comfort. They contain more 'stuff' that we purchase to enhance our lives – but that in turn adds to the energy consumption in the factories that produce these goods, both in the UK and abroad. We use more water in our daily lives – almost 150 litres per person per day – and all that water has to be purified to a level that means we could drink it, despite the fact that, of the 150 litres, we actually drink less than 10 litres.

That said, we *can* build houses that use substantially less energy but remain comfortable; we can buy artefacts that have less embedded energy; and we can use water more sparingly. We just have to change what we do and – as we are increasingly learning – we have to use better technologies to deliver all these benefits.

The current housing stock is about 26 million houses. In a 'normal' year we add about 250,000 to that number – about 1 per cent – and we lose a smaller number. We now know that we can build houses with drastically lower energy and water consumption without sacrificing the high levels of comfort we now enjoy.

However, a simple calculation shows that, with the current stock and build rates, something like 70 per cent of the houses in which we will live in 2050 are already built. What we need is a means to retrofit all the new technology into existing houses.

In 2009, the Technology Strategy Board set out to test, support and encourage the nascent market in retrofitting old houses. In conjunction with the Department for Communities and Local Government (which effectively owns about 4.5 million units of the housing stock) we ran a competition to develop ways to decrease the greenhouse gas emissions of existing houses by up to 80 per cent.

The first stage of the process was a design study. Many of the smaller architectural businesses and building contractors that might be expected to contribute to this exercise do not necessarily have the spare capacity to explore what can be done and, as we battled through the economic downturn, many were more in the mode of struggling to survive. So we used the Small Business Research Initiative (SBRI) process, which is designed to get government departments to engage with small, innovative companies, to allow us to fully fund the design studies.

We were aiming for a wide range of building types and geographical locations, so we advertised the competition widely, but even so we were surprised by the level of response – almost 400 groups of companies submitted applications to this first stage. Despite the extra money allocated from the 2009 Budget to extend this activity, we could support only about half the applications – and so 194 design studies began in the summer of 2009.

The second phase of the competition was intended to turn some of these designs into reality. The output of the design stage was assessed for performance and practicality, and 87 designs were funded for implementation. These houses are now being converted up and down the country. When they are finished, they will be occupied by real people living real lives, but will be monitored for their performance against the design specification. It is hoped that the designs will form a library of designs that can be used both in other social housing and by private owners – the designs are, after all, owned by the taxpayers!

One of the gratifying outcomes of this exercise in stimulating innovation has been its ripple effect – as many who had completed the design phase but had not won support for implementation had come to understand the business potential of their work and committed themselves to implementing it anyway.

The retrofit competition is just one of the research and development programmes that the Technology Strategy Board is leading to help business find opportunities to reduce the environmental impact of buildings. In the end the winners will be the businesses that have developed these new solutions, householders and other occupants who benefit from greater comfort and lower bills, and the environment itself.

Personal transport

Our society has come to rely on personal transport. Cars are probably regarded as a right by modern humans. They have been developed in a world where safety and comfort (not to mention speed and acceleration) are seen as more important than resource and energy efficiency. Developing the news types of cars that we will need to use in 2050 is therefore a mixture of technology and marketing.

The technology is challenging but not impossible. Implementing it in competition with existing cars would be difficult, but governments around the world are trying to support this evolution of the market. Unlike houses, the car stock turns over fast enough to be able to replace all the existing cars by 2050, but as consumers we will not buy cars that compromise the performance luxury we have come to demand without government support for the change.

The Technology Strategy Board has been working with the Office for Low Emission Vehicles (OLEV) (and its forebears) for three years to help the automotive industry develop these new cars.

The first step of the journey was to identify and start to develop the necessary technologies. It is not a simple matter to replace the internal combustion engine with any of the alternatives. The waste heat produced by the engine is used to provide heat for the passenger compartment. The mechanical motion enables the production of hydraulic pressure that can be used to power systems like power steering. And the electricity produced by the alternator is mostly regarded as free, so the efficiency of many electrical components is not maximized. Our early competitions encouraging business research and development therefore focused on developing the new technologies that would address the necessary changes in vehicle systems. We also supported a number of programmes that increased the efficiency of more conventional technologies, which will allow a more measured approach to the change we need.

The next step was to test these technologies in more real-world situations. Working with energy companies and local government, we launched our low carbon vehicle demonstrator programme in early 2009 with the aim of putting a significant number of low carbon cars on the road being driven by real people. As with the retrofit competition in housing, we were surprised by the size and quality of the applications, so much so that our initial intent to put 100 cars on the road had to be drastically upgraded and we ended up launching the results with 340 cars across the country.

These trial projects are being monitored, for both the performance of their systems and the behaviours exhibited by the drivers, so that the design of the next generation of these cars can incorporate a real understanding of how we use them.

The next stage – working with OLEV and the Automotive Council – is to help support the development of new supply chains to produce new components and subsystems. Without these supply chains, automotive manufacturers will be unable to build the tens of millions of cars that will be needed over the next 40 years if we are to answer the challenge of ultra-low carbon transport.

In the coming transformation of the way we travel, there are two other aspects worth noting. The first is that it is almost axiomatic that these cars will interact in some way with the electrical grid. Certainly, fully electric cars will need to be recharged and, unless the production of electricity is decarbonized, much of the new technology implemented in these cars will be wasted.

The second is that efficiency in travel is as much a function of our planning and the information we have available to us as it is of the motive power. We need to ensure that these cars and their drivers are fully aware of their options – how to avoid congested areas and how to manage their power with respect to geography and recharging opportunities. This will require a significant increase in the 'intelligence' of the cars themselves and much better connectivity with the infrastructure on which they travel.

Innovative businesses in the UK and elsewhere are working on many of these issues right now. The job to be done is to accelerate this process, combining the technological expertise of business with the vision of policy makers to create confidence in these huge future market opportunities, and so help innovative solutions become reality.

David Bott is Director of Innovation Programmes at the Technology Strategy Board. He can be reached at david.bott@tsb.gov.uk. For more information on the work of the Technology Strategy Board please visit www.innovateuk.org.

Part 2

Making a return

2.1

Clean tech as an investment class

Rob Wylie *at WHEB Ventures explains how clean tech appears to an investor.*

In broad terms clean tech involves finding more efficient and sustainable ways for addressing the huge challenge of a rapidly growing population's demands for energy, food and water. These resources are all interconnected, and any appropriate solutions would almost always involve the use of less energy and hence can be viewed as 'low carbon'.

One example that might not be obvious involves the UK company Exosect's approach to controlling insect pests with natural alternatives to pesticides. Trucost has calculated that 40,000 tonnes of CO_2 will be saved for every 2 million hectares of rice treated with Exosect product rather than conventional chemical pesticides.

Clean tech as an investment theme

As an investment theme clean tech cuts across almost all industrial sectors and technologies. Investment levels have grown tenfold between 2003 and 2008 to a figure of around $840 billion. There was a sharp downturn in 2009, as there was in all areas. However, the commonly held view is that this is the one area capable of sustainable growth going forward, albeit with periodic adjustments, and that it presents huge opportunities for innovation. It's rare for presidents and prime ministers to lobby on behalf of a sector and perhaps even rarer to promise to put money into it but that is what is happening with clean tech or low carbon.

Clean tech or low carbon investment can be divided into five main areas:

- *Energy generation technologies* include wind turbines, photovoltaic solar cells, wave power, biomass energy and biofuels. Until recently this has been the main interest of investors, governments and corporates alike and has been subject to some over-exuberance in investment and valuations – the solar and biofuel bubbles in the United States spring to mind. In certain areas, such as onshore wind, it is reaching the goal of grid parity in pricing. Solar is becoming highly competitive, with low-cost Chinese suppliers posing a growing threat to Western suppliers. There is evidence that government subsidies such as feed-in tariffs are now being reduced, leading to investment uncertainty. During the times when banks actually lent money and credit was cheap, the capital-intensive nature of this area did not seem to be a deterrent to some of the enthusiasts. It is now a huge problem for new developments and will hinder the further development of the less proven technologies such as wave and tidal.

  There is, however, still plenty of scope for innovation, particularly in making the more established technologies more efficient, which comes under the area below.
- *Energy efficiency* has only recently attracted high-level support, even though it perhaps should have been the first to attract attention, as it is quicker and cheaper to implement for the same level of carbon reduction. The area receiving the most interest is smart grid. Here we are seeing enormous support from governments such as the US government, which has allocated around $11 billion to the area. Its potential for scalability and the fact that it is not capital-intensive makes it attractive to investors. Innovation opportunities in this area also cover distributed generation technologies, which reduce power losses in the transmission system, and energy storage technologies, including advanced batteries, fuel cells and carbon capture and storage (where emissions from fossil fuel power stations are captured and buried underground), as well as finding ways of helping intermittent power generators such as wind become more reliable and predictable power sources.
- *Clean industrial processes* and materials can potentially be used in a wide variety of industrial applications.

  A unifying theme across the clean tech materials area is the use of technology that has the potential to reduce environmental impact, improve the efficient use of resources, reduce costs and respond to consumer demand. Examples of clean tech materials include advances in biodegradable plastics, advanced ceramics, the application of new technologies to industrial processes such as fibre-optic sensing technology, green pesticides and cleaning processes with lower environmental impacts than conventional alternatives, and nanotechnology, especially nanomaterials.

  Examples of this area include Exosect, which has developed a cost-effective way of controlling insects by using mating disruption technology. The company offers a solution for pest control in top fruit, rice and stored products, and for controlling clothes moths. This precludes or minimizes the need for chemical pesticides or insecticides in a variety of very large markets. Another company is fluXXion, a spin-out from Philips, which has taken microelectronics technology involving silicon wafers and applied it to process intensification within the chemical industry through a step change in the way that the chemical industry can strip and distil solvents from mixtures, with much smaller footprints, energy consumption and hence cost and much greater operational flexibility.

- *Waste* production equates to loss of potential profit.

  Within the EU, households, agriculture and industry generate 2 billion tonnes of waste every year. The OECD estimates that 45 per cent more waste could be generated by 2020 than in 1995. New government regulations are being implemented to enforce recycling, for example through the European Union End of Life Vehicle Directive, Waste Electrical and Electronic Equipment Directive and Landfill Directives. The application of appropriate technology could help the recovery and recycling of a significant proportion of this waste.

  One example concerns rubber recycling. Watson Brown, a UK company, has developed a mechanical process for recycling industrial rubber waste, which can no longer be landfilled, but which can then be reused at a much lower cost and energy consumption than that of virgin rubber. This is good for industry and good for the environment.

- *Water* has been mentioned as the 'new oil' in terms of opportunity, with companies such as GE publicly stating that this is an area in which they would like to develop a large business interest. However, investment figures for innovative products in this area do not as yet bear this out, despite the obvious environmental imperative.

  The world's population tripled in the 20th century and, within the next 50 years, is forecast to increase by another 40 to 50 per cent. This population growth – coupled with industrialization and urbanization – will result in an increasing demand for water. This is at a time when, as UN figures indicate, over 1 billion people already lack access to safe drinking water. The UN Food and Agriculture Organization estimates that two-thirds of the world's population will face water shortages by 2025 unless significant changes occur in water resource management. To put this into context, agriculture accounts for 70 per cent of all water use globally, and technologies exist now for dramatic reduction in its use. For instance, irrigation control systems using sensors, telemetry and software developed by companies such as AquaSpy, originally Australian and now US based, have shown savings of up to 30 per cent of total water use and up to 50 per cent yield increases.

  Hence water conservation, purification and treatment technologies and more energy-efficient desalination techniques all represent opportunities for innovators.

  However, as stated above, this area has not received as much investment as the demands for doing so would suggest. The reason for this is that many of the technologies involved in, for instance, water treatment are only incremental and not step-change improvements. The water industry is very conservative in the uptake of new technologies. Water has yet to benefit from being priced according to its full economic value. The latter is starting to change in areas that have been particularly hard hit by water shortages, such as Australia and California, with countries such as

Israel being traditionally at the forefront in developing important new developments in this area.

Opportunities abound or not?

Given the scale and breadth of opportunities and the level of government support, surely it must be a nirvana for innovators, investors and corporates. Unfortunately not. Like all other sectors the low carbon economy is just as susceptible to the economic crunch and, and in some cases, more so. The following sections give a few pertinent facts.

Changes in investment appetite

It is still a fairly new area for investment. There isn't a sufficient track record of cash-for-cash returns to help clean tech VCs raise new funds. This has not been helped by the IPO markets being essentially shut for new offerings, especially for companies not showing sustainable profits, and the M&A market being very cautious over the past 18 months. The credit crunch has also meant that traditional investors in VC funds, such as pension funds, are either not investing in VCs or doing so only if they already have a long-standing relationship and hence have not traditionally focused on this area. Finally there are now many low-cost opportunities for less risky late-stage or growth deals owing to a combination of market reality and the dearth of bank finance. This combination of factors has led to a focus by most VCs on supporting their existing portfolios and on late-stage deals. There is therefore a real danger that promising early-stage clean tech companies will fail to raise finance and fall by the wayside.

Even in the good times it should be recognized that most VCs tend to invest in 0.5 to 1 per cent of all the investment proposals they see – there is a very high attrition rate.

Changes in corporate attitudes

Corporates have increasingly made public their interest in this area, and many have developed VC activities of their own, co-investing alongside traditional VCs. The reality is that, as in other areas such as biotech, they now prefer to have a fully proven product to exploit, avoiding technical risk even if it is 'low C'. An additional characteristic of corporates in this area is that they are often utilities, and traditionally risk-averse.

Changes in exit possibilities

As stated above, the IPO markets are essentially shut to anything but companies with profitable track records and/or good prospects for growth – it has proven very risky to float to finance negative cash flow. The credit crunch has forced companies to be more conservative about how to finance and value acquisitions. This might change, but the M&A exit route in 2009 for innovative small companies was dire and perhaps can only marginally improve in 2010.

How to succeed?

Innovative companies need money, and that is now much harder to get. The quick answer is that innovators and investors have to be more innovative and take a reality check on the market. There are still huge opportunities to be had. Here are 10 thoughts that might help:

1. Be realistic about cash requirements and valuation – at least double or triple the former, and remember that having 10 per cent of something that is worth something is better than having 100 per cent of something that is worth nothing.
2. Find ways to generate profitable revenue early – it might not be in your largest market opportunity, but the learning curve on the applicability of your product will have been done.
3. Look carefully at sales lead times – these always tend to be underestimated, with corporate partners and municipalities seeming to live in another time zone when it comes to making decisions.
4. Be careful about reliance on government subsidies for economic viability. Assume they will change their minds in the current environment – they will.
5. Find an investor syndicate that will add value and has business experience. They all say they do, but unfortunately that is sometimes not the case – inexperienced investors can seriously wreck a business.
6. Be realistic about your skills to do the plan. Hire people who are more experienced and cleverer than you are – easy to find but difficult to do. It's called strengthening the team and succession planning!
7. In a similar vein, hire a useful board of independent non-execs who can genuinely open doors, are willing to do so and are strong enough to make investor directors listen.
8. Be careful of markets requiring government certification or approval – these can be very expensive in terms of delayed sales and are something that EU governments in particular seem to be reluctant to address.
9. Avoid capital-intensive projects unless it is clear how they can be financed, through either corporate or government-guaranteed support.
10. Show clearly how a 5 to 10 times return can be made within three to five years.

Dr Rob Wylie has focused on the clean technology investment area for over 20 years and is a founder partner of WHEB Ventures, which raised the UK's first broad-based clean tech VC fund in 2005. WHEB now manages two specialist clean tech VC funds, with total assets under management of £130 million. Rob is also a co-founder of WHEB's associated companies: Ruston WHEB, the clean tech executive search company; WHEB Asset Management, a fund management company that focuses on investing in listed sustainable stocks; and WHEB Infrastructure Partners, a fund for investing in renewable energy projects. Contact Rob Wylie (tel: +44 (0)20 7299 4141; e-mail: rob@whebventures.com).

2.2

Funding clean tech

In clean tech, there is double-digit growth wherever you look. But who are going to be the winners and losers, asks ***Simon Bond****, Director of the Bath Ventures Innovation Centre, University of Bath.*

The global expenditure on renewable energy projects is expected to leap by close to 70 per cent and reach £100 billion a year by 2020 according to new research by Bloomberg New Energy Finance. The flow of venture capital into clean tech outstripped that of all other sectors from 2009, including ICT and biotech, and accounted for £3.7 billion across 557 deals in North America, Europe, China and India. Meanwhile the world's most famous investors are queuing up to place very public bets on clean tech. The world's most successful investor, Warren Buffett, has made four high-profile investments in the sector in the last couple of years, and hedge fund billionaire George Soros recently announced his own plans to 'invest a billion dollars in clean tech'.

Clearly clean tech is the smart place to be in order to raise or indeed invest money. Double-digit growth is expected wherever you look. Based on current trends, renewable energy will constitute over 30 per cent of the world's installed power generation capacity by 2030. But how does this sector work? Is there a clean tech investment cycle? Who will be the winners in this sector? And who will lose?

Clean tech: another biotech or ICT?

The problem in answering these questions is that clean tech covers such a wide range of business activities and operates across such diverse markets that it is difficult to nail down a conclusive set of investment principles for it as a cohesive sector.

Investors and start-up CEOs have developed investment cycles in the biotech and ICT sectors based on the mutually understood stages of pre-revenue seed funding, rounds of subsequent funding against business development milestones and a 'value crystallization event' or pay-off centred around an IPO or trade sale to an easily indentified corporate consolidator, such as Genzyme in biotech or Cisco in ICT. Can the biotech or ICT investment cycle be applied to clean tech? The answer is yes, but not wholly.

If there is a historical comparison for clean tech investment then it is probably the communications sector, and in many ways the next 30 years of 'clean tech' will do to energy what the last 30 years have done to communications.

There are many parallels between the two sectors – the complete, global overhaul of how we make, distribute and consume energy, driven by substantial year-on-year decreases in carbon emissions, is set to define the sector in our economy in the same way that digitization drove the communications revolution to spawn the mobile telephone, the internet, call centres, fibre grids, and a plethora of digital services and media that sit on top of this new infrastructure.

The role of regulation

Crucial to the analogy is the role of regulation. In communications it was the progressive liberalization of previously state-owned telecommunications assets and the re-creation of the sector into a set of market-share-hungry, competing private companies, first in the United States and then Europe, followed by the rest of the world.

For clean tech the market is being created by self-imposed legally binding carbon emission reduction legislation and treaties that can be achieved only if investment is made into massive new energy production infrastructure like solar and wind farms, better, more efficient power distribution systems, and lower-power-consuming devices such as Energy Star-rated computing equipment and electric vehicles.

However, here is the crucial difference in the regulatory driver for clean tech that needs to be understood by the sector's CEOs and investors alike. The financial value of the communications revolution lay in being able to do more communications for less cost; the financial value of the clean tech revolution lies in reducing or removing the cost of carbon emissions – and the financial cost of carbon is not driven by business efficiency but by government regulation. This is the small print of the clean tech revolution – all its financial value depends on the appetite of national governments for continuing to drive down carbon emissions by driving up the financial cost of making these emission to companies, countries and their citizens. If any of these players lose their zeal for acting on climate change by reducing their carbon emissions – both quite abstract terms when you think of human nature and the timescales involved between climate change cause and effect – then the financial underpinnings of clean tech investment will be seriously challenged!

So how do you make sure that you're the Google rather than the Lycos of the clean tech revolution?

Three sub-sectors

There are three sub-sectors that most opportunities will fall into:

- *Generation*. New sources of renewable energy such as solar, wind and water (wave and tidal) are necessarily major endeavours and require large-scale project finance of an order that will outstrip the ROI tolerance of many investors and VCs. Supply of components, systems and devices to this market is more promising for start-ups, but these projects are often tied to national government-backed programmes, and purchasing decisions are not always transparent.
- *Monitoring*. The monitoring of energy consumption (and the subsequent action to control consumption) has been an early success in the clean tech market. Benefiting from being able to offer reductions in customers' energy bills against soaring prices, companies like EnerNOC in the United States, which provides a monitoring and savings service to businesses, has had a significant IPO. In the UK, home energy monitoring start-up Alert Me attracted significant venture capital in an otherwise difficult fund-raising market.
- *Distribution*. The power distribution grid in most of the world's leading economies is in a sorry state – losses over this 'leaky' old infrastructure mean that, for every unit of power we consume at the 'plug', three units need to be generated at the power plant. Ergo the quickest way to cut energy consumption and the associated carbon emissions by a third (or close to it) would be to install a smart grid – an intelligent network that anticipates and distributes power according to need from a multitude of generation sources, which could include variable and unpredictable wind, solar and local generators. Deliciously complicated, smart grid is a hot prospect for investors and start-ups in clean tech. National targets for smart grid have been set and contracts are being placed. The timescales of ROI are reassuringly like those of the ICT sector and, in addition to benefiting successful new entrants, smart grid is set to benefit established companies such as Landis+Gyr and Cisco as they turn their companies' traditional strengths – in metering and communications in these cases – to address new challenges.

And possibly a fourth

There's a fourth sector, services, which I will take the risk of including. As the clean tech sector develops from plans, ambitions and announcements into real deployments, I expect to see superb business opportunities develop in the provision of services. Installing, maintaining and upgrading all the new infrastructure discussed above and providing outsourced energy management services to homes and businesses are obvious examples. More unusual could be the renting of carbon-emitting products to consumers. From cars to computers, outright ownership may become too expensive as the cost of carbon embedded in the manufacturing process and end-of-life disposal starts to be reflected in the price of things that we have traditionally owned outright.

Clean tech lessons – it's the 3Rs

Clean tech is still in its infancy, and it is still too early for any conclusive lessons to have been learnt about investment in the sector. However, there is clearly a checklist of considerations that should be applied to filter clean tech opportunities. Reassuringly, that takes us back to the basics of the 3Rs: regulation, ROI timescale and replaceability.

The role of government *regulation* makes clean tech special and different. Investors and CEOs need to critically appraise the regulatory sensitivities of their business model.

ROI timescales can take a very long time, and there are few data points on consumer adoption to refer back to. Like communications, sustainable energy will be commoditized, and when more than 30 per cent of our power comes from renewables its value and price will fall.

Finally, clean tech is emerging as a sector in a globalized economy, so the specific opportunities need to be assessed in terms of their *replaceability* in the global value chain. For example, is it smart to build a wind farm in the south-west of England if marine renewable energy is further ahead and likely to be a cheaper import from Denmark?

Clean tech poses complex problems and requires sophisticated solutions, and few 'investment rules' have been proven. However, with the smart money flowing towards clean tech, I predict that more than half of the world's next 50 billionaires will make their money in this sector. The challenge is to see how many of these we can help to come from the UK.

Simon Bond is Director of the Bath Ventures Innovation Centre, the University of Bath's commercialization group. The Innovation Centre helps accelerate the development of technology-based start-up companies, both from the University's research base and from the private sector. Simon is also the founder of: Silicon South West, a network for the region's semiconductor designers and engineers; Low Carbon South West, a network for clean tech start-ups; and the open Mobile Innovation Camp, a network for mobile device application developers. Contact Simon Bond (tel: +44 (0)1225 388682; e-mail: s.a.bond@bath.ac.uk; website: www.bath.ac.uk/bathventures).

2.3

Oceans of potential

The resource is enormous, but how do you generate returns? What are the challenges for investors in moving beyond proof of concept? ***Tony Lewis, Raymond Alcorn*** *and* ***Mark Healy*** *at the Hydraulics and Maritime Research Centre at University College Cork discuss the birth of a new industry in our oceans.*

Wave energy and tidal current energy, collectively termed ocean energy, are currently enjoying significant interest from developers, investors and governments. The immense potential and opportunity has been recognized, and advances in technology and the focus on developing renewable technologies have brought ocean energy to the cusp of commercial reality, presenting attractive opportunities for investors and developers alike.

What needs to be done now to commercialize ocean energy and generate returns for developers, investors and the environment?

Potentially enormous resource meets growing drivers

The potential ocean energy resource certainly justifies its development. Wave energy is essentially a mass storage of wind energy, whilst tidal energy harnesses the bodily movement of water resulting from the gravitational pull between the moon and the earth. The International Energy Agency estimates a global resource of 8,000–80,000 TWh/year in wave energy and over 800 TWh/year in tidal current energy.[1] When compared to the 2007 world electricity production from all sources of 19,855 TWh,[2] it is clear that this is a very significant resource.

The effectiveness of available ocean energy technology dictates how much of this resource can be usefully harnessed. The World Energy Council has estimated that the economically exploitable market potential for wave energy electricity production is 140–750 TWh/year for current designs of devices when fully mature.[3] If potential improvements to existing devices are realized, this figure could rise to as high as 2,000 TWh/year, or approximately 10 per cent of current world electricity production.

It is clear that there are significant potential markets for wave and tidal stream energy generation equipment, as well as site development, construction, installation and operation services. Owing to uncertainties about future costs, estimates of the long-term potential market size of wave and tidal stream energy tend to be approximate. However, as an indication, consultants hired by the UK's Carbon Trust have estimated that the value of worldwide electricity revenues from wave and tidal stream projects could ultimately be £60 billion/year to £190 billion/year.[4] It is clear that this renewable source of energy presents a very significant opportunity for investors, and those in the sector that can succeed in commercializing the technology.

This large resource on the supply side is matched by significant drivers on the demand side. The macro-context for the global move towards renewable forms of energy has been well documented – security of supply (dwindling fossil fuel reserves, political supply risks) and global warming (statutory carbon reduction targets) being the two dominant factors. However, the particular drive to realize ocean energy is due to two main factors: the sheer opportunity of the renewable resource as outlined above, and the very valuable predictability factor relative to other renewable sources – wave energy is highly predictable days in advance, whilst tidal energy is fully predictable up to 100 years in advance. This is a significant advantage relative to other power-producing sources such as wind and solar, and could potentially be one of the most attractive, and hence valuable, sources of renewable power for grid operators.

Technical and non-technical challenges thus far

The marine environment is one of the most extreme environments for power conversion systems. It is a very delicate balancing act to engineer devices to resist the destructive forces and immense energy of waves and tides, whilst at the same time trying to harness that very same energy for conversion to electrical power. Secondly, these power stations have to be engineered to greater-than-normal levels of reliability and survivability, particularly given the extremely corrosive environment, as the difficulty of accessibility and repair means that any breakdowns can lead to major loss of income.

The challenges that have impeded the commercialization of ocean energy thus far can be classed as technical and non-technical. On the technical side, the resource has been proven and energy extraction has been proven – ocean energy devices have already successfully delivered power to the grid (eg Aquamarine, MCT, Oceanlinx, OpenHydro, OPT, Pelamis). However, survivability and commercial viability remain the two main technical challenges. Can these devices be engineered to produce power in an extreme environment on a long-term basis at a competitive cost? Cost reductions can principally be achieved by increasing efficiencies and reducing deployment and recovery costs and operation and maintenance costs.

The non-technical challenges to the commercialization of ocean energy largely revolve around the significant investor support that is needed owing to the capital-intensive nature of development. Nascent industries traditionally need government support and incentives in early development stages, and governments have been quite supportive of the industry in terms of development funding. However, the ocean energy industry, pre-commercial viability, has struggled to emerge in the absence of significant interim funding during the so-called 'valley of death'. This is the period between early-stage, low-level funding for proof of concept and later-stage utility-scale funding for pre-commercial devices. Many companies struggle to survive this period when significant commercial investor funding is badly needed. This is largely due to the fact that the long-term nature of development has not been appreciated. This has resulted in investment with either too-stringent timeline expectations leading to rushed development and subsequent problems, or drip-feed investment that has resulted in insufficient progress.

Finally, legal and administrative issues such as permitting, licences, environmental impact assessments and so on have also proven to be challenging for developers where statutory bodies have been slower than developers in reacting to the ocean energy opportunity.

Getting to commercialization and generating returns

'Smart' investment is needed to overcome these challenges and recognize the long-term nature of ocean energy development, but with potentially major returns for those who make the commitment. In the wind energy sector, for example, developer Airtricity was sold for €1.8 billion in February 2008 to utility SSE, less than 10 years after it was founded, representing a multiple of four times invested capital, and a 720 per cent increase over the initial equity fund-raising carried out in 2002.[5] Ocean energy, particularly at the 'valley of death' stage referred to above, needs investors who understand the technology and risk, but who are prepared to commit to long-term development for very significant potential returns.

What can investors do to identify the most promising ocean energy companies and technologies? Aside from standard due diligence, investors need to consider factors specific to ocean energy development. In developing the device, has the company followed an ocean energy development protocol for technical development? Non-adherence to the general format of this tried-and-tested system has consistently proven to be the downfall of many ocean energy developers. How does the developer rate against others in independent holistic reviews carried out by bodies such as the Carbon Trust or EPRI, or in evaluations such as the Hydraulics and Maritime Research Centre (HMRC)'s Developer Evaluation, which assesses every technical and non-technical aspect of ocean energy development?

For their part, developers need to work to actively reduce perceived and actual technical risk in an industry that is defined by risk. This means following and documenting thorough progression through the development protocol referred to above, and adhering to international engineering development standards. This meticulous but longer-term development ultimately leads to reduced technology risk, classification by bodies such as Lloyds and DNV, and resultant device insurance that is not only necessary but also encourages investors. With the resource and technology for extraction already proven, it is incumbent on developers now to engineer for cost and survivability. Presenting realistic assessments of the effectiveness and development stage of a technology to the outside world is also imperative. Realistic assessment enhances investor trust and confidence, and overestimating performance or timeliness in the past has been a problem that has hurt the credibility of the ocean energy industry. Finally, it could be suggested that developers should identify gaps or weaknesses in their technology and systems and seek to outsource or collaborate with other developers in order to produce effective prototypes sooner. The Marine Renewables Industry Association[6] in Ireland is an example of this, whereby industry players are addressing these issues and actively seeking opportunities for collaboration. In this industry, as with many others, it will most likely be those that are first to market, rather than those that eventually produce the perfect solution, that will prevail.

Governments with access to the ocean energy resource will need to provide support funding to developers from concept to commercialization. Feed-in tariffs and Renewables Obligation Certificates (ROCs) need to reward higher risk levels associated with a nascent industry for utilities and investors. Significant mid-stage funding is needed to support devices from proven concept to pre-commercial stage. A statutory one-stop shop is needed to minimize these administrative hurdles for criteria-meeting companies dealing with independent statutory bodies with sometimes differing time frames and objectives. Lessons can be learnt and partnerships should be developed with the wind industry, which struggled with similar problems for years, and is only now managing to secure one-stop-shop facilities that will ease planning problems whilst maintaining existing necessary stringent requirements. The Ocean Energy Development Unit[7] within the Sustainable Energy Authority of Ireland is an example of one such facility that has been established to address this challenge.

Dawning of an industry

Now is an exciting time for the ocean energy industry globally. A number of wave energy developers are approaching pre-commercial stage with increasing numbers of commercial and utility partners, whilst many are at earlier stages and are promising superior efficiency or reliability. In tidal energy, two developers are separately testing their first full-scale devices whilst selling the produced grid power in the process.

From an investor point of view, significant funding rounds for various ocean energy developers have successfully been closed recently, an extraordinary vote of confidence in an otherwise still-very-nervous capital market environment.

On the government side, those countries with significant ocean energy resources have recognized the opportunity and are providing significant support in what is now a race to secure ocean energy investment. In Europe, for example, where global ocean energy development is most concentrated, the governments of two of the countries with the most significant resources, the UK and Ireland, are both providing significant support to their ocean energy industries.

The UK has put in place a comprehensive suite of support for the marine energy industry, including up to £60 million to support the development of marine energy in the UK. This includes the £22 million Marine Renewables Proving Fund, complementing the existing Marine Renewables Development Fund, and a recently announced national Marine Energy Action Plan to develop the sector to 2030. The Crown Estate, which owns the UK seabed out to 12 nautical miles, has announced leasing agreements for 10 tidal and wave power schemes of up to 1,200 MW, costing up to £4 billion to install, for deployment in Scotland.

The Irish government is also providing significant funding to the Irish ocean energy sector. Over €26 million has been provided for developing the industry, including a national ocean test facility, a grid-connected wave test site on the west coast, a prototype fund, an ocean energy feed-in tariff, and the establishment of a national Ocean Energy Development Unit.

These are examples of countries recognizing that they are potentially the Middle East of ocean energy and need to capitalize on the opportunity to become world leaders for the development and supply of ocean energy devices. The EU, recognizing the unique ocean energy potential around its shores, is also providing significant support. The European Commission has recently announced calls for proposals to link EU-wide ocean energy R&D infrastructures such that developers can access all scales of testing with funding operated by the EU. HMRC has responded to this call and has proposed a collaborative research project with 28 partners, which is currently being evaluated.

Ocean energy certainly seems to be coming of age, with many factors and forces converging to provide the impetus and breakthroughs needed to finally reach commercialization. The opportunities for developers, investors and resource-rich countries are significant, with potentially great rewards for those that recognize the nature of ocean energy development.

Notes

[1] International Energy Agency (2007) *Energy Technologies at the Cutting Edge: International energy technology collaboration – IEA implementing agreements*, International Energy Agency, Paris.

[2] IEA 2007 Statistics, http://www.iea.org/stats/electricitydata.asp?COUNTRY_CODE=29.

[3] World Energy Council (2007) *Survey of Energy Resources 2007*, World Energy Council, London.

[4] Entec, 2005, reported in Carbon Trust (2006) *Future Marine Energy. Results of the Marine Energy Challenge: Cost competitiveness and growth of wave and tidal stream energy*, Carbon Trust, Witney.

[5] *Finance Magazine*, Ireland, September 2009, http://www.finance-magazine.com/display_article.php?i=8384&pi=142.

[6] http://www.mria.ie.

[7] http://www.sustainableenergyireland.com/Renewables/Ocean_Energy/Ocean_Energy_Development_Unit/.

The Hydraulics and Maritime Research Centre (HMRC) is a centre of excellence for ocean renewable energy and coastal engineering, providing support to the maritime industry as well as engineering R&D. The Centre is the designated National Ocean Test Facility for Ireland and is a semi-autonomous unit within the Department of Civil and Environmental Engineering at University College Cork. It provides infrastructure and research facilities to developers of ocean energy devices and coastal infrastructure. Since its establishment in 1979, the HMRC has undertaken a variety of fundamental and applied research projects, together with industrial design contracts. Contract research is also a major part of HMRC operations. Dr Tony Lewis is Director and founder of the HMRC, and has been involved in ocean energy since 1977. He is one of the founding members of the European Ocean Energy Association and has been a contracting partner on research contracts from a variety of European Commission Framework Programmes for nearly 20 years. He has been the Alternate Delegate for Ireland to the Ocean Energy Implementing Agreement under the auspices of the International Energy Agency (IEA) since 2003 and is coordinating lead author for the ocean energy chapter of the IPCC Fourth Assessment Report. Dr Raymond Alcorn is currently the Research Manager at the HMRC. He joined the HMRC from an Australian commercial wave energy company, where he spent four years as Head of Electrical Engineering, working on design, development, deployment and commissioning of full-scale wave energy plant. Originally an electrical engineer, he has been involved in wave energy for the past 15 years on various projects since obtaining his PhD in the field from Queen's University Belfast. Mark Healy is a research engineer at the HMRC and is involved in technical and commercial evaluation of ocean energy companies. He has previous experience as a research analyst with an Irish stockbroking firm and as a management consultant at an international financial services firm. He holds a BE and MEngSc in mechanical engineering from University College Dublin.

2.4

Gold rush or money pit?

***Brian Kennelly** at EarthEnergy adds up the numbers in microgeneration.*

Any textbook analysis of the market conditions for building-related renewable energy technologies will forecast an exponential market growth. The UK has a legally binding commitment for 15 per cent of our energy to come from renewable sources by 2020, which includes heating and transport fuels as well as electricity.

Over the past 10 years a number of government policies and regulations have been introduced to drive market behaviour, and these are a combination of sticks and carrots, some more effective than others. However, none has yet created the acceleration of growth necessary to meet the targets.

The typical market growth curve of any new product or technology goes through the phases of innovators, early adopters, early majority, late majority and laggards, and this model is just as appropriate for microgeneration. However, microgeneration technologies are not an emotional purchase of a 'must have' gadget that will improve our lives or impress our friends. They are an expensive, technically difficult purchase that is typically made under some form of regulatory duress and impossible to justify using normal financial models. This is why we are still languishing in the 'innovators' sector of the growth curve.

Why do I say this? The capital cost of any microgeneration technology is significantly higher than the conventional alternative and, whilst there will be ongoing cost savings typically through reduced energy bills, most technologies will take over 10 years to repay the original investment. We are a credit-based consumer society – have it now and pay for it later – and all renewable energy technologies are the complete opposite of this – pay for it now and benefit later. We all have limited credit availability, and the tendency is to spend what we have on a new car, kitchen or holiday, something

	2002	2003	2004	2005	2006	2007	2008	2009	2010	2011	2012	2013	2014	2015	2016	2017	2018	2019	2020
Building regulations	Baseline year				20% reduction c/w 2002				further 25% reduction						zero carbon				
'Merton Rule' PPS22			10/15/20% renewable energy/carbon reduction on new build – not enforced widely																
PPS1 – sustainable dev				not enforced widely															
Energy Efficiency Commitment (EEC1)	off-gas/priority group																		
Energy Efficiency Commitment (EEC2)				off-gas/priority group															
Carbon Emissions Reduction Target (CERT)							off-gas/priority group												
Clearskies grants		householders & communities																	
Low Carbon buildings Programme phase 1					Grants for householders														
Low Carbon buildings Programme phase 2						Grants for non-commercial organizations													
Code for Sustainable Homes																			
Private Sector									L3 – 25% saving			L4 – 44% saving			L6 – zero carbon				
Public Sector						L3 – 25% saving			L4 – 44% saving			L6 – zero carbon							
Energy Performance Certificate																			
Private Sector									for conditioned bldgs when built/sold										
Public Sector							Requirement to 'improve' stock												
Decent Homes				Whole house controllable heating															
Fuel Poverty				Eradication by 2010!															
Feed in tariffs (FIT)									£/kWh generation meter/export meter										
Renewable Heat Incentive (RHI)										£/kWh deemed/metered									
Carbon Reduction Commitment (CRC)									Energy Assessment/reduction & carbon trading – big fines for non-compliance										
Zero Carbon non-dom bldgs																			
Scenario 1 – off site rich												30%			37%			44%	
Scenario 2 – balancing on/off site												44%			49%			54%	
Scenario 3 – on site rich												44%			53%			63%	
Big stick																			
Small stick																			
Carrot																			

Figure 2.4.1 Timeline of drivers (carrots and sticks) to encourage uptake of building integrated renewable energy technologies

that improves our lives, not a utilitarian purchase such as a heating system that will take over 10 years to pay for itself. Unfortunately (for us in the industry), organizational behaviour tends to mirror this consumer behaviour, with few organizations looking beyond a three- or five-year horizon.

The various grant mechanisms introduced over the years have softened the blow of purchasing microgeneration to some degree, but I can't say they have actually prompted the purchase in the first place. Purchases are far more likely to be driven by personal choice (the enthusiastic amateur) or regulatory requirement, such as a condition of planning permission, the so-called 'Merton Rule' that was first introduced by the London Borough of Merton to require reduced carbon footprints in new developments. Unfortunately, it seems that far too often developers can bulldoze their way through this relatively weak 'stick'.

Dawn of a new era?

From reading the above, you may well think that the renewables industry is stuck in a bit of a rut, servicing a few small niche clients, the high-net-wealth individuals and the target-driven public sector.

But no, we really are at the dawn of a new era, and I'm not being melodramatic; after three years of gestation, the government is introducing feed-in tariff mechanisms to pay individuals and organizations alike for all the renewable energy they produce or use. This will lead to a sea change in the purchasing environment, which will create phenomenal growth in the market, developing an industry 20 or 30 times its current size by 2020.

The feed-in tariff (FiT) scheme started in April 2010 and offers a fixed payment per kilowatt-hour of electricity generated on-site from renewable technologies such as photovoltaic solar panels, wind turbines, hydro-generation, anaerobic digestion and micro-CHP (combined heat and power). The aim is for the FiT to offer standard renewable projects a 5–8 per cent return on investment.

The Renewable Heat Incentive (RHI), due to start on 1 April 2011, is even more generous, intended to offer a 12 per cent rate of return on the additional cost of the renewables over and above a conventional heating system. To keep the scheme simple to administer, the payments for small and medium-scale installations will be based on the calculated (or deemed) heat energy requirements of the building rather than through expensive metering. This also gives absolute certainty over the level of income generated over the life of the tariff.

The importance of these two revenue streams is that they transform the purchase of renewable energy technologies from expensive costs to investment opportunities.

Easy as 1, 2, 3...

There are three ways to invest in renewable energy to benefit from the new incentive schemes.

Individuals

Anyone can invest in renewable energy technologies for their own home, to provide electricity, heat and/or hot water and benefit from rates of return between 6 and 12 per cent. This revenue is tax free, so for a 40 per cent tax bracket investor installing say a ground source heat pump this provides an effective rate of return of about 20 per cent on the investment.

For example, a typical four-bedroom detached house of about 150 square metres would require a 9-kW ground source heat pump costing about £15,000, assuming a borehole-based system. This house would require about 17,000 kWh of heat energy and about 4,000 kWh for hot water, and given an RHI of 7 pence per kWh would generate an annual income of £1,470 every year for 23 years. With an additional fuel saving of about £350 compared to an oil boiler, this represents a total benefit of £1,820 per year, giving a total return on investment of £41,860 tax free!

Companies

Entrepreneurs may wish to invest in a renewable energy installation company. Currently there are only about 400 installers registered with the government's Microgeneration Certification Scheme (MCS), membership of which is a prerequisite for installers to attract payment from the incentive schemes. With the anticipated market growth required to meet the 2020 renewable energy targets, this is going to be an exciting time, with the potential for new companies to enter the market and for existing construction industry companies to diversify into renewables.

However, I would urge potential investors to act with some caution. Other European countries have gone through similar periods of accelerated growth only for the industry to be destroyed by unskilled or unscrupulous installers mis-selling products and/or leaving a trail of poor-quality installations that either don't work properly or at worst are dangerous. This kind of experience can put industry growth back years, and the UK cannot afford for such a knock-back to its growth plans for renewable energy to meet the legally binding targets. This is why regulation is so important and why the industry must produce technical standards that clearly define the level of work and skill clients can expect and provide a means to differentiate between the professionals and the less scrupulous players.

Anyone contemplating investment in a company undertaking renewable energy installations needs to carry out appropriate due diligence to ensure the company really understands the technology it is installing and is working in accordance with industry codes of practice and guidelines.

Investors

The third, and most innovative, investment opportunity in the microgeneration sector has yet to be established, but I believe will be the key to the mass roll-out of these technologies. The challenge is to address the existing housing stock, a large proportion of which is in public sector ownership of one kind or another through local authorities, housing associations and arm's-length management organizations, as well as registered charities. All of these social landlords are facing spending restrictions and belt tightening as we come out of recessions, and they have limited means to borrow money to retrofit renewable energy solutions to their houses. The solution is to form special purpose vehicles (SPVs) with private sector funding, which can install, own and operate renewable energy installations and reap the benefits of the FiT and/or RHI. This provides a win–win situation; the tenants access low-cost heat or free electricity, the landlords achieve some of their carbon-saving targets, and the investors achieve a healthy return on their investment. I see this as particularly attractive to pension investments, owing to the certainty and longevity of the revenue stream.

Investors taking advantage of this opportunity will want to team up with established installers and manufacturers having a good track record in the sector and the confidence of the client base. The key will be the degree of certainty that the equipment installed will perform correctly and remain relatively maintenance free for the duration of the tariff.

Don't all rush at once

Over the last few years a number of entrepreneurial investors have viewed microgeneration as the next dotcom. Unfortunately, to date this vision has not been fulfilled, and indeed the heat microgeneration industry finds itself in a bit of a limbo while waiting for the RHI to come into being. My advice would be to tread carefully, ensure you know the provenance of the company you are contemplating involvement with, and above all beware of the unskilled or unscrupulous.

That said, there are few investment opportunities that bring such a good rate of return with such a high degree of certainty – it has to be worth a punt!

Brian Kennelly is Managing Director of EarthEnergy Limited, the UK's leading geothermal company specializing in the design and installation of ground source heat pump systems for the heating and cooling of buildings. EarthEnergy has been operating since 1995 and has pioneered the use of heat pumps in the social housing sector in addition to its core business of larger-scale installations for schools, hospitals, offices and other developments. Contact Brian Kennelly (tel: 01326 310650; e-mail: b.kennelly@earthenergy.co.uk; website: www.earthenergy.co.uk).

2.5

Clean energy in the emerging economies

*Corporations in China, Brazil, India and South Africa are making a significant move into clean tech, reports **Kate Levick**, Head of Government Partnerships, Carbon Disclosure Project.*

The global politics of climate change have altered following the COP15 negotiations at Copenhagen in late 2009. The largest emerging economies showed a new assertiveness and willingness to make commitments, as demonstrated by the pledges captured in the Copenhagen Accord. The world gained a new acronym – the BASIC countries – to refer to the leading emerging economies, Brazil, China, India and South Africa.

Companies in BASIC countries are leading the way on investment in clean energy

In 2010 CDP published a study of clean energy investment trends among companies in the BASIC countries. The research was commissioned by the Renewable Energy and Energy Efficiency Partnership, a partnership of some 300 organizations, including 46 governments, which was established at the 2002 World Summit on Sustainable Development in Johannesburg. CDP analysed responses from companies in each country, and commissioned interviews to draw out insights into the relationship between company action and policy. The report is available at www.cdproject.net.

Companies in the BASIC countries are making large investments both in energy efficiency and in renewable energy. The scale of investment is particularly impressive in China, which in 2009 overtook the United States to become the world's largest investor in renewable energy, with overall investment of US$34.6 billion.[1] Several of the companies interviewed by CDP reported recent investment in energy-efficient manufacturing plant that equated to billions of dollars in investment, while Gree Electric Appliances reported spending US$145 million specifically on production efficiencies and product efficiency improvements. China Vanke Company reported spending US$5 million to install solar photovoltaic equipment on corporate premises, while the Beijing Deqingyuan Agricultural Science and Technology Company reported investing US$8.8 million to generate electricity from agricultural waste.

The scale of investment varies significantly across the different BASIC countries, reflecting differences between the size and growth rates of their respective economies. Out of the four countries the lowest levels of spend are seen in South Africa. However, it was noted in the course of the research that companies based there reported seeing energy security as a very high priority, owing to electricity supply problems experienced by South Africa in 2009 and expected future price rises. Therefore, increased levels of corporate investment in energy efficiency and renewable energy are expected in the coming months and years.

The Carbon Disclosure Project (CDP) enables companies all over the world to report climate change information to their stakeholders. The first annual CDP information request was issued in 2003 to the world's largest 500 companies. Today, 2,500 organizations in some 60 countries report through CDP, which represents 534 institutional investors with assets under management of US$64 trillion, as well as 50 large multinational purchasing companies and 18 UK government departments.

One of the most striking aspects of CDP's rapid growth has been increased quantity and quality of reporting by companies in countries that did not take emissions reduction targets under the Kyoto Protocol. These states typically did not move as fast as their richer peers to put national climate change legislation in place, but responses to CDP show that their major companies were beginning to think about climate change even in the absence of strong domestic regulation.

What drives companies to invest in clean energy?

When companies in BASIC countries were asked why they had made investments in energy efficiency and renewable energy, the most common answer was that these investments reflected their corporate environmental or social responsibility policy. Internal policy is not formed in a vacuum and reflects a mixture of financial and economic considerations, brand awareness and expectation of future requirements by customers, regulators and other stakeholders. It can be seen to reflect thought leadership and strategic foresight on the part of businesses and to be a proactive, rather than reactive, driver of behaviour. Internal policy on these issues can be very strong; for example, the China Vanke Company, from the real estate sector, said that '"Green Company" is the company's mission and its path to future competitiveness.'

Following internal policy, cost reduction and energy security were also very frequently cited as drivers for action. This was not surprising in relation to energy efficiency, since these projects will typically have short payback periods and will also reduce energy consumption. It was striking that these drivers were also commonly cited for renewable energy investments, even though this type of investment can be seen in industrialized countries as both risky and expensive.

What is the role of policy as a driver for corporate investment?

It is clear that government policy plays a strong role in corporate clean energy investment decisions, but it is not the only factor that companies take into account. For example, in South Africa companies see volatile electricity supply and pricing primarily as a business issue, although they are also very aware of, and interested in the effects of, new policy measures that are being put in place by the national government to address the situation.

In Brazil the response by companies to historical and current energy policy is clear. Many companies reporting to CDP in 2009 mentioned using renewable fuel in corporate vehicle fleets, reflecting the government's long-standing support for ethanol production from sugar cane. A number of the interviewed companies referenced some kind of engagement in government-backed renewable energy auctions administered by the Agência Nacional de Energia Elétrica (ANEEL) or in energy efficiency investment projects mandated under electricity supply regulations. New policies that will affect corporate behaviour are expected under the National Climate Change Plan, especially following Brazil's ambitious emissions reduction commitments made at the COP15 negotiations in Copenhagen and confirmed in the Copenhagen Accord.

The role of policy on corporate investment in China is an interesting one. Perhaps more than in the other countries studied, some companies are attentive to high-level policy signals and incorporate these into corporate policy without necessarily requiring detailed regulation. One of the companies interviewed (from the household appliances sector) said: 'Policies imply that the improvement of the product's performance in energy and environment and the improvement of level of energy production and resources utilization have become a must. Enterprises, as the main body of responsibility, must perform the duty.'

China has historically set itself ambitious national targets for energy efficiency and renewable energy generation but has taken a pragmatic approach to regulation, including a number of voluntary measures and a focus on the largest companies that have the greatest impacts. Perhaps because of the success of these measures, some companies are now seeking more specific rules and requirements. For example, the Beijing Deqingyuan Agricultural Science and Technology Company noted that: 'At present, the government encourages the voluntary actions of enterprises, but there are no relevant standards yet.' For renewable energy, China Merchants Bank again confirmed the importance of overall policy direction as well as the role of specific measures, saying: 'All these laws and regulations have shown the government's great determination in developing low carbon economy and renewable energy. The incentive policies have drawn China Merchants Bank to realize "Green is Green" – there are tremendous opportunities for a low carbon economy.'

Future developments

If there is a single message to be taken away from this research, it is that companies in the largest emerging economies are making sizeable investments in clean technology and are taking a strategic approach to this type of investment. Given that energy security and cost are expected to become a more important business issue all over the world, and that national policy is increasingly addressing both these issues and the need to reduce emissions to fight climate change, it seems safe to assume that this trend will continue. We can expect to see a great deal more action on clean energy from companies in emerging markets and should not be surprised if their investments start to compete with or overshadow those seen in the industrialized economies.

In the words of James Cameron, Executive Director and Vice-Chairman of Climate Change Capital:

> *It has always been vain and arrogant to suggest that the technological solutions to climate change will inevitably emerge from the so-called developed nations. Given the right policy frameworks and the capacity to take science and engineering skills and attach them to huge domestic as well as global markets, there is every chance that the technological breakthrough that the world requires will emerge from these so-called developing countries.*

Note

[1] Pew Charitable Trusts (2010) *G20 Clean Energy Factbook*, Pew Charitable Trusts, Philadelphia, PA.

Kate Levick has coordinated the Carbon Disclosure Project's relationships with policy makers around the world since 2008, having previously worked on international climate policy issues at BP and for the UK government's Office of Climate Change. For more information please contact kate.levick@cdproject.net.

Part 3

How the market works

3.1

The policy framework

***Roger Salomone**, Energy and Regulation Adviser at the EEF, puts the UK as a centre for clean tech under the microscope.*

Low carbon technology is becoming big business, and the competition to capture it will be fierce. Variously described as 'clean tech', 'low carbon' or 'green', this emerging sector cuts across the economy and encompasses a wide variety of industries at different stages of development. Mature industries such as energy efficiency and nuclear power are receiving a renewed impetus. Areas that were once modest parts of traditional industries – such as wind power, hybrid vehicles, alternative transport fuels and green building technologies – are rapidly maturing into multibillion-pound industries in their own right. Most dramatically, whole new industries such as marine renewables and carbon capture and storage (CCS) are beginning to emerge.

The UK clean tech market is already worth more than £100 billion per year, and manufacturing accounts for more than 30 per cent of its value, compared with less than 15 per cent for the wider economy. Amongst some of the fastest-growing areas the share is higher still. For example, manufacturing accounts for nearly 40 per cent of economic activity in the renewable energy sector. Most significantly, the UK clean tech market is forecast to grow at a recession-busting 5 per cent per year over the next few years to top £150 billion by 2015. This is four times as fast as the UK economy as a whole, which is projected to grow by around only 12 per cent over the entire period.

Unsurprisingly, the UK is not alone in its aspiration to profit from the transition to a low carbon economy and the fast-growing industries it is generating. International competition is already fierce and will probably intensify in the future. Many countries around the world, particularly the advanced economies and the rapidly industrializing economies of Asia, are pursuing ambitious plans to develop strong clean tech industries.

Governments are devoting significant financial resources to establishing home-grown industries and are actively courting inward investment.

South Korea provides a striking example. Spending in the clean tech sector accounts for $30 billion, or more than 80 per cent, of the three-year $38 billion economic stimulus package Seoul deployed in response to the global downturn. In July 2009, South Korea announced a further $85 billion investment in the sector in the form of a five-year investment programme to catalyse the development of low carbon industries such as hybrid and electric vehicles. Government investment in clean tech over this period will top 2 per cent of GDP as the country pursues its target of quintupling its global market share in the sector to 8 per cent.

A country's business environment is created by a complex interplay of a wide range of financial, legal, political, regulatory and cultural factors. Through a combination of more strategic industrial policy, better joined-up thinking from government and active engagement from industry, the UK could yet position itself as the premier location for the low carbon industrial revolution. To create a compelling business environment for clean tech companies, government needs to ensure that skills, tax and industrial policies are all pulling in the same direction. Failure to do so could leave the UK with the worst of both words – incurring the costs of the transition to a low carbon economy without taking advantage of the benefits.

Skills

A good supply of the right skills will be a major consideration for clean tech companies when they decide where to locate, invest or expand – especially at the crucial time when their skills needs change as they move from niche technology developer to volume manufacturer.

The UK will need a mix of generic and specialist skills to attract and sustain clean tech industries. A strong supply of core skills essential to modern manufacturing will be required, such as the capability to research, design, engineer and commercialize new technologies. In addition, specialist, sector-specific skills, such as nuclear engineering, will be needed.

Establishing a low carbon industrial base will not depend on developing a wide range of entirely new skill sets. Rather, core technical skills already central to many industries will need to be refined and applied in new situations and to different types of products.

Take CCS, for example, which will largely draw on expertise already available and widely used in the oil and gas, chemicals and power generation industries – subsurface and offshore engineering, the transportation of gas by pipeline and the separation of CO_2 from other gases.

The UK already has clusters of strengths in specialized skills relevant to the clean tech sector, such as offshore engineering capabilities focused on the east coasts of England and Scotland, which are transferable to marine renewables and CCS. In addition, it has strengths in areas of automotive engineering that are central to the development of hybrid and electric vehicles, such as powertrain technology and control systems.

However, future demand for most specialist skills cannot be easily or accurately predicted, especially in the rapidly evolving industries that currently characterize much of the clean tech sector. It is highly probable that new but unforeseeable specialisms and vocations will emerge as the new market evolves. What is most important is that the UK has a skills system that can respond to the market's emerging needs, in terms of both any new qualifications needed and the provider network to deliver them. Our skills architecture, as it currently stands, is not fully equipped to do this. Companies, large and small, are actively taking steps to meet their own skills requirements, but upskilling and reskilling people for clean tech industries will require flexibility in funding and qualifications. After years of policy changes, the skills system is in need of simplification. Employers are often confused by the sheer number of advisory and planning bodies in the skills system, many with seemingly overlapping remits.

Regardless of architecture, governance or funding levels, a demand-led system will deliver results only if employers are proactive and engage with training providers about the needs of their businesses and employees. Manufacturers can now explore an increasing number of opportunities available to engage with and benefit from the vocational training system.

Tax

Industry depends on activities that are sensitive to taxation, such as capital investment and innovation. Modern manufacturing is capital- and research-intensive: companies add value, create wealth and stay competitive by investing regularly in state-of-the-art machinery, product design and R&D.

This is especially true of emerging industries, which account for much of the clean tech sector, where many of these investment-intensive processes account for a disproportionate share of overall activity. Therefore, the tax system's treatment of capital expenditure and R&D can have a significant influence on the business case and the funds available for the investment needed to develop a clean tech industrial base.

In early 2010, the rate of corporation tax in the UK is 28 per cent, with a lower rate of 21 per cent applying to 'small' companies. At first glance, the headline rate might appear reasonably competitive: it is one of the lowest amongst the major industrialized economies and only a fraction above the OECD average of 27 per cent. In addition, the UK is among the minority of OECD countries to have a separate, lower rate for small companies, which often act as key innovators in an economy.

However, the competitiveness of UK corporation tax has progressively eroded over the past decade. In 1999, the UK rate was below the global, OECD and EU averages. But the situation is reversing, and the UK rate is above the average in each of these areas. The loss of competitiveness against some of the industrializing economies of East Asia has been especially marked and could be significant in the clean tech context. China, South Korea and some of the ASEAN countries are currently significant export destinations for UK clean tech companies and could offer attractive growth prospects in the future. However, many countries in the region have cut their tax rates aggressively to attract inward investment.

Cutting-edge manufacturing, in any industry, is dominated by the capital costs of plant and machinery. A major report on tax published by EEF in March 2009 highlighted how the UK's corporate tax system actively discourages the types of investments that will underpin the manufacturing products for the emerging clean tech market. The UK system fails to recognize the nature and importance of capital investment in modern manufacturing.

From an international perspective, tax allowances for R&D in the UK are reasonably competitive. In 2000, the UK introduced R&D tax credits for SMEs and extended the scheme to larger companies in 2002. The level of the tax credit available was increased in 2007. In 2010, the credits allow large companies to reduce their corporate tax liability by 130 per cent of the value of qualifying R&D spend. SMEs can reduce their tax liability by 175 per cent or, for companies not in profit, can opt to receive a cash payment of £24 for every £100 spent on R&D.

Traditional measures of tax competitiveness, such as the level of corporation tax and the level of allowances for business-critical activities, are often less applicable or relevant to early-stage companies. In particular, pre-revenue companies that have yet to commercialize their technologies, let alone generate a profit, are not eligible for corporation tax. Hence allowances that can be offset against this liability are less significant (although they could become an important consideration if and when the company starts earning revenues and making a profit). However, early-stage companies frequently play an important role in developing low carbon technologies, and there is scope to make better use of the tax system to encourage their activities. Financing the development of a technology can be especially challenging for small, loss-making companies that have yet to take their product to market.

Under the current tax system, loss-making companies can build up an allowance equivalent to their accumulated tax losses to offset against future corporation tax liabilities when they become profitable. Arguably, this allowance would be more valuable to loss-making technology developers if they could access it earlier. EEF has already called for the introduction of a 'green bond' scheme that would make this possible.

Under the scheme, loss-making developers of low carbon technologies would be able to monetize the value of the future tax allowance generated by their accumulated losses by selling bonds to investors. As well as providing financial support to companies when they most need it, the scheme would provide them with a potential alternative to ceding a controlling stake in the company in exchange for conventional equity finance.

Facilitating industrial development

Bringing new technologies to market is typically a lengthy, costly and risky process for private enterprise. Significant investments in capital and research need to be sustained over a number of years (or even decades) before revenues, let alone profits, are realized. This situation is especially challenging for SMEs, which often lack the deep balance sheets, alternative revenue streams and access to credit that larger businesses may enjoy.

Recent UK governments have shown an aversion to 'picking winners'. This has been born of the belief that it is more efficient to let the market decide which technologies to back and has been compounded by a fear of wasting resources by backing technologies that fail to live up to expectations.

However, the risk runs both ways, especially when dealing with early-stage technologies. Failure to back those that are potential 'winners' means the UK could miss out on being at the forefront of lucrative new clean tech industries such as marine renewables or plastic electronics. Despite the advantages that the UK held in terms of geography and early research, for example, it is Denmark, Spain and Germany that, by providing long-term support, are the European countries that have actually developed turbine manufacturing industries. The launch of a Low Carbon Industrial Strategy in July 2009 was a sign that policy is shifting in identifying areas of potential comparative advantage for the UK.

Innovation support

The UK and EU regulatory environments have significant attractions for clean tech innovation. Like most advanced economies, the UK has strong and well-enforced intellectual property rights (IPR) that protect the interests of innovative businesses. This is not necessarily the case everywhere. In a recent EEF survey, 46 per cent of respondents cited the protection of IPR as a challenge when operating in low-cost countries.

A key part of the EU's response to climate change is the use of product standards to drive clean tech innovation. For example, the EU is setting the pace in emissions limits for motor vehicles and has been rolling out a suite of legislation that sets efficiency standards for products with a significant impact on energy use. Being located in an $18 trillion economy at the forefront of setting environmental product standards could be a considerable spur for clean tech innovation.

Innovation is a much broader range of activities than research, development and demonstration (RD&D). Standard measures of RD&D often fail to capture areas of innovation that are crucial to manufacturing, such as process re-engineering and product design. However, it is still an important part of innovation in low carbon industries, which makes government funding for RD&D a key metric of business support for the clean tech sector.

Government support for RD&D in the UK has been relatively modest by international standards. In 2007, UK government funding for clean energy RD&D represented 0.01 per cent of GDP, half the OECD average of 0.02 per cent. The governments of the most supportive countries spend significantly more. For example, France spent four times as much (0.04 per cent), South Korea five times (0.05 per cent) and Japan seven times as much (0.07 per cent).

Public procurement

A potentially powerful but underexploited area of innovation policy in the UK is public procurement. The sheer size of the budget suggests that there should be ample opportunity to support low carbon goods and services through public procurement.

The Department for Transport's Low Carbon Vehicle Procurement Programme (LCVPP) is an example of the creative use of public procurement in the clean tech sector. The LCVPP uses the public sector's purchasing power to help accelerate the commercialization of low carbon vehicle technologies. Clear performance criteria for a low carbon van were set out, and the private sector has been given the freedom to develop a solution. The incentive is a commitment from the public sector to order a meaningful number of the winning product.

The LCVPP model should be replicated in other areas. Low carbon heating is a potential candidate. The public sector, in its broadest sense, has a vast estate with numerous buildings across the country. All these buildings need to be heated. A procurement programme to provide innovative, reliable and cost-effective low carbon heating systems for deployment in the public sector should be launched. This would provide UK heating system manufacturers with the opportunity to secure enough orders to develop their businesses and scale up production.

Planning

Difficulty obtaining planning permission for energy infrastructure in the UK has for a number of years widely been seen as a major barrier to changing the energy system. For example, applying for planning permission has typically been a long and uncertain process for wind farm developers in the UK. Unless it is addressed, this barrier to deployment could undermine the UK's ambitions to develop a clean tech industrial base. Vestas, the world's largest turbine manufacturer, cited the detrimental impact of the planning process on the UK onshore wind market when it announced the closure of its blade facility on the Isle of Wight in August 2009.

Under the Planning Act 2008, vital, long-overdue reforms to the planning process for major infrastructure projects were implemented, including power generation facilities with capacities of 50 MW or more. A presumption in favour of a range of different types of energy infrastructure will strengthen the UK's manufacturing base in planning-sensitive industries where domestic orders could be significant, such as nuclear power.

Conclusion

To complement the leadership it has shown in developing policies to reduce CO_2 emissions, government must champion a business environment that encourages and attracts the companies that are developing the solutions to climate change. Industrial policy has lagged behind initiatives to cut emissions and increase consumption of renewable energy. Until very recently no strategy was in place to exploit the industrial opportunities in the clean tech sector.

On balance, despite encouraging recent progress, the UK remains a long way from being the best country in the world for manufacturers of low carbon technology. However, there are strong foundations that can be built upon. Through a combination of a more strategic industrial policy, better joined-up thinking from government and active engagement from industry, the UK could yet position itself as the premier location for the low carbon industrial revolution. To create a compelling business environment for clean tech companies, government needs to ensure that skills, tax and industrial policies are all pulling in the same direction.

The EEF's report Under the Microscope: Is UK plc Ready for Low Carbon? *was published in November 2009. For more details, contact Roger Salomone at rsalomone@eef.org.uk. EEF is an employers' organization with over 6,000 members that is dedicated to the future of manufacturing. All its activities are designed to help manufacturing business evolve, innovate and compete in a fast-changing world. With a unique combination of business services, government representation and industry intelligence, no other organization is better placed to provide the skills, knowledge and networks manufacturing business needs to thrive. Further details are available from www.eef.org.uk.*

3.2

Sustainable investing

*The market in capital for clean tech has grown well beyond the pioneer stage, says **Penny Shepherd** MBE, Chief Executive UKSIF – the sustainable investment and finance association.*

We are on the brink of a new industrial revolution. Governments and communities worldwide are looking for ways to live successfully within environmental limits. Sustainable investors have been backing the best options for over 20 years, but now the pace and scale have accelerated. In the last few years, a new generation of investors has emerged. They want to back smart innovations that will make them money. But that isn't the whole story. Many also want to create a new economy that supports healthy societies and protects the environment. They reckon that will not only grow their wealth but protect it too – and leave a safer world for their children.

Plentiful rewards

The opportunity is clear. The threat of climate change and its repercussions across the world is driving changes not only to public policy, but also to business and consumer behaviour. The UK government, like others across the world, has national targets and international obligations to meet and, in terms of climate change solutions, by no means all the answers. Major businesses also recognize the need to invest in making their operations more sustainable. So the door's wide open for today's new generation of innovators, investors and entrepreneurs to come up with winning solutions – and, for those who are successful, the rewards should be plentiful.

The chance to reap those rewards was first spotted by far-sighted people in the City more than two decades ago. As far back as 1988, for example, the Jupiter Ecology Fund became the first UK green fund available to the public, while Impax Asset Management was created as a specialist environmental investment manager in 1998 and so has been 'investing for a cleaner future' for a dozen years. But now, as governments the world over have woken to the fact that sustainable development is an urgent necessity rather than a vague long-term aspiration, the opportunities and returns are there for the taking.

So who is investing?

Wealthy private investors have become a substantive force in the sustainable investment market. Indeed, the European Sustainable Investment Forum (Eurosif) has forecast that by 2012 sustainable investments will represent 12 per cent of the portfolios of wealthy European private investors, surpassing a trillion euros in total – unimaginable 20 years ago. According to Eurosif, this reflects both interest from successful entrepreneurs and inherited wealth that has moved to a younger generation.

Needless to say, leading wealth managers have responded. Indeed, some of the longest established have been among the earliest movers. Cazenove Capital Management traces its origins back to 1823. It has been identifying key sustainability themes for client investment since 2004. Rathbone Brothers, established in 1742, set up Rathbone Greenbank Investments to manage only ethical and responsible investments. Their team's sustainable investment track record dates back to 1992.

Meanwhile, a growing number of major pension funds are asking their fund managers to deliver clean technology investment portfolios. One such fund is the Universities Superannuation Scheme (USS), the pension fund for UK universities and other higher education institutions and one of the largest pension schemes in the UK. By November 2009, it had invested about £150 million[1] in clean technology and renewable energy. And a worldwide group of pension funds, including the UK Environment Agency's pension scheme, have commissioned Mercer, the investment consultancy, to study the implications of climate change for the types of investments they should hold in the future.

Introducing opportunities

So, today, clean technology investing has moved beyond the pioneers. A wide range of specialists are now matching clean tech business opportunities with investors. What are the areas of interest? They include renewable energy, water, waste and pollution control. The FTSE Environmental Markets Index series describes one classification. Although used specifically for stock market listed companies, it gives a good insight into the technologies seeking investment. Its classification is given in Table 3.2.1.

Different investment advisers and managers often specialize in different points in the investment chain. Some focus on early-stage investment, while others concentrate on larger or listed businesses further down the line. So an investor or entrepreneur seeking early-stage investment shouldn't expect this from a manager specializing only in stock market listed companies, or vice versa. But, at each stage, the service is essentially the same – interested investors need to be linked with the best opportunities.

Table 3.2.1 FTSE Environmental Markets Classification System

E1.0	RENEWABLE & ALTERNATIVE ENERGY
E1.1	Wind power generation equipment
E1.2	Solar energy generation equipment
E1.3	Other renewable equipment
E1.4	Renewable energy developers and independent power producers (IPPs)
E1.5	Biofuels
E1.6	Diversified renewable and alternative energy
E2.0	ENERGY EFFICIENCY
E2.1	Power network efficiency
E2.2	Industrial energy efficiency
E2.3	Buildings energy efficiency
E2.4	Transport energy efficiency
E2.5	Diversified energy efficiency
E3.0	WATER INFRASTRUCTURE & TECHNOLOGIES
E3.1	Water infrastructure
E3.2	Water treatment equipment
E3.3	Water utilities
E3.4	Diversified water infrastructure and technology
E4.0	POLLUTION CONTROL
E4.1	Pollution control solutions
E4.2	Environmental testing and gas sensing
E5.0	WASTE MANAGEMENT & TECHNOLOGIES
E5.1	Waste technology equipment
E5.2	Recycling and value added waste processing
E5.3	Hazardous waste management
E6.0	ENVIRONMENTAL SUPPORT SERVICES
E6.1	Carbon and other environmental assets trading
E6.2	Environmental Consultancies
E6.3	Diversified environmental

Source: FTSE Group, http://www.ftse.com/Indices/FTSE_Environmental_Markets_Index_Series/Downloads/FTSE_Environmental_Markets_Classification_System.pdf.

One specialist that matches business opportunities with providers of early start-up capital is ClearlySo, an online marketplace that arranges regular 'speed dating' events throughout the UK. At a typical gathering, each entrepreneur has to convince each investor that his or her venture is worthwhile, exciting and sound, and usually has five minutes in which to make the pitch. ecoConnect, a clean technology network, is another organization that supports this early stage.

For subsequent stages of investment, there are investment funds available for knowledgeable individuals. These may invest in very specific areas or be more broadly based. For example, the Triodos EIS Green Funds invest in a portfolio of sustainable UK companies in renewable energy generation and technology, energy efficiency, sustainable living, low carbon products and technology or waste recycling and reduction. The funds target companies with high growth potential that Triodos believes can deliver high returns to investors. A more focused option is Foresight Group's £22.5 million Foresight Sustainable UK Investment Fund. It is one of the largest EIS funds ever raised. It invests in clean tech infrastructure in the UK such as recycling, waste to energy and renewable energy. Invicta Capital's Invicta Biomass Fund is an even more specific choice. It invests directly into the development and operation of medium-sized biomass plants in Scotland.

The Five Fund Forum, organized by Sustainable World Capital and VB/Research, supports larger investment organizations. It helps them to select from well-established clean tech and renewable energy investment funds rather than investing directly in individual clean tech companies. The Forum holds its 'by invitation only' events in London, Amsterdam, Copenhagen and Zurich and covers a range of investment stages.

For those seeking to invest in companies listed on stock markets, the range of funds available has grown over time. Sustainable solutions funds may use a blend of environmental and social themes to select investments. The first sustainable water fund was launched in 2000, with the first clean energy fund available from 2001. Several climate change funds arrived in 2007. Some climate change funds invest in clean technology solutions, while others target companies that are leaders in managing their environmental impacts. The various approaches will tend to result in funds with different financial characteristics. As with any investment, it is important to look behind the label and understand the approach being offered by a specific fund.

Index tracking through unit trusts and exchange traded funds (ETFs) is also available, with a range of clean technology indexes launched over the last few years. The Osmosis Climate Solutions ETF, launched in February 2010, is just one instance of this trend.

Some investment managers offer investment strategies that go beyond stocks and shares. For example, Generation Investment Management (co-founded by Nobel laureate Al Gore) offers a Climate Solutions strategy that combines private investment in clean tech businesses with exposure to listed clean tech stocks; and the Cheviot Climate Assets Fund, from Cheviot Asset Management, invests in a global basket of bonds, commodities and equities across the themes of energy, food, health, resources and water.

More generally, the range of investment opportunities is growing. With food insecurity becoming a rising threat, agriculture funds are rising in importance. And sustainable forestry is of increasing interest as policy makers debate the role of forests in capturing carbon.

Today, sustainable investment boutiques are becoming particularly prominent. These small investment managers are being set up by City experts to focus specifically on the opportunities from clean technologies and other sustainable investments.

As the perils of climate change and resource scarcity become increasingly acknowledged by governments of all hues around the world, the signs are clear that low carbon and resource efficient innovation is the way forward. Today's public policies to reduce carbon and waste will be joined by tough measures to protect water and other natural resources. These will all drive the growing demand for winning technologies. The future of clean tech investment is by no means a California-style gold rush – but it *is* a sustained and sustainable opportunity to benefit financially from what are likely to be the most compelling investment opportunities in the coming decades. The bonus is that it should also help to build a better world.

Note

[1] $250 million (http://www.usshq.co.uk/UssInvestments/Responsibleinvestment/MarketWideInitiativesPublicPolicy/ClimateChange/Pages/default.aspx).

Penny Shepherd MBE is Chief Executive of UKSIF – the sustainable investment and finance association. She has over 30 years of experience in working with the finance sector, including over 15 years on sustainability and corporate responsibility issues. She has been a member of the Mayor of London's Sustainable Development Commission and spent 20 years in the computer industry assisting financial services and other companies. UKSIF, the sustainable investment and finance association, is a non-profit membership network with over 200 members. It promotes responsible investment and other forms of finance that support sustainable economic development, enhance quality of life and safeguard the environment. It organizes the annual National Ethical Investment Week to raise awareness of today's green and ethical investing options. Contact Penny Shepherd at UKSIF – the sustainable investment and finance association, Holywell Centre, 1 Phipp Street, London EC2A 4PS (tel: +44 (0)20 7749 9950; e-mail: info@uksif.org; websites: www.uksif.org, www.neiw.org).

3.3

Carbon capital and technology transfer

*The carbon markets have proved they can deploy capital to speed up the transfer of technology, but they need to know the rules by which they are playing after 2012, says **Paul Kelly**, Chief Executive Officer at EcoSecurities.*

Technology development and transfer have been cornerstones contained in many of the international climate change agreements, including the United Nations Framework Convention on Climate Change (UNFCCC) and its Kyoto Protocol. More recently, the Bali roadmap highlighted the role of technology transfer as a key component in any post-Kyoto regime. In addition, the Copenhagen Accord (signed by a limited number of countries at UN negotiations in December 2009) called for action on the development and transfer of technology with the establishment of a 'Technology Mechanism' to accelerate and support climate change adaptation and mitigation measures. Furthermore, the agreement indicated that the required increase in funding (US$30 billion in 2010–12 and US$100 million by 2020) would come from a variety of sources, with many governments engaged in the recent climate change negotiations looking to the private sector to provide a large part of this.

With the role of technology now and in the future so fundamental in mitigating the impact of climate change, this chapter examines the ways in which the Kyoto Protocol's Clean Development Mechanism (CDM), the private sector and the carbon markets have helped to promote technology transfer, and what needs to be done in order to further develop the carbon markets and increase the deployment of technology more rapidly in the future.

What constitutes technology transfer?

According to the Intergovernmental Panel on Climate Change (IPCC) special report *Methodological and Technological Issues in Technology Transfer*, technology transfer is defined as 'a broad set of processes covering the flows and know-how, experience and equipment for mitigating and adapting to climate change amongst different stakeholders such as private sector entities, governments, financial institutions, non-governmental organizations (NGOs) and research / education institutions'.

The Clean Development Mechanism

Although the CDM has no explicit technology transfer mandate, it has, over its duration, helped to contribute to technology transfer through the financing of emission reduction projects that use technologies currently not available in the host country.

The CDM, however, as defined by the UNFCCC, is a flexible mechanism that allows emission reduction projects in developing countries to earn certified emission reduction (CER) credits, where each is equivalent to one tonne of CO_2. These CERs can be sold in trading schemes such as the European Union's Emissions Trading Scheme (EU-ETS) to help industrialized countries gain some flexibility in how they meet a part of their emission reduction targets under the Kyoto Protocol.

EcoSecurities develops CDM approved emission reduction projects internationally. Each and every project goes through a rigorous registration and issuance process overseen by the CDM Executive Board (CDM EB), which is designed to ensure that emission reductions are real, measurable, verifiable and above all additional, ie they would not have occurred without the project.

For many organizations, including our own, the CDM has been perceived as an innovative way of addressing climate change, being the first truly global investment and credit scheme of its kind.

Amatitlán: a CDM and technology transfer success story

Background

Amatitlán is a geothermal project located in the Guatemalan department of Escuintla currently being developed under the CDM by EcoSecurities and Ortitlan Limitada. Most of Guatemala's electricity is derived from fossil base sources. However, the country is fortunate to have geothermal resources of around 800 MW. Prior to Amatitlán being built and going into operation, the country had only one geothermal power plant in existence.

About the project

The purpose of this project is to utilize the geological resources that exist in the Amatitlán geothermal field. This has been achieved by implementing a state-of-the-art geothermal power plant to generate renewable energy that can then be transported to the Guatemalan electricity grid. The plant utilizes three turbines to generate around 162,000 MWh of power and as a result reduces greenhouse gas emissions by around 82,000 tonnes of CO_2 per year.

The results

This project utilizes the CDM to provide carbon financing, which has allowed Guatemala to access not only additional financing to make the project viable but also state-of-the-art technology that did not exist in the country previously. In addition to reducing the greenhouse gas emissions of the country, the development of the Amatitlán project has also significantly contributed to the sustainable development of Guatemala in the following ways:

- The provision of additional employment opportunities in the local area generated approximately 500 temporary jobs throughout the construction phase and 20 permanent operational and maintenance jobs.
- The electricity portfolio of Guatemala has diversified, as the project provides access to renewable geothermal energy, which increases the stability of the power supply to customers, as it's free of seasonal or fuel-driven price fluctuations.
- A programme to reduce flooding in the area has been implemented, which includes the reforestation of the surrounding hillsides with over 5,000 trees, as well as the repairing of the local road infrastructure.

Success of the CDM

Over the past few years the CDM has been extremely successful in incentivizing the development of innovative greenhouse gas emission reduction projects in the developing world. Amatitlán is by no means an isolated example; you only have to take a look at the United Nations Environment Programme's (UNEP) Risoe pipeline to see just how effective the CDM has been at helping to mitigate climate change. As of 1 March 2010, there are 4,968 CDM projects making their way through the various stages of approval. According to the UNFCCC's website, there are 2,119 registered CDM projects that have collectively issued 395,202,168 CERs. Considering that the CDM didn't really become fully operational until 2006, this really shows what can be achieved in terms of abating climate change in a relatively short period of time.

As previously discussed, although the primary remit of the CDM is to help reduce greenhouse gas emissions, it has also played a substantial role not only in helping developing countries achieve their sustainable development goals, but also in facilitating investment and technology transfer within these countries. This point is further substantiated by the UNFCCC's 2008 report *Analysis of Technology Transfer in CDM Projects*. It examined all of the projects currently in the CDM pipeline (3,296 projects as of June 2008) and determined that, when looking at technology transfer in terms of both equipment and knowledge, over 53 per cent of projects claimed in their project design documents (PDDs) that technology transfer was taking place. Given the size of the CDM pipeline, this marks a significant contribution to the overall role that technology has played in minimizing the impact of climate change.

What next for climate change and the private sector?

What is and has been clearly evident for some time is that the private sector has a key role in helping to combat climate change. The Amatitlán example provided above shows that, when the right incentives and frameworks are established, the markets to channel significant amounts of capital investment into the right areas can be created. The problem now is that the metaphorical 2012 crossroads is almost upon us and, as yet, the rules of engagement for a post-2012 carbon market have not been defined.

Although the CDM has played a valuable role in creating a functioning carbon market, when looking at the latest projections from the IPCC and what the global community needs to do to avert a 2-degree rise in temperature, global greenhouse gas emissions need to peak no later than 2020. Such a scenario, realistic or not, implies that there is a very urgent need to quickly and comprehensively agree real ways in which the private sector can engage in a post-2012 environment, not only to make significant cuts in emissions, but also to increase the deployment of energy-efficient technologies in the developing world. The business community pushed very hard at the 2009 UN climate change negotiations, with over 900 companies requesting more commitment from world leaders to reach an agreement on climate change via the submission of a progressive statement called the Copenhagen Communiqué. The impetus within the private sector for sustainable change does exist and even more so within the communities that are involved in the carbon market. However, to fully realize the investment and potential of this group of very involved and determined stakeholders, the answer is clear. With the right signals from the regulatory community, the private sector is ready and willing to deploy the necessary capital needed to reduce current CO_2 concentrations to safer levels – we just need to know the rules by which we are playing.

Paul Kelly is CEO at EcoSecurities, a world-leading organization in the business of sourcing and developing emission reductions, and the company has spent the last 13 years focusing on climate change mitigation. EcoSecurities' emission reduction portfolio is one of the largest in the industry, covering a wide range of technology types, geographical locations and standards, including the CDM, Gold Standard and VCS. In addition, EcoSecurities provides clients with carbon management services, helping them to understand and deal with an increasingly carbon-constrained world. Contact Paul Kelly (tel: 01865 202635; e-mail: info@ecosecurities.com; website: www.ecosecurities.com).

3.4

Intellectual property for clean tech

***Nick Sutcliffe** at Mewburn Ellis discusses how to use the IP system to capture the full value of innovation in clean technology.*

Innovation is a universal theme throughout all clean technologies. From nuclear fusion to fuel cells, the development of new or alternative technologies to reduce the environmental impact of human activity sets technical challenges that require innovative solutions.

Whilst some innovative solutions in clean technologies may represent major breakthroughs, others may be more mundane modifications or incremental improvements in existing technology or may involve the application of old technology in a new context. In all cases, however, innovation distinguishes a product or service from its competitors and plays a key role in its commercial success.

Innovative solutions do not come cheap. Bringing an innovative solution to market involves a significant investment of time and resources. Capturing the full market value of this investment is vital for businesses competing in intensely competitive global markets.

Intellectual property protects innovation

Imitators selling copycat products are a serious problem for innovators marketing clean tech products. Whilst imitators benefit from the investment and ingenuity of the innovator free of charge, at the same time they reduce the potential rewards available to innovators by competing in the market.

Innovators can, however, protect themselves from imitators and reap the full rewards for their innovation using intellectual property (IP) rights. IP rights come in several different forms, and different IP rights can be used to protect different aspects of a product from imitators.

Some IP rights, such as copyright, come into existence automatically. This type of right is very cheap to acquire and, indeed, a business may be unaware of all the automatic IP rights that it actually possesses.

Other IP rights, including patents, registered trademarks and registered designs, need to be actively sought, and the application process may be tortuous and expensive. The acquisition of these rights therefore requires both a conscious decision by a business and a continuing level of commitment.

Although less grandiose than other IP rights, the trade secrets and know-how that a business necessarily acquires during its operations may be invaluable in differentiating it from its competitors. Even in the absence of other IP rights, the experience of actively developing a clean tech product is likely to give a business an edge over less-experienced competitors.

For any business operating in a clean technology field, an IP strategy that distinguishes a business and its products from the competition is likely to involve a combination of all these different forms of IP.

Intellectual property is a business asset

Intellectual property is usually associated with an offensive role: actively using your intellectual property to exclude competitors, preserving a market exclusively for you or those authorized by you to exploit.

However, intellectual property rights have other roles within the overall commercial strategy of a business. Intellectual property rights may in themselves be used to generate revenue, through either licensing or selling. Intellectual property rights, and more generally a good intellectual property strategy, may also play a key role in attracting investors. Whilst investors are generally attracted to good science rather than good patents, the absence of an appropriate strategy for protecting the good science can often be a deal breaker.

An intellectual property portfolio can also have a defensive role to play. It can deter competitors from enforcing their rights against you (for fear of retaliation), and any dispute might be settled by way of a cross-licence.

Of course, the same intellectual property rights may fulfil more than one of these roles. For example, a business may license intellectual property rights for a country in which it does not itself intend to operate, whilst retaining exclusive rights for countries in which it intends to do business. Similarly, non-core applications of a technology may be licensed out, while core applications are retained as the sole preserve of the business. This allows the business to extract the maximum value from its intellectual property.

On a wider level, by deterring the development of copycat products, intellectual property rights have the effect of encouraging competing businesses to develop their own technologies rather than copy each other. This drives innovation within the technical field as a whole.

Patents protect technical innovations

Patents are the key IP right for the protection of technical innovations. A technical innovation protected by a patent may be embodied in a commercial product and/or the processes for manufacturing or using a product.

Because it protects the underlying technical innovation, the patent protects more than just the commercial product or process, and is infringed by any competing product that employs the same underlying technical innovation, irrespective of whether or not the products look alike.

As products in clean technologies rely heavily on technical innovations to distinguish themselves from competitors, patents are likely to play an important role in the IP strategy of any business operating in this area.

Any technical innovation may be patentable

A technical innovation must meet certain legal criteria in order to qualify for patent protection. In particular, the innovation must be new and cannot be merely an obvious development of what is already known. Applications for patents undergo a rigorous examination process at patent offices around the world to ensure that patents are granted only for innovations that meet these criteria. Although this examination process is often slow, fast-track procedures are available for applications relating to green or clean technologies in some countries, including the UK and the United States.

Patents may be issued for innovations in any technical field from nuclear fusion to biofuels and may relate to any aspect of a product or process. For example, as well as a product as a whole a patent may cover a specific hardware or software component of a product or it may cover the use of a product in a particular application or process.

A patentable innovation may be an incremental improvement on a known product or a major breakthrough that opens up a whole new field, or something in between.

The technical field of the innovation and its significance to the overall technical field are not important: as long the innovation fulfils the appropriate legal criteria, it qualifies for patent protection.

Strategies for intellectual property

Protecting an innovation with a patent is expensive and, without clear focus, expenditure on patents can rapidly spiral out of control. Whether or not to pursue patent protection for a particular innovation will therefore depend on a judgement call of whether the innovation is important enough to the business plans of the business to justify the expenditure.

This decision may rest on the fundamental consideration of whether or not a business needs to be able to stop a competitor from replicating or copying the innovation, if it is to maintain its competitive advantage. Current or future revenue streams need to be considered. There is little point in focusing efforts on a product or service that is only ever going to find a small market, no matter how unique or innovative it may be, if in doing so there is no budget left for seeking protection for a less 'exciting' product or service that nevertheless accounts for a business's main stream of income. A sound intellectual property strategy focuses on key assets and avoids unnecessary expenditure on protecting products and services that are less critical to the success of the business.

It is also important to marry patent protection up with potential revenue streams. Sometimes it will pay off to focus protection more specifically on one or two particular revenue streams, rather than seeking very broad protection that may be harder and more expensive to obtain with little or no added benefit.

Management of intellectual property

The process of deciding whether or not to seek protection for a particular innovation requires serious consideration of a range of commercial issues. However, once the decision to seek protection has been made, it is important that the innovator does not switch to an automatic default mode. It is all too easy to continue to drift along the same path, even when the commercial issues may have changed, and it may no longer be appropriate.

Continual active management is essential in order to get the best value from an IP portfolio. This means stopping at every decision point and taking stock of the overall business strategy and where this particular IP right fits in. Is an application appropriate? Can you drop it? Or do you need to take more protection?

Always take the time to evaluate whether the protection you are paying for still makes commercial sense. IP that does not add value to a business is simply a drain on resources that could be better used elsewhere.

Other people's intellectual property

In all of this, it must not be forgotten that competitors may well have their own IP rights. It is important to be aware of the impact that rights of others could have: at worst, these rights could halt the activities of a business completely. Rather than simply hoping for the best, prudent businesses will have in place strategies for dealing with third-party IP rights long before any problems become critical.

These strategies might include watching the IP filing activity of known competitors. This may allow a business to work around competitors' patents or other rights and/or to consider whether it might be vulnerable to attack. Watching a competitor's IP filing activity can also provide useful intelligence about its development work.

A wise business might also consider the arguably counterintuitive possibility of publishing details of developments that it does not intend to protect itself but that it intends to commercialize now or in the future. Such publication can prevent a competitor from later securing its own protection that might otherwise foreclose your ability to commercialize your own development.

And sometimes the best defence can be possession of your own portfolio of intellectual property rights.

Green Channel for patent applications

The Intellectual Property Office offers accelerated processing for patent applications relating to inventions that have an environmental benefit. This initiative, the so-called 'Green Channel', enables inventions with an environmental benefit to be fast-tracked through the UK patent system.

The service is available to any patent applicants if their invention has some environmental benefit. There is no specific environmental standard to meet in order to benefit from the Green Channel, and it is recognized that inventions with an environmental benefit can arise in any area of technology.

The acceleration service is flexible, enabling applicants to request acceleration of any part of the patent application process. What's more, the service is free – applicants just pay the usual patent application fees. Applicants simply need to make a request in writing, indicating how the invention is environmentally friendly and which actions they wish to accelerate. The written request can be made at the same time as filing the patent application, or can be made on a later date.

It is possible to get a granted patent under this scheme in as little as nine months, if the applicant requests accelerated 'Combined Search and Examination' and publication and then responds promptly to any objections or outstanding matters. In fact, of the 200 applications accelerated under this service in its first year of operation (approximately 1 per cent of the applications processed by the Intellectual Property Office in this time), 24 patents have already been granted.

Contact the Intellectual Property Office (tel: Central Enquiries 08459 500 505; e-mail: www.ipo.gov.uk).

Recycling old intellectual property

The old adage 'There is nothing new under the sun' is particularly appropriate in the development of clean tech products. Old ideas from other technical fields may often be useful in solving new problems in clean technologies.

The patent literature is a vast and freely available resource, which may be easily searched to find these old ideas. As long as the patents are no longer in force, the ideas described in them can be freely used by anybody. Furthermore, the adaptation of an old idea for use in a new clean technology application may itself give rise to new IP.

Innovation lies at the heart of the drive towards clean technologies and will be a cornerstone of successful businesses in this field. For these businesses, the development of an effective IP strategy will be invaluable in realizing the full value of this innovation and distinguishing themselves from their competitors in the global market.

Nick Sutcliffe is a partner in Mewburn Ellis LLP, one of Europe's premier IP firms, with over 60 patent and trademark attorneys and technical specialists, covering the full range of intellectual property issues: patents (in all technology areas), trademarks, designs, industrial copyright and related matters. Nick Sutcliffe has a BSc in biochemistry from the University of Bristol and a PhD in biochemistry from the University of Leicester. He spent four years working in industrial research and development before joining Mewburn Ellis in 1997. He qualified as a chartered patent attorney and European patent attorney in 2001 and became a partner at Mewburn Ellis in 2003. His work is mainly in the biotechnology field. Contact Nick Sutcliffe at Mewburn Ellis LLP, 33 Gutter Lane, London EC2V 8AS (tel: 020 7776 5300; e-mail: nick.sutcliffe@mewburn.com; website: www.mewburn.com).

Part 4

Clean energy

4.1

Wind power

*Britain has the potential to meet 40 per cent of its demand for electricity from wind power, but will it happen, asks **Nick Medic** at RenewableUK.*

Britain is set to enter what commentators are calling 'the age of austerity', with public sector spending likely to be slashed by at least 10 per cent. It is against this backdrop that the country faces two urgent and interrelated threats. First is the very real need to reduce our green emissions by at least a third from 1990 levels by 2020. This must be done if we are to help prevent catastrophic climate change and irreversible environmental consequences. The second and more immediate threat is to our energy security. We must restructure the energy balance to secure the supplies to sustain our future demand.

Within the next 15 years a full third of the UK's existing electricity generating capacity will be permanently retired as our ageing nuclear power stations reach the natural end of their life and polluting coal and oil plants are taken out of service. Britain must find new domestic sources of energy and end reliance on expensive imported fossil fuels.

The potential of wind

Under its EU obligations, the UK has adopted a target of 15 per cent of all energy (including heat, transport and electricity) from renewable sources by 2020. The most viable way to achieve this would be to increase sevenfold our renewable electricity output. Fortunately, Britain has the most abundant wind resource in Europe. However, if we are to meet our targets, total capacity derived from offshore and onshore wind will have to increase from the 4 GW we have installed today, powering close to 2.5 million homes, to over 30 GW by 2020.

It is an ambitious push forward, but the numbers stack up. In addition to the 4 GW of installed capacity operating today, a further 9 GW are either being built (2 GW) or have planning permission and are going into construction (7 GW). A further 10 GW of schemes are awaiting planning permission, and 32 GW of offshore licences were recently awarded by the Crown Estate in Round 3.

It is clear that Britain, when compared with Europe, has a leading role to play in this sector. The UK has the potential to develop 40 GW of offshore wind power alone, almost equalling the current installed capacity of wind power in Europe. If we include potential onshore wind power capacity in the UK, which stands at around 15 GW, we reach an incredible combined wind power capacity of 55 GW. Given the best load factors in Europe, this capacity translates into approximately 160 TWh of electricity, or enough energy to power all of the UK's homes and a sizeable percentage of all UK businesses. Put another way, Britain could meet 40 per cent of its electricity demand from wind power alone.

The challenges ahead: skills and supply chain

An independent report by Bain & Company, commissioned in 2008 by RenewableUK, estimated that the UK wind sector currently employs 5,000 people. However, the report concluded that, with the right political support, the sector could provide 57,000 jobs and contribute £39 billion to the British economy by 2020. The UK wind sector is poised for extraordinary growth that will dramatically alter the dynamic of our energy supply and radically curb our carbon dioxide emissions. However, for this opportunity to be fully realized the sector must overcome a number of hurdles.

One of the key challenges facing the renewables sector as it expands is the acute shortage of relevant skills. RenewableUK is recommending that government streamlines and consolidates training provision, reducing the number of agencies, and provides employers with access to apprenticeship funding. There is also a need for a centralized wind/renewables funding stream to coordinate funding and identify and select leading training institutions. For a couple of institutions this funding should be ring-fenced.

In addition to the creation of a skilled workforce, RenewableUK has been busy on strengthening awareness of the need to build a UK-based supply chain. This will not only help to ensure that construction is quick and efficient, but also drive down costs through increased competition. In the first quarter of 2010 close to £500 million has been invested in the UK in offshore wind manufacturing.

Finance

Market stability through adequate renewable funding and financial support mechanisms, supported by a transparent regulatory framework, will be vital to the expansion of the industry. If the UK is seen as an unstable or risky market we will miss out on the huge investment necessary. Long-term market confidence is crucial to attracting business investment, and this will require mechanisms that inspire investor confidence in the

UK's renewables industry and its regulatory regime. In this area, RenewableUK believes it is vital that the Renewable Obligation system remains in place to underpin investor confidence. Any move away from it at this stage would serve only to confuse and discourage investors, causing a hiatus in projects going forward.

Also welcome is the introduction of a feed-in tariff to support the small wind systems market. For the first time, households and business will be able to get paid directly for each unit of electricity they generate on premises.

Planning

If we are to take advantage of the green energy opportunity before us, we must ensure that the planning process in the UK is streamlined and effective. In the UK the average onshore wind farm project waits 17 months for a decision by local planning authorities and even then the approved applications rate remains staggeringly low at just 25 per cent. This is in comparison to 75 per cent of large infrastructure projects such as supermarkets, housing estates and roads being dealt with within the 16-week statutory guideline period. Clearly, the system can deliver speedy decisions, so onshore wind farms need to be treated fairly and on a par with other types of planning applications.

Grid

In its current form, the UK's transmission network presents a significant obstacle to the development of the renewables sector. Getting connected to the grid is a problem faced by every type of electricity generator and one that can delay the construction and operation of wind farms. Our rising energy needs alone mean the grid will need to be extended. It was built to transmit a maximum of 75 GW of electricity; by 2020 it will need to be able to cope with 120 GW. In the case of offshore wind it is important that the Electricity Network Strategy Group's proposals, setting out a broad-brush map for new onshore infrastructure development, are implemented, with a strong single authority given the responsibility necessary for keeping it on schedule.

The network itself was designed to serve the needs of large fossil fuel power stations, situated in close proximity to the UK's major population centres. Much of the grid infrastructure is reaching the end of its life, and 60 per cent will need to be replaced or upgraded within the next decade. In addition, most renewable technologies – wind, wave and tidal – tend to be located away from established infrastructure. The National Grid needs to have a strong coordinating role and should be issuing clear advice on the need for onshore upgrades to support an offshore network and the general formation of the offshore network. We cannot allow our ageing grid infrastructure to hinder our progress towards renewable energy, and this means a fresh approach is required to meet the energy needs of 21st-century Britain.

Big task – big benefits

There is no denying the massive scale of the task ahead of us when it comes to realizing the renewable energy potential of the UK. There are difficulties and complications involved in bringing about this green energy revolution but, with the necessary support from government and other agencies, we can do this. We must not allow ourselves to become overwhelmed by the challenge, because the targets can and must be achieved. Our efforts to nurture this vitally important sector will be rewarded with great economic and environmental benefit.

The UK's plentiful supply of renewable resources – wind, wave and tidal – make the UK ideally placed to deliver an energy system that could be the envy of the world. We have the chance to revive our industrial base to create new jobs and economic prosperity, secure our energy supplies to meet the future demand and make a real difference to climate change. It is time to embrace the revolution.

RenewableUK is the UK's leading trade and professional body for the wind and marine renewables industries. Its primary purpose is to promote the use of wind, wave and tidal power in and around the UK. It acts as a central point for information for its membership and as a lobbying group to promote wind energy and marine renewables to government, industry, the media and the public. It researches and finds solutions to current issues and generally acts as the forum for the UK wind, wave and tidal industry. *Contact RenewableUK (tel: 020 7901 3000; e-mail: info@renewable-uk.com).*

4.2

Marine

Wave and tidal energy conversion are nascent technologies. ***John Griffiths*** *at JWG Consulting reports.*

As an island nation the UK has a close relationship with the sea. Since the 1970s inventors have been seeking to extract power from waves: from Salter's Duck, a bobbing device shaped like a duck, through to today's Pelamis device, a floating articulated metal snake 180 metres long. Energy extraction from flowing water began in the 12th century with water-powered mills, and carries on today with such examples as the Seagen turbine installed in Strangford Lough, County Down in 2008.

Tidal range barrages such as La Rance in France have been in commission since the 1960s, and the potential of these is being investigated for estuaries in the UK.

Interest in accessing the thermal energy of the sea in tropical regions has been ongoing since the mid-1930s using a thermodynamic cycle known as ocean thermal energy conversion (OTEC). An onshore plant today produces power and deep ocean water (from a depth of 1,000 metres) in Hawaii.

This chapter is an introduction to the natural resources, technologies, markets and commercial prospects for ocean energy.

Resources

The wave energy resource in the UK that it is feasible to develop is around 50–70 Terawatt hours per year – enough to power just over 11 million households – and is around 2.5 per cent of the potential wave energy in the world. Tidal stream energy, the most predictable marine renewable energy, would power some 4 million households in the UK and is about 9 per cent of the world resource. OTEC world resource is spread over 60 million square kilometres of ocean and would supply 340 million households

– more than 10 times the number in the UK! Ultimately these ocean energy sources are powered by the sun's heat, in the case of wave and OTEC, and by the gravitational effects of sun and moon on the seas that create the tides.

Why is this considered worth investigation and investment? Because they do not produce carbon dioxide, which tends to increase global temperatures, and they offer diversity in the energy mix, allowing a nation such as the UK to reduce its reliance on imported fuel, thereby improving the security of energy supply.

State of technology

Wave and tidal technologies are sitting where the wind technologies were 20 years ago, with a range of types (for example, there are more than 250 patents for wave devices alone) and no technology fully proven. By 'proven', we mean having the sort of reliability that an aeroplane engine is required to have, which takes about 40,000 machine-hours of operation to demonstrate.

The implication of this is that governments need to inject funding to ensure that technologies are demonstrated and so that leading-edge technologies that operate reliably and economically can be recognized. That kind of backing is often shared with syndicated investment from a range of utilities, major industrial companies, energy multinationals and a very limited number of specialized banks.

Specifically, there are a handful of wave energy conversion systems being tested at full scale in the seas off the UK, the United States, Portugal, Spain and Australia. In addition to 'sea-snake', with its hydraulic rams that link the segments together, there are heaving buoys, a huge hinged flap that is pushed down by the surging waves and released up as they pass, and a concrete container that encloses the wave at the shore and allows the captured moving air to pass through a turbine to generate power. The power range of wave devices is from around 40 kW up to 750 kW at present, with intent to reach as much as 2 MW in a single device in some cases.

Tidal devices fall into three main types – horizontal-axis rotors such as Seagen, vertical-axis turbines that consist of shaped blades mounted in rotating cylindrical frames such as the Gorlov or Darrieus turbines, and horizontal foil shapes that oscillate up and down in the flowing tidal stream. Tidal devices to date have been in the 300-kW to 1.2-MW range.

OTEC systems have been built only at small scale, from 75 kW up to 1 MW, and are heat pumps that utilize the temperature difference between the cold sea at a depth of 1,000 metres and the warm tropical surface water to drive a cycle that turns an expander or generator to produce power. A typical initial demonstrator would have 10MW power capacity and would produce some fresh water also. None have been built at this scale yet, as the equipment is large.

Key developers and important companies

The major names in wave energy technology include Pelamis Wave Power of Leith, Aquamarine Power, Edinburgh, and Ocean Power Technologies based in the United States and in Warwick in the UK, which have all deployed machines. Other companies that are at the demonstration stage are CETO and Oceanlinx in Australia, Wave Dragon from Denmark, which also has a base in Wales, and Trident Energy in Essex.

In tidal energy technology, leading names include Marine Current Turbines based near Bristol, which deployed Seagen, OpenHydro of Dublin, which has deployed in Scotland and Canada, Tidal Generation (now owned by Rolls-Royce), in process of deploying in Scotland, and Hammerfest Strom, which deployed in Norway and is about to do so in Scotland. Other companies close to deployment of devices are Atlantis Resources Corporation, based in Singapore and London, and Pulse Generation, which has deployed its oscillating foil device in the River Humber.

OTEC is being investigated by Lockheed Martin in association with the US military, and OCEES of Hawaii operates an onshore pilot plant producing bottled water and power.

Market size and prospects

The wave and tidal energy markets look set according to some analysts to be at around £300 million per annum by the middle of the decade, with a high proportion of that in the UK. The Crown Estate has just awarded leases for a total of 1.2 GW of wave and tidal installations by 2020 in the Pentland Firth and Orkney area. If that is achieved, the UK alone will invest at a far higher annual rate than £300 million towards the end of the period. The most conservative forecasts suggest the worldwide market to be at £25 billion per year by the end of the decade. Over that period ongoing R&D will figure almost as large as commercial deployment of devices.

Economics

The economics of ocean energy at present are such that subsidy is required for 20 years to develop volume in the market. At present there are feed-in tariffs in some European countries as high as £0.22 per kWh. In the UK, and specifically Scotland, the Scottish Renewable Obligation Certificate (SROC) is awarded for every 0.2 kWh of electricity from wave and for every 0.33 kWh of electricity from a tidal stream source. An SROC is worth roughly 5p in today's market. The costs of wave and tidal energy are such that this level of subsidy is necessary at present to stimulate the market.

However, that will not always be the case, and as more devices are manufactured and deployed in commercial volumes the unit costs will fall. Some commentators suggest that the cost reduction will be as much as 20 per cent for every doubling of the number manufactured once the first 50 MW or so have been installed. The most conservative analysts suggest that the reduction is perhaps only 8 per cent with every doubling. This 'experience curve' effect is expected to result in a fall in cost over the next 40 years to the 7–10p per kWh range around 2050.

OTEC power could be competitive in price in isolated communities where the current prices paid for power generated from imported diesel oil are in excess of £0.2 per kWh. It is understood that there are some 30 clusters of island communities in the tropical zones where this is likely to apply, triggered by the oil price resting around $75 per barrel.

The long-term cost of ocean energy in developed countries appears set to be highly competitive with the true cost of new nuclear power. True cost in this context includes the full cost of nuclear reprocessing and storage of radioactive wastes produced over hundreds of years.

Opportunity

Ocean energy therefore represents a huge opportunity for investors, manufacturers, offshore installation and maintenance organizations and utilities over the next few decades. There is a strong synergy in the skill base and material requirements with the offshore oil and gas industry, which will be in decline in north-west European waters over that period.

The inventive and innovative skills required to bring about mass deployment and the cost reductions described will need to be sourced from the oil and gas industry as well as an influx of new engineers and technicians who must be trained to replace an ageing workforce in that industry. There is significant opportunity to breathe new life into fabrication and assembly facilities that were mothballed during the decline in the North Sea reserves. There are increasing calls for a 'new manufacturing phase' in the UK, and ocean energy offers just that opportunity whilst also securing the energy supply mix on an acceptable trend in the light of the need to reduce greenhouse gas emissions.

John is a Chemical Engineer, with 43 years experience as a General Manager, Consultant, Project Manager and Engineering Manager as well as in a range of Operational and Technical roles in: Marine Renewable energy; Oil and Gas Design; Operations and Project Management; Contracting (Engineering and Construction on and offshore); Consultancy and Studies. Contact John Griffiths (tel: 020 8947 0052; e-mail: jwg@jwgconsulting.com).

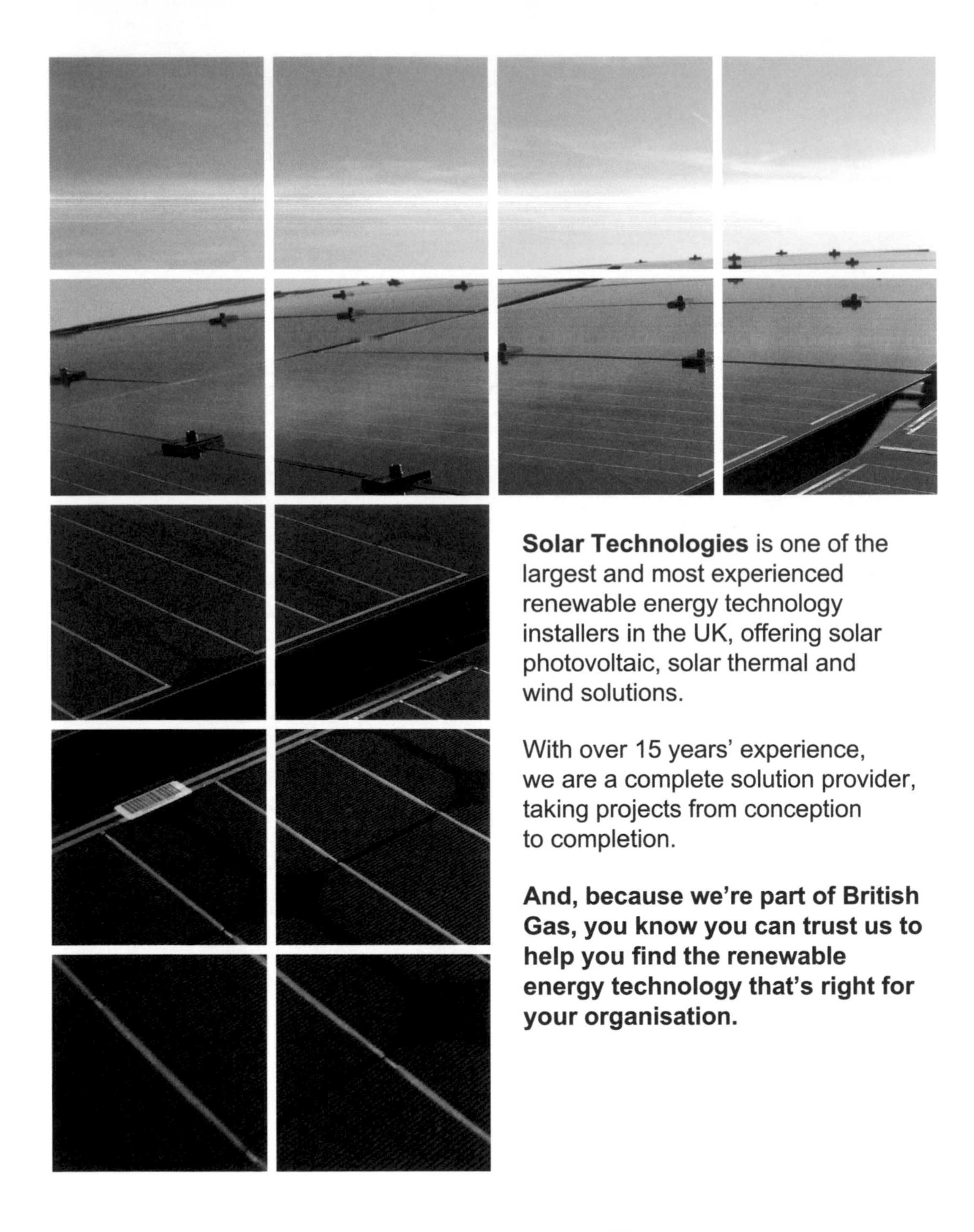

Solar
Technologies
Part of British Gas

4.3

Solar

*Globally, the case for using solar technology to generate your own electricity is up and running, reports **Barry Marsh** of Solar Technologies, part of British Gas.*

Harnessing the power of the sun directly rather than releasing stored solar energy in the form of fossil fuels created millions of years ago offers an increasingly cost-effective and popular way of involving companies, organizations and individuals in producing their own 'green' energy. Using technologies such as solar photovoltaic cells and solar heating systems will help the UK meet its targets of reducing carbon emissions.

Solar photovoltaic

A solar photovoltaic (PV) panel is made up of cells of one or two layers made from a semiconducting material such as silicon. When light shines on the cell, it creates an electric field across the layers, causing electricity to be generated. This electricity is then converted from a direct current (DC) to an alternating current (AC) before being used in the office, factory, home or other site.

In recent years, economies of scale coupled with technological advances have led to solar photovoltaic systems becoming ever more affordable. For example, there were falls in the cost of photovoltaic panels of around 50 per cent over an 18-month period to spring 2010.[1] Incentives from government, such as the new feed-in tariff (FiT) for England, Scotland and Wales, have helped create a more advantageous financial platform for investment decisions to be made.

Compared to other countries, the UK has been slow to take up solar PV systems; for example, Germany has 200 times as many installed systems. Globally, the amount of solar PV installed generation capacity has been showing massive growth. In 2006 it increased by 19 per cent, by 62 per cent in 2007, by 110 per cent in 2008 and by 20 per cent in 2009 – reaching 7.3 GW.[2] In the UK, the introduction of the FiT is expected to encourage the market to grow from the 22 MWp installed during 2009 to 250 MWp during 2011. The UK is expected to follow the German experience, where capacity increased from 40 MWp in 2000 when the German feed-in tariff was introduced to 850 MWp in just six years.[3]

Already, companies involved in the installation of solar PV systems have reported increases in interest from potential customers. The collaboration between energy suppliers and installers, leading in some cases to acquisition, may help to reassure consumers about the merits of solar PV.

Demonstrable expertise in this marketplace, coupled with the reassurance of a large, well-known brand, may encourage many more businesspeople and homeowners to invest in what is still quite a high-entry-cost product. The feed-in tariff also provides considerable reassurance over rate of return and builds confidence that the investment is sound financially as well as environmentally.

Solar PV panels can be placed on most south-facing building surfaces, or those that face anywhere to the south of due east or due west. Typically located on roofs, they can also be placed on external walls, sun shades, conservatories or anywhere that the building's design lends itself to. In selecting suitable locations, the installer will ensure that the panels would receive as much light as possible and have no large obstructions such as other buildings or trees causing shadow. The more light the panels can receive, the more electricity will be generated.

A typical solar PV installation would involve the electricity being generated on-site being measured by an approved 'total generation meter'. This reading is the basis on which the FiT is paid to the generator. If you generate electricity using solar PV you will be paid a fixed amount for each kilowatt-hour you produce – even if you consume that electricity yourself. Any you do use will, of course, reduce the amount you need to import from the energy market. If your installation generates more electricity than you need at any time, you can sell it to the energy market, either by negotiating directly with a purchaser or by taking advantage of a fixed-rate payment. In this context, the increasing involvement of the energy suppliers means that FiT arrangements can be arranged for the client by the installation company – removing another layer of complexity for the customer and hence potentially removing a barrier to investment.

Solar heating

A new initiative being developed for England, Scotland and Wales by the Department for Business, Innovation and Skills would see similar incentives to the FiT scheme being introduced for generating heat from renewable sources. One technology that would benefit from such a scheme is solar heating, which, in the UK at least, is difficult to justify economically in most circumstances.

Many UK people's experience of solar heating panels comes from holidays in countries bordering the Mediterranean, where solar heating is often used to heat water for holiday apartments. The technology is simple – the sun heats up a collector, the heat from which is transferred to a water system that preheats domestic hot water through a heat-exchange cylinder.

However, in recent years, the design of the collectors and the systems has been improved. While most simple, DIY-type systems will work to some extent, the greatest heating benefits are achieved when the property, system and collectors are matched to each other. Well-known heating system manufacturers are entering this market, including Worcester Bosch working in partnership with British Gas.

As a result of their holiday experiences, many UK consumers may believe that the greatest markets in Europe for solar heating must be in those warmer countries such as Spain, Italy, France and Greece. These countries come only second, third, fourth and sixth respectively in terms of their percentage of the overall European market. Germany comes in first with 44 per cent of the EU and Switzerland marketplace. (Incidentally, fifth place goes to Austria.)[4]

So it is clear that, even in northern Europe, there is a huge potential for this form of solar technology if the necessary financial incentives can be put in place.

Conclusion

By far the most popular form of microgeneration so far in the UK, solar photovoltaic and solar heating systems are not yet ready to face full exposure to the market without substantial help from government. This is due to a combination of factors, including the costs of installation and the general lack of awareness among consumers of the savings that could be made. Many people are not prepared to accept a pay-back period of more than a couple of years when investing in their home.

The recent launch of the feed-in tariff for solar photovoltaic and the proposed introduction of the Renewable Heat Incentive for solar heating have the potential to radically change the market dynamic for these products in the UK. Once the products are established, economies of scale will enter the equation, along with sustainable consumer demand. Put together, this will mean that the industry can demonstrate that it can economically contribute to the UK's quest to meet its carbon-saving targets.

Notes

[1] *Financial Times*, 10 May 2010.
[2] Solarbuzz (2010) *Marketbuzz 2010*, Solarbuzz, London.
[3] IMS Research.
[4] European Solar Thermal Industry Federation (2009) *Solar Thermal Markets in Europe*, May, European Solar Thermal Industry Federation, Brussels.

Barry Marsh is the General Manager of Solar Technologies, part of British Gas. With a background in the construction industry, he had his first experience of integrating solar PV technology into buildings in 1993, while working for a national building contractor. He has led Solar Technologies to become one of the largest and most experienced renewable energy technology installers in the UK. For further details contact Solar Technologies (tel: 01794 830154; e-mail: solarsales@solartechnologies.co.uk; website: www.solartechnologies.co.uk).

4.4

Nuclear power

***Roane Knowles-Rapson** of the National Nuclear Laboratory reviews the next generation in nuclear power.*

The geopolitics of the 21st century has brought to light some dominant realities of specific relevance to global energy policy:

1. By 2050 the global population will have grown from the current 6 billion to 9 billion. In a world where a vast disparity between wealth and poverty already exists, unmet human needs could multiply proportionately.[1]
2. By 2050, as countries seek to meet the needs of expanding populations, global energy consumption will have doubled or even tripled. It is forecast that in this narrow period humankind will consume more energy than the total used in all previous history.[2]
3. The global rate of energy-related CO_2 emissions, already over 30 billion tons a year (or 950 tons a second), is still growing.[3]
4. To stabilize greenhouse gases, at least a 50 per cent reduction in global emissions is required.

These realizations deliver two very salient points: that humankind is in desperate need of vast amounts of energy, and that this energy must be clean. It is widely accepted that nuclear power as an energy source free from direct emissions will help to mitigate climate change. Today 436 commercial nuclear power plants operating in over 30 countries produce 15 per cent of the world's electricity.[4] Should this portion of energy be generated by fossil fuels, there would be an increase of over 2 billion tons of carbon dioxide emissions each year.[5]

In addition to being a clean energy source, nuclear power can also address the other two main features of energy policies around the globe: ensuring security of supply and maintaining economic competitiveness by keeping energy prices at an affordable level. Although exact figures are a point of much debate, nuclear power is capable of providing power at a comparable price to the best coal plants – perhaps even surpassing them in the future. Atomic energy, whilst primarily used for electricity generation, can in the future provide secondary functions that will facilitate greater reductions in emissions. These include the desalination of water in arid countries, process heat for industry and, in the long term, the production of hydrogen for use in the transport sector (cars, fuel cells and so on).

The wide-ranging benefits of nuclear power have led to what is being coined a global 'nuclear renaissance'. Existing nuclear states are considering, planning or already building new fleets of reactors. In addition, many non-nuclear countries have shown keen ambition to implement civil nuclear programmes. The future will see an increase in not only global nuclear-generating capacity but also the international access to nuclear power and its inherent benefits. The next generation of nuclear power possesses several advantages over its predecessors but is also faced with numerous challenges that must be overcome in order to succeed.

A new generation of reactors

Across the world's nuclear reactors, 13,000 reactor-years of cumulative operating experience have allowed nuclear power to become more efficient.[6] Although fewer nuclear power plants are being built now than during the 1970s and 1980s, those that are operating produce more electricity (see figure 4.4.1). In 2005, production was 2,626,000 GWh. The increase in the six years to 2005 (218,000 GWh) is equal to the output from 30 large new nuclear plants. Yet between 1999 and 2005 there was a net increase of only two reactors (and 15 GWe). The rest of the increase is due to better performance from existing units.[7]

This extensive experience has allowed for the development of the new generation of reactors currently being built. The first of the Generation III reactors was built in Japan, and Generation III-plus reactors are currently being built in France, Finland (EPR) and China (AP-1000), with more already ordered in countries such as the UAE (APR-1400) amongst others. The new generation of reactors are more efficient, operate for a minimum of 60 years before life extensions (as opposed to 30 for earlier generations) and have new features designed to further strengthen their already well-proven safety performance. Traditional reactor safety systems are 'active' in the sense that they involve electrical or mechanical operation on command. Some engineered systems operate passively, eg pressure relief valves. Both require parallel redundant systems. Inherent or full passive safety depends only on physical phenomena such as convection, gravity or resistance to high temperatures, not on functioning of engineered components. It is the latter 'passive' safety systems that are found in such new-build reactors as the AP-1000.

These new commercial reactors are larger than their predecessors and require huge capital investment to build. Whilst the long-term result is still an economic and affordable source of power, the initial outlay is not feasible for smaller grids and developing countries. This has led to a focus on small reactors (up to 300 MWe) that can operate as solitary units or as a fleet of units. Additional capacity can be added as and when needed, suiting growing economies that have neither the funds nor the immediate need for a 1,000-plus MWe reactor. Small reactors are already in existence and have been operating since 1976 in a remote corner of Siberia. They provide heat and electricity to the local population.[8]

With inspiration being taken from naval uses, small self-contained modular reactors are receiving a lot of attention for wider uses in developing countries. These countries are those that lack the complex established logistical and regulatory infrastructure required for traditional civil nuclear programmes. Reactors such as Babcock & Wilcox's 125-MWe mPower modular unit is designed to be manufactured and then transported to site as a prefabricated unit.

Further into the future, Generation IV reactors will boast further efficiency and safety features. These reactors will also boast the ability to produce hydrogen on a large scale, as well as minimizing the amount of waste produced by burning spent fuel *in situ*. Generation IV reactors are still on the drawing board at present and are unlikely to be operational before 2030.

A new generation of acceptance and support

One of the key issues in the nuclear industry is the slump experienced in new-build over the past two decades. The Chernobyl accident of 1986 led to a substantial reduction in the pace of the industry because of safety concerns. In fact the accident that occurred would be impossible in Western reactors and was a result of (known) design deficiencies, procedural violations and lack of a safety culture. Since then, however, public opinion of the industry, aided by public culture, has been one of fear and uncertainty. This has been and is one of the largest challenges that the industry has had to contend with to date.

Public and political favour has returned to the industry in recent years with a greater understanding brought about by a culture of transparency. Regulatory reform and greater focus on waste management and disposal issues have been instrumental in winning back confidence. There is, however, a long way to go before the memories of Chernobyl, Three Mile Island and the caricatured barrel of fluorescent green sludge are seen as irrelevant to the modern industry.

Since 11 September 2001, the receding concerns of the safety of nuclear power generation have been replaced with concerns of terrorism and nuclear proliferation. International cooperation and the International Atomic Energy Agency's regulatory frameworks have helped to ease the worries that illegal nuclear arsenals and terrorist attacks pose. The risks have become an intrinsic part of licensing, with all new reactors rigorously inspected for structural integrity and containment in the event of an attack. International cooperation and an increased focus on peaceful nuclear technology for the global good will need to continue in order to prevent the proliferation of potentially dangerous nuclear materials. The UK has set up a National Nuclear Centre of Excellence, hosted at the National Nuclear Laboratory, which will act as a hub for

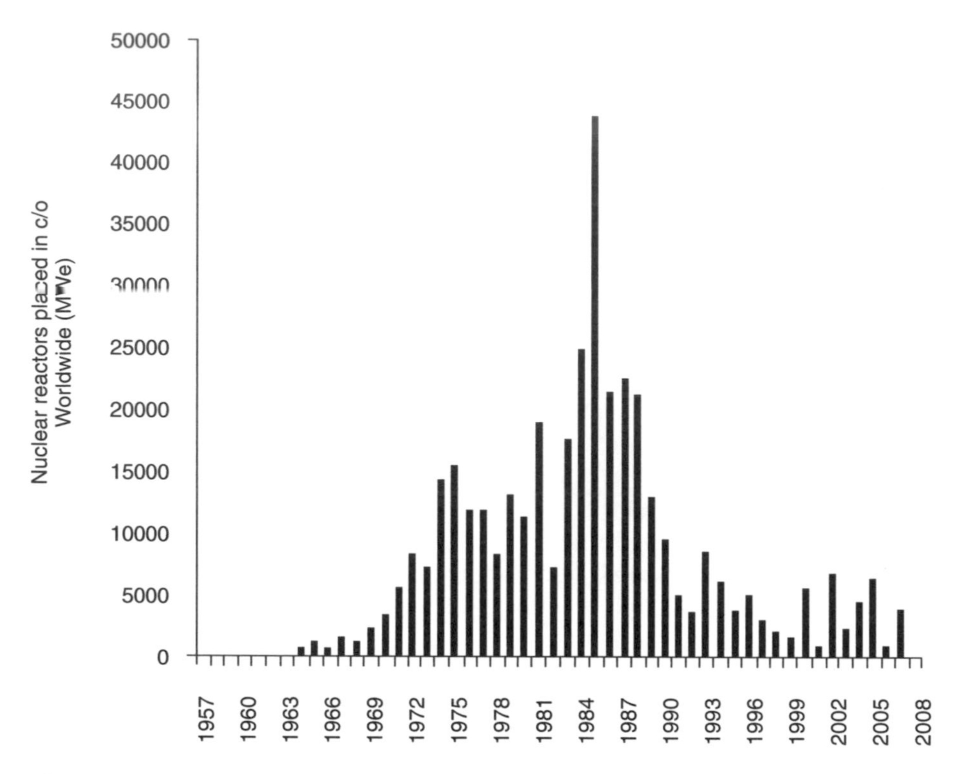

Source: World Nuclear Association (2009) Safety of nuclear power reactors, http://www.world-nuclear.org/info/inf06.html.

Figure 4.4.1 Capacity of nuclear reactors placed into operation (MWe)

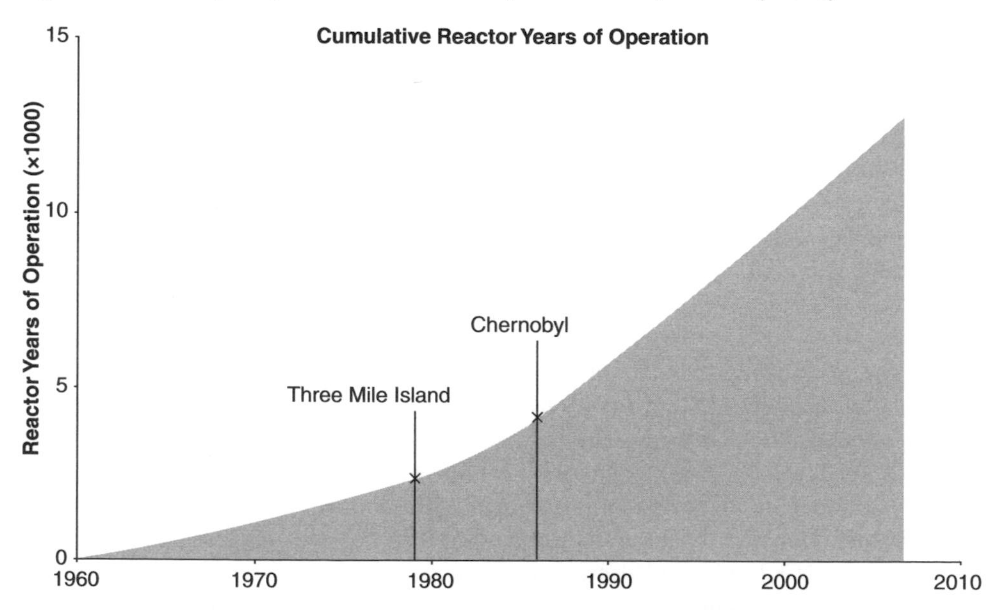

Figure 4.4.2 There has been extensive experience gained since the occurrence of the two most serious nuclear accidents in history

Fuel	Immediate fatalities 1970–92	Who?	Normalized to deaths per TWy* electricity
Coal	6400	workers	342
Natural gas	1200	workers & public	85
Hydro	4000	public	883
Nuclear	31	workers	8

**Basis:* per million MWe operating for one year, not including plant construction, based on historic data, which are unlikely to represent current safety levels in any of the industries concerned.

Source: World Nuclear Association (2009) Safety of nuclear power reactors, http://www.world-nuclear.org/info/inf06.html.

Table 4.4.1 Details of worldwide fatalities by power industry

future peaceful nuclear research. Increasingly the public debate about the future of nuclear power recognizes the progress made in removing technological obstacles in the four major areas of concern: reactor safety, long-term management of nuclear wastes, control of radioactive materials and nuclear proliferation.

A new generation of skills

The skills base required to sustain a successful nuclear industry has also taken a blow in the past 20 years. The industry for various reasons became an unattractive career path and in the UK at least received considerably less funding for research. Consequently the UK industry today possesses a vast amount of world-class knowledge and expertise embodied within an ageing workforce. In the UK there were over 7,000 experts involved in nuclear R&D in 1990; by 2004 this had dropped to fewer than 1,000, mostly working for the National Nuclear Laboratory. Indeed this is part of a larger national skills shortage in the technical areas of science, technology, engineering and mathematics.

In recent years the situation has been eased through motivated recruitment programmes, as well as government-supported schemes. The UK's National Skills Academy for Nuclear (NSAN) is tasked with establishing and developing the national skills base. NSAN is supported by the top companies and organizations involved in the industry; together they are helping to ensure the UK's nuclear future. Based in Munich, a similar European body has recently been set up to integrate knowledge from across the continent. The European Nuclear Energy Leadership Academy (Enela) will begin its initial programme in early 2011.[9] These are just two of many such efforts aimed at attracting new talent into the industry. Once the workforce is replenished, the challenge will lie in ensuring that the years of expertise are transferred and not lost.

Conclusion

Nuclear power is the only CO_2 free energy source available at the gigawatt scale. New advanced Generation III+ reactors are already under construction with more on the way. Developing the next Generation IV reactors will be the next step in establishing nuclear as the sustainable source of energy for future generations. The education of new scientists and engineers is of crucial importance in the realization of tomorrow's nuclear science and technology. Their input will be essential in finding innovative and robust solutions.

Notes

[1] World Energy Council (2007) *The Role of Nuclear Power in Europe*, World Energy Council, London.

[2] J. Ritch, Director, General World Nuclear Association (2002) Turning a corner in history: Global cooperation on nuclear power in an era of sustainable development, Speech presented in Moscow, May.

[3] Energy Information Administration (2009) *International Energy Outlook 2009*, http://www.eia.doe.gov/oiaf/ieo/emissions.html. Calculations by author.

[4] European Nuclear Society (2010) Nuclear power plants worldwide, http://www.euronuclear.org/info/encyclopedia/n/nuclear-power-plant-world-wide.htm.

[5] World Nuclear Association (2009) Climate change and nuclear power: Blog action day '09, http://www.world-nuclear.org.

[6] World Nuclear Association (2009) Nuclear power today, http://www.world-nuclear.org/info/inf01.html.

[7] Energy Business Reports (2007) *Global Nuclear Power Outlook and Opportunities*, Energy Business Reports, United States.

[8] World Nuclear Association (2010) Small nuclear power reactors, http://www.world-nuclear.org/info/default.aspx?id=534&terms=small+reactors.

[9] For more information visit http://www.enela.eu.

The UK's National Nuclear Laboratory (NNL) offers an unrivalled breadth of technical products and services to its customers across the whole nuclear industry. Covering the complete nuclear fuel cycle from fuel manufacture and power generation, through to reprocessing, waste treatment and disposal, and including defence, new nuclear build and homeland security, NNL provides these services supported by an impressive range of links with international research organizations, academia and other national laboratories. In supporting the national interest, NNL offers commercial technologies for customers and trusted technical advice to government. Its team of highly skilled employees specialize in providing tailored solutions with the right balance of innovation for successful project and programme delivery. For further details contact Keith Miller, Head of Marketing (tel: 01925 289960; e-mail: keith.x.miller@nnl.co.uk).

4.5

Energy from waste

***Andrew Williams** at M+W explains how energy from waste is playing an essential role in the UK's commitment to deliver 15 per cent renewable energy by 2020.*

Until recently, the quantity of municipal waste generated in the UK was rising year on year, with almost all of the UK's municipal waste ending up in landfill. Recent changes in public attitudes towards the environment have led to a fall in the quantity of household waste generated per person, and an increase in recycling and composting from 14.4 per cent in 2002 to 37.6 per cent in 2008.[1] Together, this has contributed to a fall in the amount of waste going to landfill; however, in 2009, we still landfilled over half of our waste, some 13.8 million tonnes in England alone.[2]

In 2007, Defra published the *Waste Strategy for England*,[3] detailing how England can manage waste sustainably and reduce the quantity of waste going to landfill, in order to meet the EU Landfill Directive.[4] The Strategy detailed how a waste hierarchy should be adopted in order to reduce the consumption of natural resources by the prevention of waste, the manufacture of products with fewer natural resources, and the reuse of products or recycling of their materials. Where reduction, reuse or recycling is not possible, energy should be recovered through the combustion or thermal treatment of the waste, with any final residual waste being disposed of in landfill.

There are concerns that recovering energy from waste would detract from recycling. However, experience in countries such as Germany, Sweden and Denmark[5] illustrates that the recovery of energy from residual waste is compatible with high levels of recycling, as part of an overall waste management strategy.

In order to utilize municipal solid waste (MSW) as a fuel in an 'energy from waste' (EfW) plant, the MSW requires processing to remove non-combustible materials and recyclables such as papers, plastics, glass and metals. If the waste has a separate stream with a high biological fraction such as food waste, it is possible to utilize a biological process called anaerobic digestion to generate methane, which can be used in a gas engine to generate electricity. The remaining material, such as contaminated packaging, food waste, green waste and wood, forms the basis of the fuel. The energy in the MSW can be recovered via three main thermal processes:

- combustion;
- gasification;
- pyrolysis.

Combustion

Combustion involves burning MSW at temperatures in excess of 850°C with sufficient oxygen to fully oxidize the waste into carbon dioxide and steam. The process converts almost all of the chemical energy in the waste into thermal energy. The thermal energy can then be used to generate either hot water, for distribution in a district heating system serving residential areas and industry, or steam, which is used to generate electricity via a steam turbine. If useful heat is recovered from the steam cycle, the process is known as combined heat and power (CHP). Any non-combustible materials such as glass, metal and stone, along with a small amount of residual carbon, are discharged as bottom ash.

Combustion is an established process widely deployed for the treatment of MSW and can offer a number of benefits as part of a waste management strategy. These include up to a 90 per cent reduction in the MSW volume, the destruction of pathogenic organisms, a reduction in the quantity of organic materials in landfill and the opportunity for energy recovery from the heat generated during combustion.

The use of combustion for the thermal treatment of MSW is widespread across Europe, with around 23 plants in the UK burning 3.3 million tonnes (12 per cent) of MSW.

Gasification

Gasification is the partial thermal degradation of a carbon-based or organic material in a reduced-oxygen atmosphere. Gasifiers generally operate at temperatures from around 700°C to 1,000°C with pressures up to several bar. Since the gasification process is mainly exothermic, once started with an external energy source, the reaction is self-sustaining, or autothermal, using the energy of the waste itself.

The reaction products of the gasification of MSW are a synthetic gas (syngas), comprising hydrogen, carbon monoxide, methane and a range of other hydrocarbon gases, and a solid residue, known as char, comprising non-combustible materials with a small amount of carbon.

The oxygen for the reactions is provided by air, oxygen-enriched air or steam. Depending on the gasification process, the MSW feedstock and the oxygen level, the net calorific value of the syngas can range from around 4 MJ/m^3 to 14 MJ/m^3. The syngas can be used as a fuel gas in a conventional boiler to produce high-pressure steam, which can be used to generate electricity via a steam turbine. Alternatively, the syngas can be cleaned and conditioned and used as a fuel gas in a gas-engine-based power generation system.

The components of the syngas can also be used as building blocks in the chemical industry; in particular, the Fischer–Tropsch process can use the hydrogen and carbon monoxide in the syngas to produce synthetic fuels such as diesel. Other examples include the use of hydrogen for methanol production.

As a thermal process, gasification has been around since the 18th century. In the UK, the gasification of coal to produce 'coal gas' for industry and domestic use started in the 19th century and continued through to the late 1960s. It was only when natural gas was discovered in the North Sea that the coal gas plants were shut down. Coal gasification is still used throughout the world for the production of chemicals and synthetic fuels.

There are few MSW gasification plants currently operating in the UK, but there are a number of large-scale MSW gasification plants planned for construction. For example, the proposed East London Sustainable Energy Facility (ELSEF)[6] in Rainham is designed to process around 100,000 tonnes of solid recovered fuel (SRF) and generate around 20 MW of electricity.

Pyrolysis

Pyrolysis is a medium temperature thermal process that involves the thermal degradation of carbon-based or organic materials, in the absence of added oxygen. The process involves using an external heat source to heat the waste in a sealed vessel to temperatures between 350 and 800°C. This results in the breakdown of the organic compounds, generating a carbon-based char, oils and syngas. The output of a pyrolysis reaction is dependent on the reaction time, temperature and pressure. 'Slow' pyrolysis can yield high levels of char, whilst 'fast' pyrolysis yields high levels of oils and syngas.

The syngas generated in a pyrolysis reaction comprises carbon monoxide, hydrogen and methane along with a range of volatile organic compounds. The condensable fraction of the gas can yield a liquid known as pyrolysis oil made up of tars, waxes and oils, which is suitable for use as a fuel oil for heating.

More complex processing of the pyrolysis oil, using catalytic cracking, can produce higher-quality oil that can ultimately be used as a transport fuel. The pyrolysis oil can also be gasified to form a syngas, comprising mainly hydrogen and carbon monoxide, which can be used as building blocks or, using the Fischer–Tropsch process, to produce synthetic fuels.

The pyrolysis process is widely used throughout the world for the production of coke for the steel industry, but, as with gasification, pyrolysis is not used for the large-scale thermal treatment of MSW. There are a number of specialist pyrolysis plants operating in Europe within the chemical industry, but few waste pyrolysis plants operating in the UK.

Investment and the Renewables Obligation

In order to incentivize investment in emerging EfW technologies such as gasification and pyrolysis for the generation of renewable energy in the UK, the government introduced the Renewables Obligation Order (RO) in 2002.[7] This obligated electricity suppliers to source a proportion of their energy from renewable sources. Under the RO, accredited renewable energy generators are issued with Renewable Obligation Certificates (ROCs) for each megawatt-hour (MWh) of eligible electricity generated each month. If an electricity supplier does not have sufficient ROCs to meet its quota, it has to pay a fee into a buy-out fund. The proceeds of this buy-out fund are then paid back, on a pro rata basis, to those suppliers that have met their obligation.

Following extensive consultation, the government reformed the RO in 2009.[8] The principle feature of the current RO is the concept of ROC banding – the awarding of a different number of ROCs per MWh of electricity according to the type of technology that is used to generate the electricity.

Under the banding system, established technologies such as landfill gas and sewage gas are eligible for 0.25 and 0.5 ROCs respectively, with reference technologies such as onshore wind, hydroelectric and EfW plants with CHP receiving 1 ROC, whilst emerging technologies such as advanced pyrolysis and gasification receive 2 ROCs. Since ROCs increase the electricity revenue significantly, they act as an incentive to encourage investment in emerging technologies. In addition, commitment to the RO has been extended from 2027 to 2037 to ensure that investors have long-term security.

In conclusion, EfW systems that comply with the Waste Incineration Directive (WID)[9] can be an environmentally low-risk method for reducing the quantity of MSW going to landfill, thus meeting the UK's obligations under the EU Landfill Directive. EfW can also play an essential role in the UK's commitment to deliver 15 per cent renewable energy by 2020 under the EU Climate and Energy Package.[10]

Notes

1 Department for Environment, Food and Rural Affairs (Defra) (2009) Municipal waste statistics, November, http://www.defra.gov.uk/evidence/statistics/environment/wastats/index.htm.
2 Defra (2009) Municipal waste statistics, November, http://www.defra.gov.uk/evidence/statistics/environment/wastats/index.htm.
3 Defra (2007) *Waste Strategy for England 2007*, May, Defra, London.
4 Directive 1999/31/EC of the European Parliament on the landfill of waste.
5 European Commission's Eurostat Statistics Database http://epp.eurostat.ec.europa.eu/.
6 East London Sustainable Energy Facility (ELSEF), http://www.sustainablelondon.co.uk/new/.
7 Statutory Instrument 2002 No 914, The Renewables Obligation Order 2002.
8 Statutory Instrument 2009 No 785, The Renewables Obligation Order 2009.
9 Directive 2000/76/EC of the European Parliament on the incineration of waste.
10 EU Climate and Energy Package 2009, http://ec.europa.eu/environment/climat/climate_action.htm.

European engineer Andrew Williams, CEng MIMechE is an energy specialist with M+W UK. He can be contacted at andrew.williams@mwgroup.net. M+W UK, part of the M+W Group (formerly M+W Zander), is a leading EPC/turnkey contractor involved in the construction of high-tech and process-driven facilities. The company has evolved into a leading turnkey provider of waste processing, energy from waste and energy production, established through forming strong working relationships with a series of leading technology providers. M+W Group ranks among the market leaders in various market sectors, including energy, semiconductors, photovoltaics and pharmaceuticals. M+W Group GmbH, Stuttgart manages the global activities of the group as a holding company. The group has three main divisions of Facility Solutions, Process Solutions and Product Solutions, and generated revenues of some €1.74 billion in the business year 2008, with a workforce of approximately 4,500. M+W Group is owned by the Austrian Stumpf Group, which is globally successful in the areas of high-tech engineering, smart and renewable energy, real estate and technology investments. Contact Charlotte Storer (tel: +44 (0)1249 455150; e-mail: charlotte.storer@mwgroup.net; website: www.mwgroup.net).

4.6

Biomass

You can profit from biomass, but can you handle it, asks ***Professor Mike Bradley****, Director, Wolfson Centre for Bulk Solids Handling Technology, University of Greenwich.*

Biomass is everywhere, and there are many ways to make money out of it. Traditionally, you could burn it to make steam or electricity for sale, claim a feed-in tariff and sell the ash on the side as a fertilizer. For some fuels you can even charge a gate fee instead of paying for them.

Recently there are many more process options. Domestic waste can be processed into refuse-derived fuel (RDF) for sale, and the recyclables (steel, glass, aluminium, etc) recovered for sale. Alternatively you can pyrolyse it to make oil for fuel, or even a feedstuff for plastics manufacture. Forest residue can be compressed into high-value wood fuel pellets, which are growing in popularity; they are now cheaper than gas to heat your house with.

All these are commercial reality. Many of the processes are proven and can be purchased easily, but many more are in development and will hit the market in the next couple of years. All are capable of delivering a profit, but there is one common challenge amongst all these disparate processes, which practical experience has shown us is very often where the profits get lost. This is in the handling and flow of the biomass material into and through the process, which always seems to be given far less consideration than the actual conversion process, even though in reality it often brings as big, or even bigger, challenges.

A typical biomass process plant is shown in Figure 4.6.1.

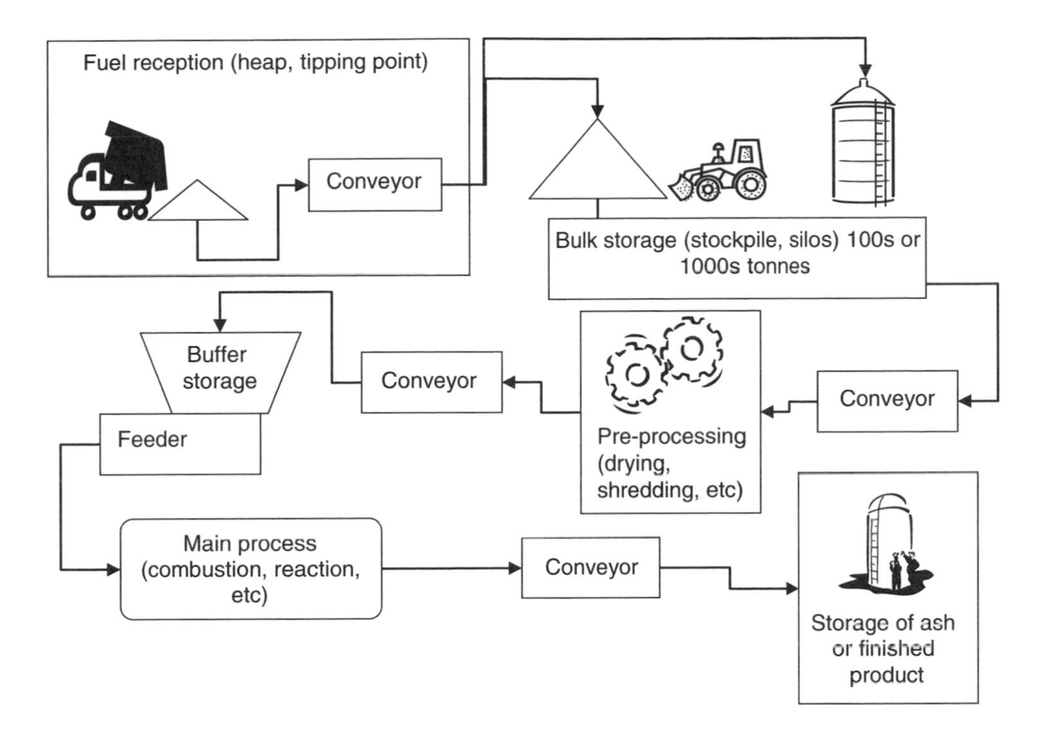

Figure 4.6.1 A typical biomass processing plant – note there are more conveyors and storage systems than there are actual processes!

Getting reliable flow of bulk solids is a trickier business than most plant constructors give it credit for – 60 per cent of novel solids processing plants don't reach full capacity even two years after start-up, and cost on average over twice the money budgeted in the business case for construction[1] – but biomass can be amongst the worst.

What is it about biomass?

Industry has handled solid fuel for years. The coal-fired power station has been with us for well over a century, and engineers have got the measure of the efficient handling of coal. But the introduction of biomass handled in large quantities has led to major losses and station downtime owing to fuel-handling system problems.

Examples of common handling problems with biomass

Here are a few of the most common problems that the Wolfson Centre has been asked to troubleshoot in biomass handling:

- poor discharge from silos or hoppers ('arching' or 'rat-holing');
- irregular or inconsistent feeding;
- dust evolution, and biohazards from this ('farmer's lung');

- breakdown of pellets in handling;
- caking (hardening) of materials in storage, from fermentation or mould formation;
- ash heating and hardening following conditioning with water.

All these, and many more common problems, lead to unplanned shutdowns and often expensive plant modifications, seriously denting the marginal profitability of biomass processing and utilization.

Why the problems?

Recent research at the Wolfson Centre has started to throw light on why many biomass materials are so troublesome for flow. It is often because of the particle shapes; whereas coal and other 'ordinary' bulk solids tend to have particles that are roughly spherical or block-shaped, often with irregularities, many biomass materials are long and thin (chopped straw or miscanthus) or flat and leafy (shredded sheet material like paper, plastic and card). When they are subjected to stress from a weight of material above, they 'knit' or 'mat' together, which makes them hard to move. Many have a low density, so gravity exerts only a small force on them to make them flow. Many are susceptible to biological attack, leading to heating and mould formation. Even after burning, the ash from biomass material behaves quite differently from the ash from coal combustion, so ash-handling systems developed from the coal tradition do not work with biomass ashes.

Choosing the right solutions

There are plenty of solutions available for moving, conveying and feeding biomass materials; there is at least one machine option that works for every material. However, many of these machines work only with a narrow range of materials, and it is hard to be sure you choose the right option. Those with the ability to handle the widest range of materials are much more expensive and may make the project uneconomic. From this it will become obvious that making a system that is reliable yet affordable requires a careful choice of the right equipment.

Furthermore, experience shows that the equipment manufacturers are not always as well informed as the buyer expects them to be, when it comes to advising on the right 'tools for the job'. They may be experts in equipment design and manufacture, but you can't really expect them to know about the way in which every possible material they might meet will behave – it is up to buyers to make sure they select suitable solutions.

Feedstock variability

Many biomass streams are effectively 'waste' materials. They are often not made to a close specification, and vary from day to day in particle size, dust content, water content, etc, much more than most bulk materials. Many are seasonal, so their properties vary – and so do their prices, so it may be desirable to use different feedstocks at different times of year.

Longer-term variation in price and availability is an issue. If all the wood-pellet-fired generation stations currently in planning in the UK are built, demand for pellets will outstrip supply by a factor of three; pellet prices will go sky-high, and these facilities will have to burn other feedstocks, for which their fuel-handling systems are not designed!

Know your enemy

The messages are:

- All biomass materials handle differently; many are inherently variable.
- Most conveying, feeding and handling systems can cope only with a restricted range of materials; those with wider capability are more expensive!
- Often, facilities designed around one feedstock will have to change to another to maintain profitability.
- It is up to buyers, not equipment suppliers, to make sure they choose the right equipment for the materials they are to handle.

Few systems that handle biomass start up and run correctly straight away – many need an extended period of development during which retrofit and lost opportunity costs are incurred, sometimes for a year or two before they get to full operation.

To give yourself a better chance of success:

- Assess, before embarking on a development, what the feedstock is likely to be – not just now, but in the future. Consider the influence of other developments on availability and price.
- Recognize the importance of ensuring the feedstock will flow reliably between reception and process. Don't make the mistake of spending all the time and effort on the conversion (combustion, pyrolysis, etc) and leave the material handling to the engineering contractor.
- Above all, *get the feedstock characterized for flow*, not just the favoured material but a range of other options too. This will identify handling equipment that will work from the outset.
- Ensure the contractors take account of flow property characterization in the equipment they buy, because experience shows they often buy more on price than on technical suitability!
- Before changing the feedstock, get the proposed new material characterized, to see if it will go through the handling system you have bought. If not, it's probably best to look elsewhere for suitable feedstock instead of persevering in trying to put a 'round peg in a square hole'.

The good news? Recent research has started to deliver meaningful characterization techniques, and these are available to industry. Technical papers from the Wolfson

Centre (www.bulksolids.com) and the Materials Handling Engineers Association (www.mhea.co.uk) are especially valuable sources of information and should be consulted for further details.

Note

[1] E. Merrick (1990) *Understanding Cost Growth and Performance Shortfall in Novel Process Plants*, RAND Corporation, Santa Monica, CA.

Mike Bradley is the Director of the Wolfson Centre for Bulk Solids Handling Technology at the University of Greenwich, the UK's leading centre for research and independent consultancy in materials handling. His team at the University of Greenwich specialize in all aspects of storage, handling, conveying and processing of loose bulk materials, and provide troubleshooting, system design and product development services to the industry around the globe. For further details contact Mike Bradley (e-mail: m.s.a.bradley@gre.ac.uk).

4.7

Microgeneration

***Barry Marsh** of Solar Technologies, part of British Gas, discusses the case for turning generation on its head and for generating power locally either at home or in your business.*

Energy market observers and government[1] agree that microgeneration technologies have a part to play in helping the UK meet its commitments to tackling climate change. At the same time, they can help bolster the reliability of energy supplies and provide affordable energy for heating. But there are several obstacles that need to be overcome before this can become a reality.

Currently, most of the UK's electricity is generated in large power stations that burn a fossil fuel (coal, gas or oil), use nuclear technology or harness water or wind power on a grand scale. Often these power generators are necessarily constructed some considerable distance from centres of population, so their energy has to be transmitted using miles of cable.

Microgeneration is a concept that turns all that on its head. Electricity is generated locally, in people's homes or at their businesses, either using purely renewable sources or making better, more energy-efficient use of fossil fuels. As well as potentially reducing the need for massive investment in new power plants, generating electricity closer to home reduces the amount that is 'lost' through the miles of overhead and underground cable between the power station and the user of the electricity.

The Energy Act 2004 defines microgeneration as 'the production of heat and/or electricity from a low carbon source' and specifies maximum size limits of 50 kW electricity and 45 kW thermal.

The UK's microgeneration industry is still at the early stages of market development, with each of the technological options at different stages. Some remain in the product development stage, while others are ready now for the mass market.

A number of barriers exist, which are common to all microgeneration technologies – these include the typical high initial capital costs, issues such as planning, and a lack of consumer awareness of what can be achieved.

There are several technologies that can be grouped together as 'microgeneration':

- solar photovoltaic;
- solar thermal hot water;
- ground source heat pumps;
- air source heat pumps;
- wind power;
- wood-fuelled heating (biomass);
- micro-CHP.

These technologies could be classified as zero or low carbon compared to 'traditional' ways of generating power.

Of these, solar photovoltaic, solar thermal hot water, wind and biomass are discussed in more detail elsewhere in this book.

It is estimated, on the basis of the information available, that just under 100,000 microgeneration units had been installed in the UK by the end of 2007.[2] Most of these were solar thermal units and solar photovoltaic systems – the latter contributing to an overall estimate of 16 MW of electricity-generating microgeneration connected to the national electricity grid.

Table 4.7.1 Approximate cumulative number of microgeneration installations by 2007

Grid-connected PV	2,300
Grid-connected micro-CHP	200–1,000
Grid-connected micro-wind	1,100
Grid-connected micro-hydro	65–75
Solar thermal	90,000
Biomass boilers	500–600
Ground source heat pumps	745–2,000
Air source heat pumps	over 150
Estimated total	95,000–98,000

Source: Element Energy (2008) *The Growth Potential for Microgeneration in England, Wales and Scotland*, June, Element Energy, Cambridge.

One interesting research finding is that householders differentiate between different types of microgeneration system, depending on their purpose. Many people see roof-based microgeneration technologies such as solar photovoltaics, solar thermal and micro-wind as being different from other technologies that provide all the heat needs of a house, such as micro-CHP or heat pumps. It appears that people make decisions on investing in technologies that merely supplement the energy sources for a home in a different way to deciding about those that make a substantial contribution.

Heat pumps

A ground source heat pump is a system that takes heat from the ground and converts it into usable heat for a home, office, factory or other building. In the summer, it extracts waste heat from the building and 'sinks' it into the ground, keeping the building and its occupants cool.

Unlike other technologies such as wind or solar, ground source energy is stable and predictable. For example, the temperature of ground water extracted using a borehole 200 metres underground in the UK is typically 12°C all the year round. Using a water-to-water heat exchanger, this energy can be used to heat water for heating and hot water to around 50–60°C.

Air source heat pumps work in a similar way, using the outside air as a heat source in winter and a heat sink in summer. Even when the temperature plummets to as low as −15°C, an air source heat pump can still extract usable heat energy.

Heat pumps are becoming increasingly popular as the technology becomes better known. While the UK remains a relatively small market, across Europe total sales increased by almost 50 per cent from 2007 to 2008. Thanks to a subsidy scheme, sales in France more than doubled over the same period.

Micro-CHP

Micro-combined heat and power systems generate electricity at the same time as heating a house, small office or other small building. Between 14 million and 18 million UK households are thought to be suitable to have micro-CHP units installed.

A detailed technology trial by the Carbon Trust revealed that micro-CHP technology could cut CO_2 emissions for small businesses by 15 to 20 per cent when installed as the lead boiler in places such as care homes, housing schemes and leisure centres. For households, current technologies are better suited to larger homes of three bedrooms or more, or older housing stock where it is not currently cost-effective to improve insulation, such as houses with solid brick walls. In such homes, micro-CHP could realistically result in savings of between 5 and 10 per cent.

A Society of British Gas Industries (SBGI) report estimates that micro-CHP products could displace 30 per cent of traditional domestic boiler installations annually by 2015.[3] This could provide carbon savings of 0.4 Mt a year by 2015, rising to 1.1 Mt per annum by 2020.

There are currently two types of micro-CHP system – those using a Stirling engine and those using fuel cells.

The Stirling engine was invented in 1816 by Scottish inventor Robert Stirling. Coupled with a high-efficiency condensing boiler, it generates electricity while the boiler is producing heat for the property. The more heat is produced, the more electricity is generated, which is why they are considered more efficient when installed in larger, less well-insulated properties.

It is the other way around for micro-CHP systems based on fuel cells – here, heat is generated as a by-product of electricity generation. Fuel cells can work on hydrogen or natural gas, the latter making this technology immediately accessible by UK households with a gas central heating system. It is estimated that fuel cell boilers powered by natural gas produce up to 2.5 tonnes less CO_2 per year than a standard boiler and could cut household carbon emissions by up to 50 per cent.

Conclusion

There have been many initiatives designed to transform the market for new microgeneration technologies, and new ones continue to be introduced. However, as yet, the market has not reached a state where the technologies can successfully stand on their own merits. While, on the whole, the technologies are proven and manufacturing capability is sufficient to support sustained growth, the industry remains fragmented. It also requires significant investment to build the necessary installation infrastructure to facilitate large-scale roll-out.

It is important we create the right environment for manufacturers, installers and other stakeholders to make the necessary investment in their business infrastructure. To allow this to take place the sector requires certainty. It requires strong signals from government that there will be continued and sustained support to drive the desired transformation.

Notes

[1] Department of Trade and Industry (DTI) (2006) *Power from the People*, DTI microgeneration strategy, DTI, London.
[2] Element Energy (2008) *The Growth Potential for Microgeneration in England, Wales and Scotland*, June, Element Energy, Cambridge.
[3] Society of British Gas Industries (SBGI) (2006) *Micro-CHP: Updated market projections*, SBGI, Kenilworth.

Barry Marsh is the General Manager of Solar Technologies, part of British Gas. With a background in the construction industry, he had his first experience of integrating solar PV technology into buildings in 1993, while working for a national building contractor. He has led Solar Technologies to become one of the largest and most experienced renewable energy technology installers in the UK. For further details contact Solar Technologies (tel: 01794 830154; e-mail: solarsales@solartechnologies.co.uk; website: www.solartechnologies.co.uk).

Part 5

Low-impact buildings

5.1

Construction resource efficiency – the way ahead

*The construction industry may be a massive consumer of material resources, but is also leading the way in terms of effective resource management, says **Katherine Adams**, Principal Consultant at BRE.*

'Resource efficiency' means exactly what it says – being more efficient in the resources we use, whether they are materials, energy or water. It's common sense! By using less we save money on the inputs, eg buying materials, and also on the outputs, eg reducing waste. We can also look at using waste as a resource (ie as a raw material), therefore reducing our demand on natural resources. This chapter focuses on construction material resource efficiency and the associated reduction of waste where significant improvements and associated benefits can be made.

What is the issue?

The construction industry consumes a large amount of material resource. In 2005, this was estimated to be 376 million tonnes; 80 per cent of this was from primary sources (ie not from recycled or secondary/industrial by-products). When we produce a material or a product, there are impacts associated with this, including the energy used to extract and manufacture it and the associated transport. This is known as the embodied energy and can vary depending on the type of material. For instance, a kilogram of bricks has 0.2 kilogram of CO_2 embedded, whilst general insulation has a figure of 2.6 kilograms of CO_2 for every kilogram. Reducing our resource usage links closely to climate change. Combined with this, the industry also generates an estimated 110 million tonnes of waste per year; not all of this is related to products used within new construction. Roughly two-thirds will be demolition or excavation waste. However, wastage rates for materials can be high. For example, contractors often quote that 25 per cent of plasterboard (one in four boards) can be wasted.

More attention is being paid in terms of government policy. This includes looking at the sustainable consumption and production arena whereby, in the construction area, product roadmaps for windows and plasterboard are being developed looking at the impacts (both negative and positive) of these products across their life cycle and how they can be improved. On the waste side, a joint industry and government target has been set to reduce construction, demolition and excavation waste to landfill by half by 2012 based on a 2008 baseline; this equates to over 6 million tonnes.

How can resources be managed more efficiently?

A supply chain approach should be adopted for the better management of resources and waste. Each part of the supply chain can undertake resource efficiency actions within their own sphere of influence. If I am a manufacturer of a construction product, then I can influence how much raw material is used in my product, if it is 'recycled' and if my product can be recycled at the end of its life. I can also look at opportunities to encourage waste minimization. An example of this is the Knauf Eco Door Jamb, which enables a full sheet of plasterboard to be used for a door opening, rather than cutting a hole in a sheet, which obviously reduces waste. I can also look at how the product is packaged to ensure that the product arrives at the site in good condition but also that the packaging is optimized and can be either reused or recycled. An example of this is Lafarge; by changing the plastic packaging on their plasterboard products, they have achieved a 78 per cent reduction in weight. I can also look at the options of taking back surplus goods or offcuts, and more and more manufacturers are offering this as a service.

If I am a designer, then I can look at using materials that have a lower environmental impact, including a higher recycled content, and investigate opportunities to design out waste, such as designing to standard sizes, using prefabrication and assessing the potential for deconstruction of a building at the end of its life. For example, by carrying out a design review for a new-build hotel, nearly £400,000 of savings related to waste minimization were identified, equating to over 3,000 tonnes of waste.

A contractor can consider the best ways of reducing waste by not over-ordering and managing materials appropriately on-site. Clients can influence the whole process by setting targets relating to resource efficiency and encouraging the supply chain to work together. Key to all of the above is ensuring that all of the actions can be measured in their effectiveness and that the objectives are shared. An example of a project that BRE worked on a number of years ago, but that still has an important message to give, is the housing development of Greenwich Millennium Village. This project was driven by a target to reduce waste by half (which was met) – this provided a common goal and focus for the project team. The key lessons learnt included having a good understanding of why the waste was produced, what it was and how much to drive change. This involved establishing what the key waste products were, when they were likely to arise in the construction process and what actions both on-site and off-site needed to occur and by whom to achieve greater resource efficiency. A supply chain focus was essential, with subcontractors contractually obliged to minimize waste, a partnering arrangement with the waste management company, and suppliers taking back materials and packaging.

The importance of measurement

The old adage of 'To manage something you must first be able to measure it' certainly rings true for resource efficiency. At BRE, this is something we have focused on for a number of years through our SMARTWaste system. This is a web-based tool to prepare and implement site waste management plans. From this system we have developed benchmarks for how much waste is produced for different project types and for waste types. This enables industry to forecast waste and set targets for reduction. It is an absolute must for a company to understand the quantity and types of waste that are generated, how waste is managed and the associated cost. In terms of cost, then, companies should really start to measure the true cost of waste. This is the cost of the wasted materials, the associated labour costs and the disposal costs. This can be over 10 times more than just the disposal costs. This surely provides an incentive for a real focus on resource efficiency.

What does the future hold?

Resource efficiency is becoming increasingly important because of both environmental and cost considerations. From a technological point of view, new developments include products and systems that help to minimize waste and that can be deconstructed and reused at the end of their life. Products also need to be designed with durability in mind and using less harmful substances. New technologies are needed to help recover the waste streams of the future such as composite materials. Supply chains need to work together to eliminate waste, which will require a different way of thinking. The future will be 'resource efficient'. Will you be?

BRE has been building a better world for almost 90 years through cutting-edge research, consultancy and testing services. Its unrivalled knowledge in regard to sustainability and innovation is now used across the construction industry and in the corporate world, creating better buildings, communities and businesses. BRE is part of the BRE Group of companies owned by the BRE Trust, a registered charity. The profits made by BRE go to the BRE Trust, the largest UK charity dedicated specifically to research and education in the built environment. See http://www.bre.co.uk/. Contact Katherine Adams (tel: 01923 664478; e-mail: adamsk@bre.co.uk; website: www.smartwaste.co.uk).

5.2

Zero carbon development

*The foundations have been laid for all new-builds to become zero carbon, explains **Sarah Youren**, a planning specialist at Sarah Youren Planning Solicitors.*

The government has committed the UK to reduce its carbon emissions by 80 per cent against 1990 levels by 2050. Emissions from the way we heat, cool and power our buildings are an important contribution to this, as 17 per cent of UK emissions are from non-domestic buildings and 27 per cent from our homes. This goes some way towards explaining the latest push to create zero carbon development to minimize our future impact on the environment.

What does zero carbon actually mean?

'A zero carbon home is one whose net carbon dioxide emissions, taking account of emissions associated with all energy use in the home, is equal to zero or negative across the year'.[1] It covers both regulated emissions, ie from systems integral to the function of the building and that are controlled through Building Regulations on heating, cooling, water heating and lighting, and unregulated emissions, such as those from appliances.

For new non-domestic buildings, zero carbon means that the net actual carbon emissions from a new building are zero over a year, taking account of typical behaviour. The definition does not include the overall building carbon footprint, such as links between the building and transport networks, logistics, water use, embodied energy and construction energy. In terms of energy use within a building it will include use of electronic equipment in offices and use of refrigeration in supermarkets. It will not include energy used for industrial processes, lifetime carbon impact of technologies, ie the emissions associated with manufacture as well as use, transport emissions, actual behaviour of people occupying the buildings, green tariffs or offsetting.

It will include as a minimum all emissions currently regulated by Building Regulations, and the government is considering the case for bringing some currently excluded building services such as lifts and escalators into the regulatory standard. The current proposal is to add a factor of 10 or 20 per cent of unregulated emissions on top of the regulated emissions in order to arrive at the target for non-domestic buildings.

What will the new rules apply to?

New-build residential development

New homes currently make up less than 1 per cent of the housing stock. However, the government has calculated that, if we build the number of homes that it is anticipated we will need in the UK to cope with predicted levels of demand, then by 2050 as much as a third of the total housing stock will be post-2008 buildings. This is the rationale for making more stringent changes to new-build than to existing housing stock. The sheer amount of new housing required should make it worthwhile to invest in developing new environmental technology and produce economies of scale to reduce the cost, thereby enabling it also to be introduced in existing housing stock.

Changes to Building Regulations

For new-build residential development the government proposes to improve the energy/carbon performance set out in Part L of the Building Regulations, with a view to achieving zero carbon housing within 10 years. This will be done in three steps: 1) a 25 per cent improvement in 2010 compared to 2006; 2) a 44 per cent improvement in 2013; and 3) zero carbon in 2016.[2] The government believes that achieving this target will save at least 15 million tonnes of carbon dioxide emissions per year by 2050. The changes will involve strengthening the requirements in relation to insulation, ventilation, air tightness, heating and lighting fittings. The first changes to Part L are anticipated to come into force in October 2010.

Changes to the planning regime

At the same time the government has published PPS1 on climate change, which encourages the setting of a framework for development to achieve zero carbon outcomes. PPS1 states that all new development should take account of landform, layout, building orientation, massing and landscaping to minimize energy consumption, including maximizing cooling and avoiding solar gain in the summer, and be planned so as to minimize carbon dioxide emissions by looking at how all aspects of development, together with the density and mix of development, support opportunities for decentralized and renewable or low carbon energy supply.

Code for Sustainable Homes

The Code for Sustainable Homes is a voluntary code that is intended to promote higher environmental standards in housing. It considers energy/carbon and also other sustainability issues such as water, waste and materials. Whilst the Code itself remains voluntary, it is used as a condition of funding for the Homes and Communities Agency National Affordable Housing Programme, on other government projects and by local authorities when they want to set sustainability-based planning conditions on housing developments. It was introduced in 2007, so is still relatively new, but already nearly 2,000 post-construction Code certificates had been issued by the end of November 2009, with over 300,000 homes registered to be built to Code standards.

Existing residential development

Energy performance certificates are now mandatory when selling or renting residential property. They provide buyers with detailed information about the energy performance of their home, together with a report on actions they can take to reduce carbon emissions and lower their fuel bills. It is too early yet to tell whether this information will have any great effect on the decision-making process of potential buyers.

Commercial development

Measuring energy performance for non-domestic buildings is complex. The diversity of the non-domestic building stock poses challenges in measuring and comparing energy efficiency. The range of activities accommodated within non-domestic buildings is huge, from occasional community use to full-time care homes. A further complication is the use of buildings by several occupiers, who may have multiple sources of heating and cooling and differing levels of intensity of use.

Anticipated timescale and measures for carbon reductions

In the Budget 2008 the government announced its ambition that all new non-domestic buildings should be zero carbon by 2019, with the public sector leading the way, with schools from 2016 and other central government estate from 2018. The government recognized that regulation is needed to achieve this ambitious target. However, given the current economic crisis it also recognized that it was important to consider the costs and potential consequences of such regulation on economic recovery for the construction sector. In November 2009 therefore the government consulted on policy principles, seeking views on the implications these will have on viability for individual developments and sectors.[3]

A key aspect of this is to address zero carbon strategies at the design and build stage, as the structures and technologies can then be locked in for the lifetime of the building and it can reduce future more complex and expensive retrofit measures. The government recognizes that the market is not driving low carbon buildings through a price premium at present, so the only way to achieve zero carbon is through regulation. It also recognizes that the energy costs of commercial buildings are often a small proportion of a company's total cost base, so incentives for low carbon construction are not always sufficiently strong. Regulation can also reduce the cost of low and zero carbon technology by increasing demand for it, thereby stimulating new markets for new technologies.

The proposed approach is to use a hierarchy of energy efficiency, followed by on-site or linked low or zero carbon technologies, followed by off-site allowable solutions. In terms of energy efficiency the government intends to set energy efficiency standards for non-domestic buildings at the highest practicable level based on a Kwh/msq/year measurement. Work is currently under way to define this level, including an appropriate differentiation for different types of building and to determine the timing and phasing of its introduction.

In order to make it easier for developers bringing forward mixed-use schemes the government proposes that the same technologies will be permitted for non-domestic buildings.

Energy performance certificates

Energy performance certificates on the sale and letting of non-domestic buildings are now mandatory. The occupier is given a report detailing the improvements to the building that the assessor recommends should be carried out in order to improve the building's energy performance.

The CRC Energy Efficiency Scheme

This is a mandatory UK cap and trade scheme focused on large commercial and public sector organizations to secure further savings of 4.4 million tonnes of carbon dioxide emissions per year by 2020. It will apply to organizations rather than to buildings. However, it should provide an incentive for large non-energy-intensive organizations to reduce carbon emissions from their own buildings. The scheme started in April 2010.

How do you achieve zero carbon development?

The definition of zero carbon development includes energy use during the year from appliances within the home or office. This means that developers will have to explore zero and low carbon sources of electricity supply, which is an area that is currently outside the control of Building Regulations. For most developers this will be a new area, requiring new technical skills and understanding of a new regulatory system.

The government has made it clear that solutions to zero carbon for both domestic and non-domestic buildings are acceptable at the development level rather than for each individual unit. Development-wide solutions such as district heating, combined heat and power or a wind turbine producing energy for the whole development site, for example, could be used to meet the requirements.

For residential development the government has stated that any type of technology that has a physical connection to the development, even if the technology is wholly or partly located away from the development site itself, will be acceptable. The standard assessment procedure will be updated to take account of this type of technology.

For non-domestic buildings the government is encouraging developers to look at introducing more efficient systems, fabric improvements, passive cooling, better control systems, better building management, building-level low and zero carbon technologies and development-level low and zero carbon technologies. Only if it is clear that these are not delivering the necessary carbon reductions or that the cost is disproportionate will it be acceptable to look at low and zero carbon technologies away from the development.

Rising to the challenge

Some companies, such as Zed Homes, are already rising to the zero carbon challenge by focusing their entire business strategy on building low and zero carbon developments.

Ashford Borough Council has teamed up with Hyde Housing Association to create a zero carbon affordable housing scheme. The Ashford Borough Council executive portfolio holder for housing, Councillor Peter Wood, said: 'This exemplar housing scheme would place Ashford at the forefront of environmentally sustainable development and present a beacon of excellence for other local authorities and housing developers.'

In London BioRegional Quintain and Crest Nicholson are developing a zero carbon scheme at Gallions Park. They are employing a host of measures, including renewable energy, energy-efficient architecture, natural materials, integrated waste management, on-site food growing and green transport measures such as car and cycle clubs.

One of the key issues now faced is how to ensure that the additional benefits of low and zero carbon buildings are appropriately reflected in the valuation of buildings in the future, and both the government and RICS are actively exploring this.

Notes

[1] Written statement by Minister for Housing and Planning John Healey MP on 16 July 2009.

[2] Department for Communities and Local Government (2007) *Building a Greener Future: Policy statement*, Department for Communities and Local Government, London.

[3] Department for Communities and Local Government (2009) *Zero Carbon for New Non-Domestic Buildings: Consultation on policy options*, 24 November, Department for Communities and Local Government, London.

Sarah Youren is a solicitor and Director of Sarah Youren Planning Solicitors. She advises on all aspects of planning and environmental law from inception to construction of a project. Her clients include private developers, funders, local authorities and government organizations. She has a particular interest in sustainable development and helps clients obtain planning permission, evaluate environmental impact assessments, negotiate planning and infrastructure agreements and acquire sites through compulsory purchase. On the environmental side she offers skilled and commercial advice on issues such as flooding, contaminated land, waste, water pollution and energy generation. For further details contact Sarah Youren at Sarah Youren Planning Solicitors, Unit 11 Bridge Wharf, 156 Caledonian Road, London N1 9UU (tel: 0845 481 8136; website: www.sarahyouren.com).

5.3

Domestic refurbishment

To retrofit the UK's housing stock will take innovation, says ***Richard Hartless*** *at BRE's Centre for Housing Best Practice and Low Carbon Futures.*

The UK housing stock is the oldest in Europe and consists of some 25 million dwellings. It is currently responsible for nearly 150 million tonnes of CO_2 per year, which is 27 per cent of the UK's greenhouse gas emissions. Following recommendations from its Climate Change Committee (CCC), the government has set a target of an 80 per cent reduction in CO_2 emissions (relative to 1990 levels) by 2050, which is a cornerstone of the Climate Change Act 2008.

Improving our existing housing stock is therefore key to the UK meeting its climate change commitments. Unfortunately, the average dwelling currently achieves an energy performance certificate (EPC) rating of only D/E, and over 5 million dwellings (nearly a quarter of the stock) achieve only an F or a G. To put this into perspective, in order to achieve an 80 per cent reduction the average EPC rating for the stock will have to be Band B or better, something that only a few hundred thousand dwellings (only 1–2 per cent of the stock) currently achieve.

Government sees energy efficiency as playing the major role in carbon reduction up to 2020, and the challenge here is the development of 'whole-house' refurbishment, involving an energy audit, installation (including all cost-effective measures) and financing.

Integral to this whole-house approach is the need to deal with so-called 'hard-to-treat' (HTT) homes. These are dwellings that have features such as solid walls, no lofts or not being on the gas network, or that are high-rise flats, etc. Such dwellings actually constitute a substantial proportion (43 per cent, ie about 10 million dwellings) of the stock and are responsible for half of domestic CO_2 emissions. By their very nature they are also expensive to treat and, accordingly, they have not so far been subject to refurbishment in a major way.

Barriers to meeting the challenge

To deliver this requires a step change in refurbishment. For the UK to meet its 2050 target requires 650,000 whole-house refurbishments each year, a major increase on the current level of activity. This requires significant up-skilling and mobilization of resources by the construction industry, as low carbon skills within the industry are still in their infancy in the UK. A number of the challenges and barriers are highlighted in the government report *The UK Low Carbon Industrial Strategy*:[1]

- The industry needs to be equipped with the skills for retrofitting existing dwellings, using more innovative low carbon construction methods and materials. This is particularly relevant to solid wall insulation if we are to achieve significant improvements cost-effectively whilst retaining our traditional housing stock.
- Not only is technical capability important, but there also need to be greater understanding and prioritization of low carbon imperatives from designers and clients, as well as senior facilities and building managers. Research shows a continuing need for information, advice and guidance across the whole sector.
- Because of under-investment the construction sector is fragmented and supply chains are often unwilling to make use of innovative materials or processes that require investment in skills and equipment. This is partly due to cautious clients, insurers and mortgage lenders, and partly a reflection of the project-by-project basis of much of the industry's employment.
- Adoption of innovation has traditionally been slow, but with the increase of low carbon legislation the construction sector recognizes the need to innovate to maintain as well as expand its current market position. However, there remains a serious information failure within the industry as to the scale of the necessary shift.

Business opportunities to address barriers

Advice and guidance

Providing robust guidance for householders (some two-thirds of dwellings are in the owner-occupier sector) is important, and this needs to be tailored towards individual house types. Web and telephone advice is already available, but this needs to be extended, and an example of this is the T-Zero model (http://www.tzero.org.uk/), where users can enter a handful of key variables to define their dwelling and it recommends packages of energy efficiency improvements. These measures are categorized by carbon saving, cost and cost-effectiveness to allow users to make an informed choice.

Home Energy Advisors will be a trained body of personnel able to provide tailored advice to householders on energy efficiency improvements. It is likely that many of these could be drawn from the Domestic Energy Assessor (DEA) community, who currently produce EPCs, which are required whenever a home is sold or rented. Given that some 6,000 EPCs are produced every day, there are plenty of opportunities to provide advice. Many large retailers, including DIY and trade outlets, see significant opportunities in providing domestic refurbishment advice and guidance.

Innovative products and technologies

Whole-house refurbishment requires the use of innovative materials in many instances. We are familiar with loft and cavity wall insulation, but these alone are insufficient to meet our carbon reduction targets, and it is estimated that many of the available lofts and cavities will be filled over the next three to five years. As noted above, there are a large number of solid walls that need to be insulated, and these may well need innovative products. At BRE, we recommend a 'fabric first' approach, ie ensuring a well-insulated building envelope before integrating microgeneration technologies, as this is generally more cost-effective and will last longer.

Some particular products of note are being used to insulate solid walls. Aerogels are very thin insulating materials that were originally developed by the space industry for use in astronauts' suits. These allow solid walls to be insulated internally with only a small loss of floor area compared to conventional materials, and this can be very important to householders living in small Victorian and Edwardian terraces. Vacuum insulation panels (VIPs) are also available for insulating the building fabric, and these too can provide an efficient thermal envelope.

Vacuum technology has also been used in the development of innovative energy efficient windows. Triple-glazed windows are available, but they may not be appropriate in some dwellings because of their bulky size, and there are particular problems in heritage areas where sash windows need to be retained. Glass panes can be constructed of two sheets separated by a vacuum of 0.5 millimetre (the sheets are held apart by very small beads), and when installed as a sash window they can produce the same overall performance as standard double glazing.

Having achieved a highly insulated envelope the dwelling requires efficient services for heating and hot water. Highly efficient gas condensing boilers are already widely used, but low carbon technologies such as ground and air source heat pumps can deliver space heating. Provided the building envelope is sufficiently airtight the dwelling can be ventilated using mechanical ventilation with heat recovery. There are also innovative products that extract the heat from waste water, and these can reduce a dwelling's hot water demand.

The final stage is the use of microgeneration technologies such as solar thermal hot water systems, which can provide up to a third of hot water demand, photovoltaic (PV) panels and micro-wind turbines mounted on suitable roofs that generate electricity, and biomass boilers that burn wood logs or pellets. All of these can reduce a dwelling's carbon emissions and ultimately could help to deliver a 'zero carbon' home.

Further information can be found in the Energy Saving Trust's *Sustainable Refurbishment* guide (CE 309), which can be found at http://www.energysavingtrust.org.uk/business/Business/Housing-professionals.

Overall opportunity

Despite the size of the refurbishment challenge, it provides significant business opportunities for the construction industry and other interested stakeholders. The government estimates that there could be 65,000 jobs from 2013 to 2020 in industries installing and manufacturing the technologies necessary to meet carbon reduction commitments, and potentially several times more in wider sectors and down the supply chains. Work undertaken for the Federation of Master Builders (FMB) suggested that the market for 'green' refurbishments could be worth £3.5 billion to £6.5 billion per year.

BRE has for many years provided technical advice on domestic refurbishment and has prepared much of the guidance for the Energy Saving Trust in this area. Further, BRE is currently undertaking the refurbishment of a Victorian terrace at a BRE site, which will showcase a wide range of sustainable technologies and is the flagship project of a large number of refurbishment exemplar projects around the country. For further details see http://www.rethinkinghousingrefurbishment.co.uk/.

Note

[1] HM Government (2009) *The UK Low Carbon Industrial Strategy*, Department for Business, Innovation and Skills and Department of Energy and Climate Change, London.

Richard Hartless is an Associate Director at the Building Research Establishment (tel: 01923 664143; e-mail: hartlessr@bre.co.uk).

BRE has been building a better world for almost 90 years through cutting-edge research, consultancy and testing services. Our unrivalled knowledge in regard to sustainability and innovation is now used across the construction industry and in the corporate world creating better buildings, communities and businesses. BRE is part of the BRE Group of companies owned by the BRE Trust, a registered charity. The profits made by BRE go to the BRE Trust, the largest UK charity dedicated specifically to research and education in the built environment. (website: http://www.bre.co.uk/).

The University of Edinburgh – a living laboratory

'Social responsibility is implicit in what the University of Edinburgh does', asserted one senior academic at a round table discussion in 2008. 'Our purpose is to contribute positively to society and enhance well-being.' 'Ah, but', said others, 'how are we evidencing the benefits we provide?' That led the University's Sustainability and Environmental Advisory Group (SEAG) to evolve a 10-year Social Responsibility and Sustainability Strategy,[1] which was formally adopted by the University Court in February 2010. We realized we had to make our commitment more explicit and to formulate a dialogue that embraces learning and teaching, research and knowledge exchange as well as people, services and infrastructure.

The strategy will guide us over the next decade. The 2010 implementation plan includes:

- developing an MA in sustainable development commencing in 2011;
- embedding social responsibility and sustainability issues into taught programme review processes;
- delivering a Transition Edinburgh University project aiming to cut carbon emissions from the 37,000 students and staff by 10 per cent – delivering on the 10:10 campaign undertaking;
- establishing a 'New Enlightenment' programme of public engagement with the local community, city-region and other partners to understand and respond to global challenges;
- establishing a network of research-experienced alumni across the world to engage in and contribute to the University's research, knowledge exchange and teaching.

Further specific actions include a sustainable procurement plan, climate action plan, greening ICT, low carbon estate development, waste reduction plans, biodiversity action plans, action on business travel and action on food choices.

As a research-led University – rated in the top 20 internationally – Edinburgh offers an extraordinary range of courses. They include Master's programmes in clean technologies and in international development studies and novel courses at the forefront of medical education.

Vice-Principal Professor Mary Bownes, who chairs SEAG, said: 'This strategy builds on our successes delivering practical environmental improvements and will cement our position as a destination of choice for both undergraduate and postgraduate taught courses and for collaborative research partners.'

Founded in 1583, Edinburgh is one of the largest and most esteemed universities in the United Kingdom. By the 18th century, the University had established a world reputation, which it retains today. It boasts a long line of famous alumni – from Sir Walter Scott to Charles Darwin – and notable rectors, including Winston Churchill. Given its venerable past, not to mention its historic landmark architecture, the University may appear a bastion of tradition. Yet the institution stands at the forefront of development in many subjects, including medicine, microelectronics, biotechnology and climate change.

The University has distinguished itself as a leader in energy and sustainability practices. Edinburgh launched an 'environmental initiative' in 1990 that has evolved into a comprehensive energy and sustainability programme. A major component of the sustainability agenda has been the introduction of three campus combined heat and power (CHP) installations, an investment of £12 million since 2003. Widely recognized for its outstanding commitment to energy efficiency, the University of Edinburgh was honoured in 2004 with a Green Energy Award for Best Environmental Initiative, presented by Scottish Renewables. In 2007 the UK National Energy Efficiency Award was also bestowed on the University.

Sustainability focus

This story began with the University's appointment of an energy manager in 1989. The following year the University hosted a conference on energy management in higher education institutions, which prompted adoption of an environmental policy with three themes: environmental teaching, environmental research and environmental practices.

The latter evolved into a comprehensive sustainability programme run by the University's Estates and Buildings – responsible for managing over 250 buildings on five campuses. Estates and Buildings is charged with promoting a more sustainable university and reducing the university's environmental and carbon footprint. This involves making most effective use of natural resources, promoting whole-life costing to contain utility costs, supporting continuous improvements in campus infrastructure, contributing to the University's missions of promoting excellence in research and teaching, and liaising with others such as the Scottish Environment Protection Agency to promote best practices on campus.

These activities have paid off for the University of Edinburgh. Since 1989, more than 5 per cent of the University's utilities spend has been invested each year in energy efficiency projects, delivering cumulative savings of £10 million.

Three energy centres

Driven by its commitment to sustainable practices and the imperative to reduce carbon emissions and to contain an annual utilities bill grown to £10 million, the University has installed state-of-the-art CHP systems on three of its five campuses since 2003. Ageing steam systems have been replaced with high-efficiency boilers and three spark-ignition gas engines.

Pollock Halls of Residence

Edinburgh's first CHP project was the 2003 installation of a GE Jenbacher engine to operate as the lead boiler serving the Pollock Halls of Residence, home to more than 2,000 first-year undergraduates. Three existing boilers continue to provide top-up and standby heating capacity. This system supplies heat to houses with 1,400 study-bedrooms and to administrative offices and refectory buildings.

Since installation, the Pollock Halls system has cut annual carbon emissions by 450 tonnes. The £1 million project was funded in part through a grant from the Community Energy Programme, jointly managed by the Energy Saving Trust and the Carbon Trust, established to help business and the public sector reduce carbon emissions.

King's Buildings

Next, the University turned its attention to the 50-year-old steam heating system at the King's Buildings campus, home of the College of Science and Engineering. Four different options were considered:

1. Scrap the existing central system and install individual boilers in each building. This would have been expensive and intrusive and would have involved a higher price for firm gas.
2. Strip out old boilers and steam pipes and install a CHP system with low-temperature hot water distribution. This had the lowest life-cycle cost, with only 5 per cent standing heat losses versus 30 per cent losses from the old system.
3. Replace the existing central plant with CHP, but retain the existing steam distribution system. This was still inefficient, with high heat losses and the problem of how eventually to replace the ageing pipes.
4. Maintain business as usual, with only replacement of steam boilers in future years. This would have meant being stuck with an energy-inefficient distribution system and constrained for future firing options; this option had the highest life-cycle costs when taking into account rising fuel prices.

The University chose option 2, as this provided the lowest whole-life cost. The old system – four steam boilers plus pipes in walkway ducts – was stripped out to make way for the CHP technology. This includes a 2.7-MWe engine and two 7.5-MWth hot water boilers. More than 1.4 kilometres of steel pipe were installed, all with thick mineral fibre insulation sealed in a flexible cover.

The system reduced annual fuel bills by £450,000, with even greater savings achieved when reduced employee costs are taken into account. These free up scarce budgetary resources for building improvement projects elsewhere. Financing for this £4.3 million CHP project included a second Community Energy grant of £1.63 million.

The King's Buildings CHP project was the largest energy efficiency upgrade in the UK university sector at the time of its installation in late 2003 and achieved the Best Energy Efficiency award in the 2004 Green Energy Awards.

George Square

The University's third CHP project, completed in 2005, included replacing 50-year old steam boilers with a trigeneration system to heat and cool 14 buildings on the George Square campus occupied by the College of Humanities and Social Science. This includes a 1.6-MWe GE Jenbacher 612 CHP engine, two 6-MW and one 3MW boilers, a 600-kW absorption chiller exploiting by-product heat to cool specialist laboratories in summer, and 75 cubic metres of thermal storage.

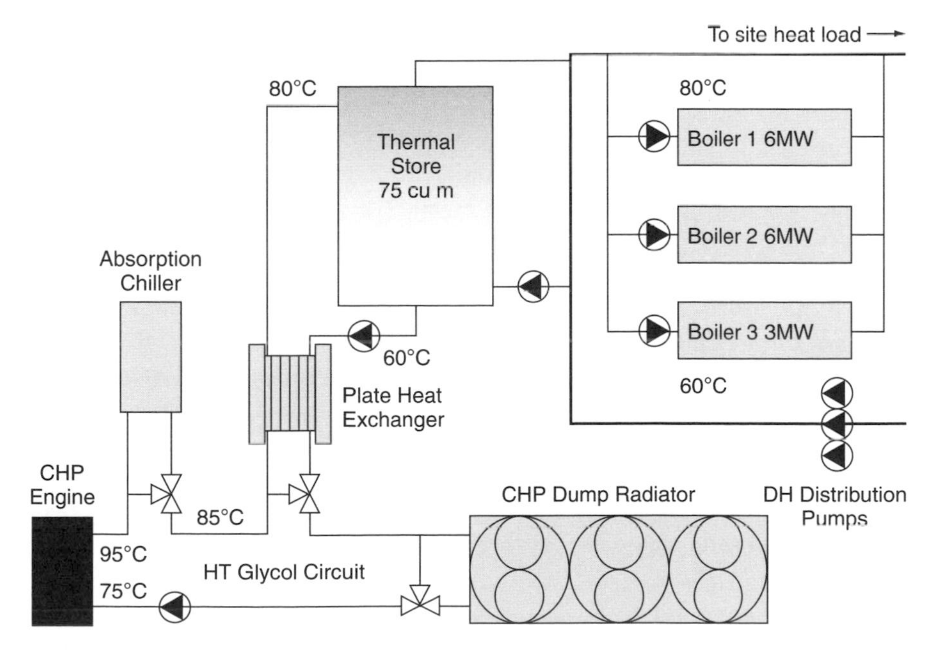

Figure P5.1 George Square trigeneration – a low carbon campus energy centre

This innovative £7 million installation was supported by a £2.7 million Community Energy Programme grant. The importance to the University of optimizing overall energy efficiency is reflected in the fact that £1.9 million of the budget was allocated to building controls that allow heating and ventilation equipment to be remotely controlled to optimize comfort conditions while minimizing energy costs and emissions. There are now more than 450 microprocessor-controlled panels in University buildings, monitored and managed from maintenance offices.

Annual savings now generated by the three units amount to over £1.4 million, enabling the original loan to be paid off entirely and accruing annual carbon savings of nearly 8,000 tonnes. The University is now considering a major extension of its George Square system to serve a further 15 or more buildings in the central area.

On a day-to-day basis, Estates and Buildings staff continue to help the University minimize its environmental impact and maximize energy efficiency. They play an active part in national networks to share best practices with other UK universities and maintain an innovative approach to building a sustainable university, determined to stay a successful international research leader for another 400 years.

If you are a graduate of Edinburgh and interested in collaboration in our alumni network, or if you think your organization can collaborate with the University in our aim to become a living laboratory tackling the global challenges, please contact Mary Bownes, Vice-Principal and Professor of Developmental Biology (Mary.Bownes@ed.ac.uk) at the University, or the author.

Note

[1] Social Responsibility and Sustainability Strategy 2010, www.seag.estates.ed.ac.uk.

David Somervell is Sustainability Adviser at the University of Edinburgh. Trained as an architect, he was attracted to energy policy issues following the near meltdown of the Three Mile Island reactor. He joined the University as Energy Manager in 1989. A founder member of the UK-wide Environmental Association for Universities and Colleges, he is currently Vice-Convener of the Scotland Branch. He has represented the University on the Business Environmental Network, the Edinburgh Sustainable Development Partnership and the Advisory Board for the Universities and Colleges Climate Commitment for Scotland. He can be reached at David.Somervell@ed.ac.uk.

Part 6

Transport

6.1

The shift to low carbon vehicles

What are the challenges and opportunities, asks ***Greg Archer****, Managing Director, Low Carbon Vehicle Partnership.*

Geopolitical drivers of future vehicles

The geopolitical challenges of peak oil, energy insecurity and climate change are focusing the attentions of governments and business on reducing demand for and dependency on petroleum in transport. Global energy demand for transport is expected to double by 2050, largely driven by growing markets for cars and trucks in the industrializing economies – notably China, India and Latin America. By 2050 the number of vehicles is expected to quadruple to nearly 3 billion. Transport already accounts for over a quarter of global greenhouse gas emissions. If transport demand continues to track rising GDP, the business-as-usual scenarios will lead to an unsustainable future of escalating oil prices, instability and accelerating climate change.

Fortunately, existing and emerging vehicle technologies and fuels can radically decarbonize road transport, but will take time to match the convenience, price and appeal of current vehicles. The vehicles we drive, how they are manufactured and by whom are evolving rapidly, creating business opportunities, challenges and risks.

There are regulatory pressures for more efficient cars

The technology transformation is being accelerated by global regulation of vehicles and fuels, fiscal stimuli for lower carbon alternatives, and substantial public and private investment in research, development and demonstration. In the European Union, which has set the most demanding targets, new car efficiency should increase by a third by 2020. Regulations are also in preparation for vans and trucks. Similar regulatory trends are occurring in every major vehicle market, although their stringency varies. An accelerating trend towards better fuel economy is now fixed after decades in which market trends and the profits of manufacturers depended upon producing larger, heavier and higher-performance cars.

Customer preferences are changing

Regulatory requirements for more fuel-efficient vehicles are being complemented by changing car-buyer attitudes and preferences. A combination of factors is changing the market, including higher fuel prices, recession, fiscal incentives and greater environmental awareness and concern (recently set back following the 'Climategate' controversies surrounding the Copenhagen climate conference). In the EU, new car fuel efficiency has improved by around 20 per cent in the last decade, with a recent quickening in progress.

Messages concerning the sustainability and efficiency of vehicles have increasingly wide market appeal, and vehicle manufacturers are responding and driving sales of lower carbon cars through adapting their marketing practices. Most manufacturers have introduced more environmentally friendly vehicle ranges or brands, such as Ford's Econetic and Volkswagen's Bluemotion. Fuel efficiency/low carbon is now the third most common message in car advertising. There has also been a switch in advertising expenditure in favour of more fuel-efficient models. In surveys, around 80 per cent of car buyers say that the efficiency of the vehicle was an important element of their purchase choice – although there remains relatively poor understanding of the scale of the potential fuel cost savings. On average, the most efficient models in each market segment are around 30 per cent better than the segment average.

To help consumers choose more efficient models, consumer information is improving. In the UK, 94 per cent of new car dealers now voluntarily display an energy-efficient label on all new cars as part of an agreement brokered by the Low Carbon Vehicle Partnership (LowCVP). A complementary scheme for second-hand vehicles has attracted over 2,300 dealer sign-ups. Comparative data on cars and vans are also available from a range of websites. Choosing a more efficient vehicle and driving it 'smarter' and less often are also part of the UK government's 'Act on CO_2' campaign to promote low carbon choices, and the EU is introducing new legislation to strengthen vehicle advertising practices.

The efficiency of petrol and diesel vehicles can be doubled – at a cost

A range of technologies are being employed that have the potential to double the efficiency of current petrol and diesel engine vehicles. For example, the use of low-rolling-resistance tyres, LED lights and improved aerodynamics cumulatively provides around a 10 per cent improvement. The adoption of advanced engine technologies, new transmissions and turbo-charging enables better, smaller engines to use 20 per cent less fuel with similar performance. The UK Climate Change Committee has predicted that by 2020 around three-quarters of cars will be some form of hybrid (using electric motors in addition to the engine, such as in the Toyota Prius). Hybrids can be up to 15 per cent more efficient. The costs of technologies to improve vehicle efficiency are strongly debated, but for a doubling of efficiency it is likely to add several thousand dollars to the price of a new car.

Substantial investment by automotive manufacturers complemented by research and development support from governments has aided the introduction of these technologies. New companies are also emerging to compete with established supply chains – some are university spin-outs, and others are management buy-outs or new start-ups. These companies face formidable challenges in financing and demonstrating that their technologies are effective and robust and can be manufactured cost-effectively. They also need to access established supply chains. To facilitate this, some of the best clean tech automotive SMEs were recently identified through a competition run by the LowCVP. Through a Technology Challenge, an expert panel identified the most promising SMEs, providing training and unique networking opportunities with prospective partners. Winners included: Clean Power Technology, whose RegEnBoost trio of turbo-charging technologies enables a 1-litre; and Libralato, which has designed a revolutionary new rotary engine that is a third more efficient, lower cost and half the weight of current models. Oxy-Gen have developed a system that enables a petrol engine to operate 15–30 per cent more efficiently by using an advanced form of combustion made possible by precisely controlling the air supply to the engine.

Electric cars

Improved (lithium-ion) batteries have raised the prospects for electric vehicles (EVs): silent, with zero tailpipe emissions and running costs a fraction of those of petrol cars. Using current grid electricity, EVs also cause only 75 per cent of the carbon emissions of equivalent petrol cars (in the UK), and this will decrease further as electricity generation is decarbonized through the use of renewable energy.

At present, batteries are prohibitively expensive, adding at least $10,000 to the cost of a small car, have a range of only about 75 miles and concerns over their lifetime. Costs need to fall by around a factor of five for EVs to be cost-competitive, and there is considerable uncertainty about how quickly costs will fall. Despite these uncertainties, governments and the automotive industry are strongly investing in EVs. Nissan, the most ambitious of the major car manufacturers, has predicted that by 2020 one in five of the vehicles it sells will be electric. This includes the Nissan Leaf, to be manufactured in Sunderland alongside a new battery manufacturing plant, which forms the cornerstone of a new ultra-low carbon regional development area in the north-east of England.

Consumer acceptability, especially 'range anxiety', presents a major barrier to EV uptake. EV drivers become anxious when a third to a half of the battery has been used, reducing the effective range. Aggressive driving styles and the use of air-conditioning and heaters also significantly reduce range. Recharging at home, ideally off-peak overnight, and at work makes commuting possible. For longer journeys the viability of fast-charging stations remains to be proven, and battery-swap stations would require a common specification of battery. Whilst some countries, notably Israel and Denmark, are adopting this model (operated by Project Better Place), in open markets competition between battery suppliers and manufacturers is now fierce, with multiple specifications. One solution will be extended-range plug-in hybrid vehicles, such as the forthcoming Vauxhall Ampera, which use an on-board generator to continuously recharge the battery.

Drivers heavily discount the lower running costs of EVs, and the capital costs will remain prohibitive for early adopters. As a consequence many governments are introducing generous incentives (£5,000 in the UK) and the installing of recharging infrastructure (the UK has made available £30 million). New business models are emerging, with the battery and possibly the whole vehicle leased, and electric vehicles adopted by car clubs. Monthly mobility services offering an EV, access to recharging and occasional use of another vehicle for longer journeys may evolve. EVs offer huge potential, but the early market is likely to be small and largely restricted to second cars. Beyond 2020 this market is likely to grow strongly as battery prices fall and new technologies emerge.

Alternative fuels

The transformation of the fuels market will be no less radical. With reducing demand for petroleum in mature markets (caused by efficient cars and the addition of biofuels), energy companies are increasingly exiting low-margin refining and distribution businesses in developed economies to release cash to invest in new emerging markets. Simultaneously new regulations in the EU and the United States are requiring new investment to decarbonize transport fuels and, in the EU, have encouraged dieselization.

Biofuels offer potential benefits for diversified energy supply, lower greenhouse gas emissions and the creation of new agricultural markets supporting rural development. Using food crops for transport fuels also presents a moral dilemma: is it right to grow food crops for fuel with millions starving and a growing population? With increased agricultural productivity, there is probably sufficient land for biofuels to sustainably supply 20–30 per cent of global transport fuels and biofuels markets are rapidly expanding globally.

Biofuels can provide a sustainable contribution to the transport fuel mix, but only if the right crops are grown in the right places, in the right ways. Differentiating between the best, acceptable and unsustainable biofuels is possible, as demonstrated by the reporting schemes developed by the LowCVP and operated in the UK since 2008.

But at present few, if any, countries have adopted adequate regulations to ensure biofuels are sustainably produced; there is little evidence that mainstream business is willing to pay more for sustainably produced fuels.

New technologies such as producing fuels from forest residues or green waste are under development but unlikely to achieve a significant market share until well beyond 2020. In the longer term, algal biofuels offer the potential for a ubiquitous carbon-neutral fuel, but remain, like hydrogen-fuel-celled vehicles, a relatively distant prospect, with mass market adoption unlikely before 2030. Biofuels can provide an important contribution to decarbonization of transport fuels, but the rush to meet short-term targets for supply in the absence of adequate controls is causing harm to both the environment and vulnerable people, thereby undermining biofuels' credibility.

Opportunities and challenges

There is little doubt that geopolitical pressures, coupled with new technologies, are decarbonizing vehicles and fuels and will continue to do so at an accelerated pace. Vehicle fuels and technologies are increasingly diversified and will offer a bewildering range of choice to car buyers in terms of both the vehicles and the form of purchase. This offers challenges for both consumers and manufacturers seeking to optimize research and development expenditure and investment in new models. In this diversified market there will undoubtedly be both technology and company winners and failures. The ultimate outcome will be more expensive vehicles that are less dependent upon dwindling and ever more costly supplies of oil and that emit less carbon. In the short to medium term, oil, however, continues as a key energy source for the growing vehicle parc.

The Low Carbon Vehicle Partnership (LowCVP) is a UK-based multi-stakeholder partnership of over 150 organizations working to accelerate the shift to low carbon vehicles and fuels. Further details are available at www.lowcvp.org.uk.

Electric vehicles

***Huw W Hampson-Jones**, Chief Executive Officer of OXIS Energy, sets the scene for the next generation of electric engines.*

Electricity versus oil, the early years

Believe it or not, at the beginning of the 20th century a great debate took place between the advocates of electric power and those who favoured the internal combustion engine (ICE) powered by petrol. History tells us which technology was adapted to widespread acclaim and the making of millions of dollars for the oil-producing countries of the world. One hundred years later, the debate is again being aired, and this time with a difference: with the knowledge of the finite nature of petroleum resources and the desire to move towards cleaner energy to limit pollution in our metropolitan cities on a worldwide basis.

In October 2009, over 2,000 cars a week were entering Beijing city roads. Both India and China, in comparison with Europe and the United States, still have a considerable amount of growth left in the market for new vehicles. In April 2010, the price of petrol in the UK reached £1.20 a litre, and the same trends can be seen in Europe and the United States. What are the implications for the future of electric-powered vehicles?

Enter new compounds

In the early 1970s a relatively unknown commodity was being studied, in the 1980s a prototype was developed, and in 1991 Sony launched its first commercial product based on this new commodity. The commodity was lithium, and throughout the 1980s and early 1990s lithium was combined with other chemicals to create what is now known as lithium-ion rechargeable batteries. Throughout the world millions upon millions of batteries have been produced using lithium-ion. The use of this battery in personal computers is extensive, and in the last few years it has been looked at for use in the automotive industry, but there is a significant problem with its use – that of safety. Additionally, there is the extensive use of cobalt in these batteries. Cobalt, which is expensive as well as being carcinogenic, presents problems for pollution as well as safety.

Simply put, the current lithium-ion rechargeable battery technology has run its course and, in the long term, is not suitable for use in the automotive industry. Its energy capacity is limited, which is a severe restriction when powering vehicles for several hundred miles or more. A typical lithium-ion battery for cars is limited to about 100 miles. In addition, because it is made up of a specific combination of compounds, it is volatile. Its volatility gives rise to considerable risk of explosion. The use of so many compounds leads to low energy capacity at considerable expense and toxicity. Thus, there is considerable consumer anxiety regarding lithium-ion-powered vehicles.

Battery technology for electric vehicles: its changes, potential and economics

Over the last 10 years, with the rising demand for vehicles in the newer economies of the world, in particular India and China, countries that are dependent on imports of oil to fuel their vehicles, there has been a growing trend globally to evaluate new sources of renewable energy to power vehicles.

Cars have already been powered by hybrid engines, a mixture of petrol and electricity. However, there is a move away from petrol to full electric engines powered by rechargeable batteries. For example, Mercedes-Benz have a car known as the Smart ForTwo Electric Drive. The car is capable of being powered by an electric engine for up to 84 miles. Few people realize that electric vehicles are quite nippy; this is because electric motors can deliver their torque (pulling power) instantaneously. However, the key advantage of this kind of car is that it can be recharged using overnight electric tariff for under £2. Try filling your current petrol tank for that amount!

The potential for electric vehicles is widespread. Take China, for example: currently there are over 100 million electric bikes (e-bikes) in use, with over 20 million new bikes sold each year. Each e-bike battery, on average, has 9 kilograms of lead and lasts for only one year. Every year approximately 600,000 tons of lead are used to power e-bikes.

If a new battery can be created that is capable of generating long-distance travel for cars, is lighter in weight and is cleaner in its use, the applications for the use of such a technology are likely to be widespread in the automotive, two-wheeled vehicle and defence sectors. If this battery technology can be provided at a much reduced cost compared with petroleum or the current chemical compounds used in existing lithium-ion, then we believe there is a case for widespread use of this battery technology for the electric vehicle market globally.

Next generation of rechargeable batteries – powering the future

Since 2005 OXIS Energy, based in the UK, has been spearheading the development and creation of a new lithium rechargeable battery. OXIS believes that vehicles powered by the use of its battery will be able to travel in excess of 300 miles, thus allowing electric vehicles to go further than current lithium-ion technology. Now this provides a very different proposition to the man or woman on the Clapham bus!

Not only has OXIS developed this technology, but it is also moving towards mass production to ensure that two-wheeled and four-wheeled electric vehicles will be able to take advantage of this technology throughout 2010–13. This is when OXIS expects mass production of electric vehicles to take effect in the world market.

The technology has been developed in the UK by a group of international scientists and is in the process of being rolled out. Empirical evidence proves its energy density is at least four times greater than that of the old lithium-ion battery technology. In addition, since the OXIS battery uses only ordinary chemical compounds, it has been proven to be inherently safe – so safe it satisfies the automotive sector's strict requirements for safety on the roads. It is also biodegradable, and therefore much safer for the environment, unlike lead acid, cobalt and old lithium-ion batteries.

OXIS has embarked on discussions with the world's leading automotive manufacturers for the use of OXIS technology in the modern pollution-free electric vehicles. OXIS is also working with two-wheeled electric vehicles (disabled scooters, golf buggies, scooters and motorbikes) manufacturers to raise the awareness of the OXIS battery. This increased energy power, coupled with its lightness of weight, is an important development in the next generation of electric vehicles. An electric vehicle may come off the production line weighing 2.5 tons but, at present, in order to power it, it will currently need another 1 ton of battery.

In summary, OXIS has developed the next generation of lithium battery technology, which is extremely safe for consumers to use. It is non-toxic, does not cause pollution and is recyclable. Moreover, it has the necessary energy to power electric vehicles for long-distance travel. It does all this at a fraction of the weight needed for current battery technology.

OXIS will establish its own production resources in the UK, and it is export led. Over 20 million electric bikes are sold in China alone. In Taiwan, where there is a population of 23 million, there are 11 million scooters and only 12,000 are electric. The global market for electric vehicles is large and rapidly growing, and current forecast estimates for the battery market globally is *circa* $60 billion by 2020.

In undertaking these tasks, OXIS is already employing highly trained graduates with skills in chemistry, physics and mechanical and electrical engineering. The future is bright; the future is electric.

Huw W Hampson-Jones is Chief Executive Officer at OXIS Energy Ltd, Culham Science Centre, Abingdon, Oxfordshire, UK (tel (office): +44 1865 408338; e-mail: huw@oxisenergy.com).

6.3

Aviation fuel

***Douglas Blackwell**, Managing Director at Bio Partners, discusses the developments in alternative fuels that are encouraging airlines to lift their target for use of renewables.*

We're all polluting our planet. Everything we touch in our homes, at work and on the journey in between has been made in processes that dump CO_2 into the atmosphere. Scientists may debate the exact amount of damage we're causing and the long-term effects, but the fact remains: every minute of every day we're releasing greenhouse gases (GHG).

Aviation seems like an obvious culprit, with vapour trails scarring our clear blue skies. Despite technology that enables us to sit at a home computer having simultaneous videoconferences with people in Los Angeles and Sydney, we love to fly. It's a preference that's producing a lot of turbulence these days.

Aviation's supporters point out that flying is responsible for just 2 per cent of global CO_2 emissions. Even so, the industry is in the process of making a remarkable turnaround, fostered by external regulation and internal determination. It provides a good and clear example of what's possible.

The science is simple: every tonne of aviation fuel burnt produces 3.15 tonnes of GHG. Aviation's industry body, IATA, has responded in a number of ways, including programmes to reduce fuel burnt and testing renewable biofuels. Encouraged by past success in cutting CO_2 emissions, IATA recently increased its former target to use 6 per cent of renewable-source fuel by 2020 to 10 per cent by 2017.

Cap and trade

A big spur for the aviation industry is the impending threat of emissions limits and trading. The EU's Emissions Trading Scheme caps the amount of GHG that countries can release and operates a market for excess amounts and shortfalls. The airline industry will be roped in from 2012 onwards. The effect on airlines will be colossal, with an additional billion euros in carbon costs added to their fuel bill.

To meet the challenge, leading aviation players are cooperating to develop alternative fuels that cut GHG emissions and satisfy criteria for sustainability. They are working to a new fuel specification in which renewable fuel, synthetic paraffinic kerosene (bio-SPK), is blended 50 per cent with regular Jet A1.

Test results are encouraging. They show that bio-SPK has nearly identical fuel properties to jet fuel and has performed successfully in tests carried out by Continental Airlines, Air New Zealand and Japan Airlines. Rigorous analysis of the results shows no adverse effects from using the 50/50 blend but does show a cut in CO_2 emissions of 60 to 65 per cent, as well as a 1.1 per cent saving in fuel consumption on long-haul distances.

Food or fuel?

So biofuels look set to save the aviation industry a great deal of money in fuel costs and carbon charges, but are they sustainable? The answer may partly come from certification schemes such as the Roundtable on Sustainable Biofuels (RSB), which developed a sustainability standard for biofuel production.

The RSB is a global initiative coordinated by the Ecole Polytechnique Fédérale de Lausanne (EPFL) in Switzerland, in which all stakeholders within and outside the supply chain can participate (farmers, non-governmental organizations, oil companies, airlines, experts, governments and intergovernmental agencies). All these actors share the concern of the sustainability of biofuel production and processing. The RSB develops a third-party certification system based on the biofuel sustainability standard, embracing environmental, social and economic principles and criteria.

The RSB standard looks at GHG emissions themselves, as well as conservation, water, air, waste management, human rights, social development, food security and land rights. The objective of the RSB is to provide a credible tool that ensures better biofuels for biofuel buyers, regulators and the public over the entire supply chain of growing, extracting, refining and supplying.

IATA's focus is on an alternative biomass fuel that can be produced sustainably without harming food production or fresh water usage, and can cut CO_2 emissions by 80 per cent. Preferred alternative feedstocks include Camelina and Jatropha. The latter, while not widely known, is proving to be one of the most promising.

The *Jatropha Curcas* plant is a perennial bushy tree that grows within the tropical belt in arid conditions. The nuts it produces as seeds give four to five times as much oil as canola (rapeseed), as much as 30 to 35 per cent of their own weight. Not only is it immensely productive, but Jatropha is a true, sustainable, alternative biofuel. It grows in marginal soils, so it doesn't steal land from food production. The tree doesn't need to be fertilized or burnt back after harvest. Jatropha, which is inedible to humans and animals, is refined into pure bio-diesel and bio-aviation fuels. The end-product seedcake can be heat- and pressure-treated to make animal feed or turned into fuel to replace wood.

Carbon in chains

Jatropha was one of the components of the 50/50 blend tested by airlines. As a fuel it works. But if it is to prove sustainability and secure a much-prized accreditation, the growers need to be diligent agriculturally, commercially and socially. Growers including Anglo African Farm Ltd, the growing associate of Bio Partners Ltd, have found themselves extending their business downstream into oil extraction and refining. The reason is that the aviation industry will not buy fuel from a non-accredited source, because nothing less than fully certified fuel will gain exemption from carbon emission charges.

To gain accreditation, biofuel suppliers must show they have measured every aspect of carbon capture from day one of planting through to the aircraft's fuel tanks. Growers must measure the entire carbon custody chain above and below ground, including harvesting, transport, extracting the Jatropha oil and refining it into bio-SPK.

Currently, Anglo African Farm's process produces a 68 per cent saving of GHG emissions before transport and refining. Over time, plantations grow more canopy sucking in more carbon. That, plus precise auditing and production techniques, is likely to boost savings up to around 88 per cent, higher than IATA's 80 per cent target. At this level, biofuel is extremely attractive. If the airline uses an 88 per cent certified fuel, it can prove it has cut its carbon dump by that amount.

Sustainable for everyone – community development

Using alternative-generation feedstock may limit the food-for-fuel argument, but may not be sufficient to address all impacts. The RSB is currently developing an approach to address indirect impacts of growing biofuel feedstocks, especially on GHG emissions, local communities and wildlife habitats.

As an example of the level of effort producers put into meeting sustainability targets, Anglo African Farm allocates a third of its 12,500-hectare Jatropha plantation to local communities. Of this share, it teaches local farmers how to efficiently grow maize and legumes – both for local consumption – plus a section of rain-fed Jatropha, which is sold back to Anglo African Farm for cash. As well as providing hundreds of jobs, the main plantation pays rent to local chiefs, and 5 per cent of profits from the sale of the crops go to a community uplift programme to improve living standards.

Because transport has to be included in the carbon cost of biofuel, production of Jatropha oil and its subsequent refining have to take place as close to source as possible. In Africa, river transport on barges is preferred over road haulage. Plantations are sited not solely on available land, but where transport links exist to oil extraction and refining facilities. These installations, again, represent rare and important investments in parts of Africa that suffer from extreme poverty.

As the enterprise begins to produce biofuel on an industrial scale, other investors will be encouraged to begin planting nearby. Buying in from other growers is an important element in the economics of the business model and for supplying the huge need of the aviation industry for biofuel.

The scale of the need

IATA's director-general, Giovanni Bisignani, has said that IATA expects the aviation industry to use 10 per cent biofuel to power aircraft by 2017. The current annual usage is 250 billion litres. With annual growth in traffic of 5 per cent, the industry will need 351 billion litres of jet fuel by 2017 from conventional hydrocarbon sources.

The target of using 10 per cent biofuel in the form of Federal Aviation Administration (FAA)-certified J50 blend fuel – 50 per cent hydrocarbon kerosene and 50 per cent bio-kerosene (bio-SPK) – will require 17.5 billion litres of bio-kerosene. This will need 45 million tonnes of Jatropha oil seed in production by 2017, covering a land mass of 10 million hectares. IATA's other preferred biomass sources (algae and Camelina) will augment supplies, but not by enough. Clearly, then, if the aviation industry is to meet its own targets, production of bio-feedstocks must be ramped up on a colossal scale.

Federal and EU regulators will continue to put financial pressure on CO_2 emissions. Industry bodies have set themselves ambitious targets to cut GHG emissions. Biofuels have proven themselves in performance as technically sound, drop-in fuels for aircraft. They reduce immensely the carbon output of flying by better fuel performance and much lower CO_2 emissions.

Biofuel will keep us flying, responsibly. Its most useful source, Jatropha, will bloom across the arid grasslands of Africa. The seeds of this humble plant will help roll back the advance of climate change, keeping our aircraft in the skies, taking us to our business meetings and our beach towels to holidays in the sun. And, as a bonus, Jatropha will bring prosperity to some of the poorest people on earth. I call that progress.

Douglas Blackwell is Managing Director of Bio Partners, the project managers for Anglo African Farm Ltd. The company invests in Jatropha plantations, community programmes, oil extraction, and refinement of bio-SPK for the aviation industry. For more information e-mail: info@bio-partners.co.uk.

Part 7

Land and water use

7.1

Water technology

There are a host of processes and services in which clean technologies could be introduced, says ***Ian Bernard****, Technical Director at British Water.*

Water is a simple but fascinating compound. It falls from the sky, is a universal solvent and is essential for all life, but if it is contaminated or is in short supply it can cause death. There is plenty of it around. The world's oceans hold 97 per cent of all surface water, glaciers and the polar ice caps hold 2.4 per cent and, apart from a small fraction of a percentage bound in biological organisms and created products, the remaining 0.6 per cent is present in surface waters (ie rivers, lakes and ponds).

The animal kingdom, including humans, throughout history has sought out water resources to drink and has over thousands of years settled and lived beside rivers, lakes and seas, convenient for a water supply to drink, irrigate crops, wash, travel by boat, trade and fish for food. This integral relationship with water still exists, but although major towns and cities are still situated next to water we have developed water distribution systems so that water is transported to our houses, offices, factories and agricultural land. We now buy manufactured goods and foods, and the importance of water and its value in manufacturing and food production is lost.

As with all life forms, human beings produce liquid and solid wastes and with increased urbanization these wastes are disposed of in a water system (sewerage). These wastes are flushed away with potable water, and this sewage enters the sewerage system, where gravity and pumps deliver it to a sewage treatment works for treatment.

Fundamentally, water is vital for our continued existence and, with an increasing world population, urban migration and climate change effects, it is becoming more important as a resource. The clear message from the European Commission's (EC) Water Supply and Sanitation Technology Platform (WssTP) is that water should be managed by integrated water resources management (IWRM) (ie within the water cycle). It has been estimated that by 2025 more than half of the world population will be facing water-based vulnerability. A report in November 2009 suggested that by 2030, in some developing regions of the world, water demand will exceed supply by 50 per cent. Unfortunately, water is often taken for granted, and unless we find technological solutions to provide a water supply for everybody then there is the potential of mass migration, with the prospect of a water war resulting.

The water industry

The water industry is an intriguing industry, fragmented into many aspects because of the water cycle and evolution of separate different water sectors. Water moves continually through a cycle of evaporation or transpiration, precipitation and run-off, usually reaching the sea. Water management covers the whole water cycle, including agriculture, industry, utilities, marine, flooding, drought management, etc. The main water industry services (ie utilities) provide drinking water and wastewater services to households and industry. Water supply facilities generally include abstraction facilities, reservoirs, rivers, groundwater sources, cisterns for rainwater harvesting, a water supply network, water treatment facilities, water storage tanks and towers, and water pipes. Wastewater services include collection sewers, sewerage, pumping stations, waste treatment works, sludge treatment and disposal, and effluent discharge facilities.

In Europe, irrigation, urban areas and manufacturing industries are the main areas driving the demand for water. According to the European Commission, water consumption at EU level is divided among the following sectors:

- *agriculture*: 69 per cent;
- *public water supply*: 13 per cent;
- *industry*: 10 per cent;
- *energy (cooling in power plants)*: 8 per cent.

These industries can either abstract directly from surface and groundwater resources or receive a potable supply from a water utility.

The water industry (utilities) supplies 150 litres per person per day (l/p/d), and the government is targeting a 13 per cent reduction to 130 l/p/d by 2030. Also, recent work has shown that the 'embedded water' is about 3,400 l/p/d. Much of the embedded water that we consume, about 70 per cent of our water footprint, comes from other nations, as we import goods and services into our country.

The message here is that there is huge scope for water savings and for reducing our water footprint or carbon footprint either in embedded water or in potable water supplies.

Water technology investments

Water technology investments are critical right now, and time is running out. Investors want to see strong evidence of water investment opportunities, in which high-growth, innovative technologies generate significant returns. However, those types of investments are rare. There is a water crisis on the horizon, and the government, the public sector and the private sector are not ready.

Some companies are starting to look at their non-water-related technology and turning it towards water, such as using LED technology for water treatment. More companies can start thinking about their products in terms of what it can do for water technology.

On economic grounds there is a clear positive correlation between access to safe water and GDP per capita. If we find clean technological solutions for providing safe water, we can prosper and improve society and the environment. And maybe governments will appreciate that water is more important than energy. The scarcity of water will elevate prices, and users will recognize the value and begin to control and reduce usage.

Water technology

Traditionally water infrastructure systems in the industrialized world are highly centralized, heavily regulated and, without competition, slow to risk new technologies. These systems are often old and expensive to maintain. There is a trend to decentralize water treatment and wastewater treatment, which gives obvious savings in 'pumping energy', but it can obviate the need to spend capital on new assets to increase hydraulic capacities in sewers or water mains.

The rapid emergence of desalination throughout the developed world is indicative of this ongoing crisis in water supply. Depending on how costs are calculated, a tonne of water (1 m^3) produced by desalination will cost 40–50p. This is seen as expensive water, but perhaps is not if compared with a litre of bottled water at £1 a bottle.

Reliable and robust sensors enabling real-time monitoring, forecasting and control systems are needed to control and manage both quality and quantity in all aspects of water systems.

Resource recovery, in particular nitrates and phosphates, is being looked at. Energy from wastes (anaerobic digestion, or AD) has been a conventional process in water utilities since the mid 1970s. Now incentives are driving utilities to develop AD plants that produce more biogas to produce energy.

Clean technologies

To utilize clean tech processes, the goal should be to reduce carbon and water footprints in a sustainable way, ie they should have a societal benefit and an environmental benefit as well as an economic one. With regard to the potable water and sanitation services water utilities, there is a host of processes and services where clean tech technologies could be introduced. (See Table 7.1.1.)

Table 7.1.1 Examples of needed water technologies

Water Processes	*Examples of Needed Technologies*
Water resources (quality and quantity):	
	Atmospheric water generators
New water resources	Catchment planning resources
Protect existing resources	Novel SUDS drainage
Treat G/W contaminated resources	*In situ* biological treatments
Water treatment:	
Enhance existing processes	Efficient membranes
New processes	Low energy filtration
Reduced energy	New 'no waste' processes
Utilize renewable energies	Efficient desalination/resource recovery
Disinfection (reduced chemicals)	Energy recovery systems
	Recover potential energies and wind/solar energy
	Efficient pumps/mixers
	Non-chlorine-type disinfectants
	Nanotechnology
Water distribution:	
Detect and repair leaks	*In situ* leakage detect and repair systems
Pressure control	
Water demand:	
New water-saving devices	Reduced-water-using devices
Advanced smart metering	Wastage detection/usage measurement
Wastewater Processes	*Examples of Needed Technologies*
Sewerage:	
Improved pumping systems	More efficient pumps
Control systems	Increase hydraulic capacity
Energy recovery	Heat, hydro-kinetic and potential energy recovery
Prevent exfiltration	Leakage detection and control
Sewage treatment:	
Enhance existing processes	Reduce efficiencies and effectiveness
New processes	New biological and physical processes
Reduced energy/aeration	Anaerobic processes
Energy recovery	Resource recovery
Sludge treatment:	
Resource recovery	Digestate treatments
Energy from waste	Improved biogas production

Environmental Water and Other	*Examples of Needed Technologies*
Effluent:	
Resource recovery	Nutrient usage – algae production Nutrient recovery
Flooding and stormwater:	
Control systems Asset protection devices	Real-time monitoring, forecasting and control systems Hydro-kinetic and potential energy recovery Stormwater infiltration
Alternative sources:	
Rain water harvesting	Smart collectors/treatment systems
Water reuse and recycle	Simple management and treatment systems
Other:	
Irrigation	Automatic/drip/moisture sensors
Cooling towers	Optimization software

There are some technologies being developed that are innovative and meet the clean tech criteria. Examples include:

- generation water from the atmosphere as a new resource;
- *in situ* biological treatment of contaminated groundwater to recover a polluted resource;
- solar-driven membranes for desalination;
- resource recovery from desalination brine wastes;
- 'no waste' water treatment processes;
- *in situ* water pipe leak detection and repair systems;
- smart water meters with burst recognition capabilities;
- heat, hydro-kinetic and potential energy recovery;
- algae production in sewage treatment effluents;
- moisture sensors for drip irrigation.

Water is an important resource, essential for a healthy life and environment. With advancing climate change, increasing populations and urban migration we are approaching a crisis scenario with a water scarcity. In order to tackle this crisis we need to develop new and innovative water technologies to reduce the water demand, increase supplies or reduce costs in a sustainable and environmentally friendly manner. The introduction of clean tech technologies will take us along the right path.

For further details visit www.britishwater.co.uk.

7.2

Wood technology

*The extraordinary increases that we have already seen in agricultural productivity are coming to forestry, says **Mats Johnson** at SweTree Technologies.*

Climate change has generated a unique global awareness of how well, or badly, we use our resources, thus starting a debate on how we should use them in the future. This is an opportunity for change. Will we have enough renewable raw materials in a sustainable way in the shift from an oil-based society?

The need to decrease our dependence and use of oil-based products, whether for energy or materials, is increasing the demand to enhance the production and use of renewable resources for these purposes. At the same time the human population is expected to increase by approximately 50 per cent over the next 40 years and, furthermore, many of the developing countries will evolve into industrial countries in this period. Altogether this will lead to a large increase in the global demand for renewable resources such as wood for both energy and materials purposes. However, we cannot expect that this demand could be met through large changes of land use; historically this has been very difficult for humans. This means that the same land area needs to produce more where this is possible, yet in a sustainable way. We need improved methods for forestry, faster-growing trees and new methods of using cellulose fibre to a greater extent in plastic materials.

Over the last 10,000 years there has been a tremendous increase in the productivity of many agricultural plants. The same remarkable improvements have not, however, been realized for trees. The reason for this is that most trees flower very late (15–20 years is not uncommon) and irregularly and therefore tree breeding is, relative to that for many agricultural crops, slow. However, there is no reason to expect that the breeding potential is smaller in trees than in any crop plant. New biological and chemical knowledge about trees and wood, emanating from many academic research labs, strongly indicates that we can expect trees with improved traits to grow radically faster where there are good conditions for the supply of water and nutrients and that many new materials can be made based on cellulose fibre.

To make this possible we need to use trees with improved traits, just as we use agricultural crops with improved traits. With considerably higher production of wood in selected geographical areas we can also to some extent ease the pressure on the natural forests to deliver these products. There are several examples in the world where land of formerly devastated rainforests has been converted to plantation forests and replantations of rainforest in a good mix, which has thereby enabled improvements of both productivity and ecological assets. An interesting side effect of increasing the growth of wood in a specific area is that, as a consequence, carbon dioxide is taken out of the atmosphere, ie there is an increased carbon sink.

So far the interest for using new biological knowledge to improve wood growth is the highest in the developing countries and in countries that have come a long way to becoming industrialized countries, eg Brazil and China. It is the logical result of the general driving forces in these countries for improved ways of living, as well as their particular knowledge and strong companies in these fields, combined with the decision competence in these companies. This also includes support from governments at different levels.

For the old industrial countries the lack of government support and less entrepreneurial driving forces will hinder this development in certain geographical areas. This is most notable in Europe. However, it will make it very difficult for Europe, where land is more locked up than in other areas of the world, to be able to use more wood as a renewable resource. This will conserve Europe's need for oil, as well as hinder technology development in this knowledge area based on skills in Europe.

Some examples

The publishing of the first genome of a tree (the poplar) has made it possible to a greater degree to elucidate the functions of the genes in trees. In collaboration with Umeå Plant Science Centre (UPSC), SweTree Technologies has tested carefully selected genes for their function. This knowledge can be used for marker-assisted breeding, a technique that is commonly used for agriculture crops but has yet to be implemented for forest trees owing to several practical limitations, such as the abovementioned late flowering time. The genetic knowledge can also be used to directly tune a tree's own use of its genes, specifically gene by gene. Such trees are now being tested in the field in several parts of the world, and this technology can be expected to develop into a biotech revolution for the supply of wood for any purpose. In this way the same benefit as that shown in regular breeding programmes can be achieved, but much more efficiently and with a much higher precision, using the biotechnology methods. Achieving the same improvements with regular breeding may take a very long time, 50–100 years, illustrating the clear benefit of direct breeding using biotechnology.

Based on Professor Torgny Näsholm's work at UPSC in Umeå, Sweden, we know that many plants, including trees, prefer to take up the growth-limiting nutrient nitrogen in the form of organic molecules such as amino acids, in particular arginine. Plants treated with arginine show larger and more well-developed root systems, and such plants are thus better prepared for quick establishment and rapid growth, enabling higher rates of survival when planted. A faster start to forest plantations means more wood per hectare over the whole growth period.

Cellulose fibre, one of the main constituents of wood, is a polymer that can be used for many purposes, just like oil-based plastics. In today's context there is a tremendous opportunity to develop different chemical solutions to expand the use of cellulose fibre for many more applications where presently oil-based plastics are used. Already there have been presentations of cellulose fibre materials ('paper') stronger than iron. Cellulose fibres are mixed in different ways into materials used in many applications, eg cars. We will see, for example, plastic bags, clothes, parts of electronic products and new building materials being made from cellulose in the future. We can even expect the next Kevlar to be cellulose fibre based using nanotechnology. One research centre focusing on this is the newly founded Wallenberg Wood Science Centre at the Royal Institute of Technology (KTH) in Stockholm.

Since 2004, Mats Johnson has been CEO of SweTree Technologies, a company catalysing the shift from an oil-based society to one based on renewable resources such as wood using new biology and chemistry knowledge about wood. Mats has made a career in the biotechnology field working for companies such as Pharmacia Biotech, Amersham Pharmacia Biotech and KaroBio, mainly in different business leading positions but also in R&D. His technical background is in biotechnology from the Royal Institute of Technology (KTH) in Stockholm, Sweden. Mats can be contacted at mats.johnson@swetree.com.

Part 8

Carbon removal

8.1

Geo-engineering

*It is time to start taking a serious look at technologies for cooling the planet, say **Colin Brown** and **Tim Fox** at the Institution of Mechanical Engineers.*

Many initiatives and campaigns over the last 20 years have called for action and investment to reduce the production of 'greenhouse gases'. Despite this we are still going in the wrong direction. Whilst the focus must continue to be on reducing our emissions so as to deal with the root cause of global warming, the reality is that we have not been successful so far. The failure to get a legally binding multinational agreement at the climate change talks in Copenhagen in December 2009 did not help. In the meantime we need to understand the consequences of our failure and consider what other actions we might take.

We are fast approaching a critical point in dealing with climate change. The consensus is that we cannot allow global average temperature to rise by 2 °C above pre-industrial levels. If we do – and many predict this will happen within the next few decades – we are told we will face dramatic and irreversible changes to our climate.

A technology that cools the planet to compensate for greenhouse gas emissions could therefore prove to be extremely useful. In the short term it could buy us the time we need to implement emissions reduction solutions at the scale required. Although unlikely to be a cost-effective approach, geo-engineering does have the potential to remove all current carbon dioxide emissions from the atmosphere. This would allow all emitters to continue 'business as usual' and yet avoid the damaging effects of global warming by instead footing a large bill each month for the new 'air cleaning' industry. Ironically, however, the cost of an industry to maintain the status quo may well be difficult to recover. In a way it is the true absolute cost of mitigating climate change, but in allowing continued emissions rather than reducing them we will need to be clever about the economics and carbon equivalence of what we are doing.

Technologies

Typically geo-engineering technologies fall into three categories. These are:

1. extraction of carbon dioxide from the atmosphere as a direct reversal of the emission process;
2. direct reflection of solar radiation back into space, or shading of the planet to reduce the amount of heat that is available;
3. interference with the detailed heat transfer mechanisms in the atmosphere to try to increase the natural heat loss processes.

The engineering focus is on those technologies in category 1. Those in category 2 require devices of such vast size to be effective that they are likely to be energy-intensive to deploy and very expensive. Those in category 3 involve irreversible actions that raise concerns over their long-term legacy, which means they rightly need much careful thought. On the other hand, 'cleaning devices' in category 1 have a natural and attractive logic.

There is no shortage of geo-engineering ideas, but engineering assessments of their practical feasibility are in short supply. To begin to redress this balance the Institution of Mechanical Engineers (IMechE) has undertaken an initial assessment in its Cooling the Planet programme.[1] Of the many options reviewed, the two most promising are artificial trees and algae-coated buildings.

Artificial trees

Research has started into building machines that, like trees, can remove CO_2 from the atmosphere. Unlike trees using photosynthesis, however, these artificial trees would use a reversible chemical reaction that operates thousands of times more quickly. This reaction occurs when air passes through the device (the tree) and CO_2 sticks to a sorbent material (the leaves). The CO_2 is then removed and buried underground in the same way as is proposed for the carbon capture and storage (CCS) technology under development for coal-fired power stations.

Prototype designs based on current technology, with an area footprint the size of a standard shipping container, could capture around 1 tonne of CO_2 per day and cost an estimated $20,000 each. With further refinement and technology development it is conceivable that 100,000 'trees' could be deployed to capture the UK's entire non-stationary and dispersed emissions (that is those from the transport sector and from dispersed sources such as homes, light industry and remote communities).

The operating costs are not yet clear but would include the powering of the device and the transmission and underground storage of the carbon dioxide it produces. It seems likely, however, that if a realistic carbon price emerges, and the credits from this process are traded, there is potentially an economic business to be had.

Algae-coated buildings

Algae naturally absorb CO_2 through photosynthesis. This second option introduces algae into the urban environment through the use of tubes that are fitted to the outside of buildings. The algae are periodically harvested from these tubes and can be used for biofuel and as the feedstock for the production of a fertilizer that sequesters the carbon. The advantage of this proposal is that unlike artificial trees it produces products that can be sold directly. Also, no additional land is required and hence it will not affect existing and future food production or other important land uses.

Algae would be harvested as fuel before they start to decay or die. This prevents the carbon being released back to the atmosphere during decomposition and allows it to be processed for energy directly. Algae have a high energy content, with a value per unit mass, at 18.5 to 35 MJ/kg, that rivals that of coal (which averages at 24 MJ/kg) and exceeds the energy density of wood, wastewater sludge and agricultural by-product. In the concept assessed by the team at the IMechE the algae provided fuel to a generator or combined heat and power (CHP) engine, and the exhaust CO_2 from that process was fed back to the next batch of algae in combination with air, thereby ensuring a low carbon solution.

Moving forward

In response to these challenges, the IMechE has developed the following recommendations to help the technologies become reality:

- *Obtain government support for geo-engineering research.* In common with many greenhouse gas reduction technologies, all geo-engineering technologies rely on carbon pricing or similar intervention to make them economic. There is no free market drive for them to exist and consequently they are characterized by immature technologies. There is therefore a need for central support of a programme of geo-engineering feasibility research and development. Moreover at the early stages this should be in an international context because of the similarity of the challenges facing a wide range of countries. As little as £10 million per annum could provide us with a more reliable quantitative understanding of the effectiveness, risks and costs of geo-engineering as well as the ethical, governance and moral perspectives associated with it. Importantly this research would need to bring together climate scientists and modellers, engineers, economists, social scientists and philosophers to ensure we understand the impact of the technology.
- *Use the resources we already have.* The UK is already a world leader in climate modelling and impact studies, as well as mitigation and adaptation research. Investors and businesses are fortunate to have access to the Tyndall Centre, working with the Hadley Centre, together with a range of world-leading research institutions and universities. The UK is therefore ideally placed to lead, coordinate and deliver geo-engineering research.
- *Pilot promising schemes.* Schemes that show the most promise should be funded through to demonstrator phase to enable their potential to be assessed and for the

best schemes to become ready for commercial deployment. Such work requires investment in new modelling capabilities, tools and pilot-project scale engineering studies.

- *Adopt a realistic roadmap.* Carbonization and decarbonization of the global economy can be accurately predicted because of the time delay in building capital infrastructure to make any significant changes to our trajectory. Building on existing knowledge of mitigation and adaptation, we can best achieve the climate change targets through a transition incorporating geo-engineering.
- *Maximize the commercial opportunities for UK plc.* Develop a partnership between industry and government policy based on mutual confidence. We should build on public research spend into geo-engineering through commercial investment in private development and demonstration. We can avoid the uncertainties through committing to a long-term policy that means the business opportunity of geo-engineering (which can only be based on market intervention) can become a reality.

Conclusions

There are many better options than geo-engineering for avoiding the impact of dangerous levels of global warming. Using generation from renewable and other low carbon sources to meet the increasing electricity demand is eminently more sensible than capturing CO_2. The reality unfortunately is that we need to do both. The overall target for reductions in emissions we have set ourselves is on an unprecedented magnitude and unlikely to be achieved in the timescale necessary. However, there are some unexpected benefits from following both. Firstly, if artificial forests are located in proximity to carbon storage sites, they are likely to be remote from populations and hence be more readily accepted. Secondly, air-capture units and algae farms could most likely be designed, developed and deployed on a timescale significantly ahead of the implementation and delivery of a comprehensive programme of vehicle electrification and the full electrification of the built environment. This would help pace emissions reduction at an achievable rate. Moreover, even when the latter has been achieved, it will still be necessary to continue to extract the CO_2 emitted by aircraft, ships and the other remaining non-electric vehicles, as well as continue to clean up past emissions.

Note

[1] Institution of Mechanical Engineers (2009) *Geo-engineering: Giving us the time to act*, Institution of Mechanical Engineers, London.

The Institution of Mechanical Engineers is the fastest-growing professional engineering institution in the UK. Its 80,000 members work at the heart of the country's most important and dynamic industries. For further details see www.imeche.org.

8.2

Carbon capture and storage

***Judith Shapiro** at the Carbon Capture and Storage Association reviews the development of technology for removing CO_2 emissions and putting them underground.*

Carbon capture and storage (CCS) is urgently needed as a fundamental part of the global fight against climate change. Both developed and developing countries rely largely on fossil fuels to provide energy, and demand for that energy is ever increasing. By capturing approximately 90 per cent of the CO_2 from large point sources such as power stations CCS has a crucial role to play in tackling greenhouse gas emissions whilst maintaining security of supply. The International Energy Agency has estimated that, to halve global emissions by 2050 (widely believed to be required to limit the temperature rise to 2 °C), CCS will need to contribute one-fifth of the required emissions reductions, both in the power sector and in the industrial sector.

In addition, the UK is now committed to ambitious targets for CO_2 reduction (34 per cent by 2020 and 80 per cent by 2050) following the adoption of the Climate Change Act in December 2008, and the Committee on Climate Change has also recommended that electricity should be largely decarbonized by 2030. CCS must be deployed alongside other low carbon options if we are to meet these climate change goals in the urgent time frame required.

It is important to note that CCS is the only low carbon option for many industries beyond the power sector, including in steel and cement production. It also has exciting potential for producing carbon negative power when used with biomass. In addition, CCS enables clean production of both electricity and hydrogen, which will be essential for decarbonizing sectors such as transport and heating.

What is CCS?

CCS involves the capture of carbon dioxide from power stations and industrial processes and then compression, transportation to the point of storage, and injecting the CO_2 into deep underground geological structures. There are several methods of capture: post-combustion, pre-combustion and oxyfuel (see Figure 8.2.1).

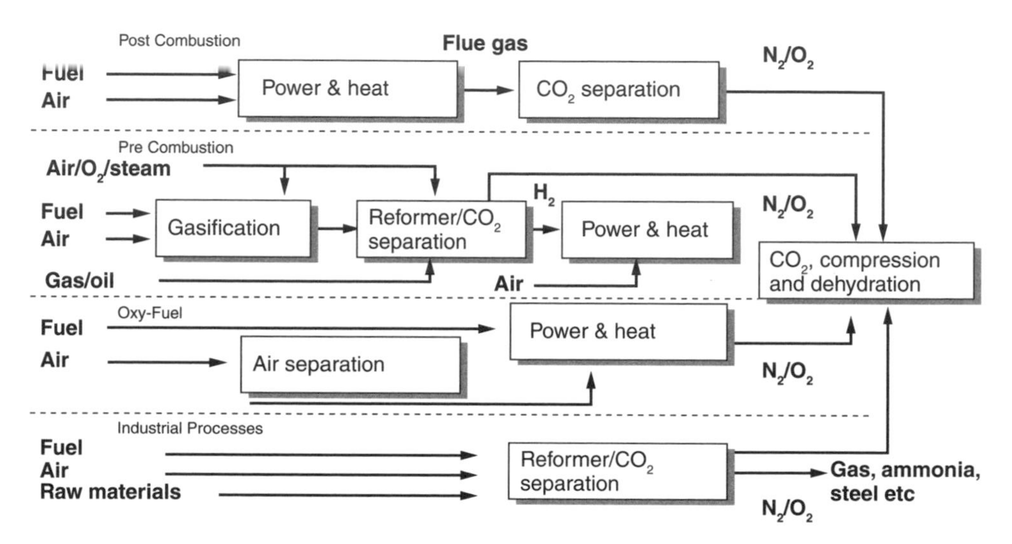

Figure 8.2.1 CO_2 capture processes

The most common form of carbon dioxide transportation for the volumes that will be needed is pipelines. However, there is also potential for shipping carbon dioxide, particularly in the early stages of CCS deployment. The final stage of CCS is permanent storage in underground geological structures. Carbon dioxide is typically injected about 1–2 kilometres below the ground or under the seabed, either in depleted oil and gas fields or in deep saline formations – essentially porous rock that is soaked with salt water, which is then displaced by the injected carbon dioxide.

All the parts of the CCS chain have been tried and tested in other industries around the world for many decades, and the next stage is now urgently to begin building commercial-scale, integrated projects. Important learning should be taken from projects such as Statoil's Sleipner project in the North Sea, which has been successfully separating out CO_2 (for natural gas processing) and injecting for permanent storage since 1996.

Challenges and positive steps

At the moment, the major barriers to the development of CCS are regulation and funding. Long-term political commitment is needed to develop the framework by which companies have the certainty to invest in projects. The UK, in particular, has made considerable progress in developing regulation for CCS over the past few years, and had a strong influence over the development of an EU directive for CO_2 storage, which was agreed in 2008. The UK currently has the most stringent regulation in place for CCS of any country in the world, requiring all new coal-fired power stations to demonstrate CCS on a proportion of their capacity, as well as a requirement for any new combustion plant over 300 MW to be built carbon capture ready (this is fuel neutral).

With such a strong framework for CCS in place, the UK is in a good position to take an early lead on CCS. In addition, the UK benefits from existing experience in relevant areas to CCS (such as power and process engineering, offshore oil and gas operations and project management) and abundant storage resources under the North Sea. Current estimates show that the UK continental shelf is likely to have enough capacity for 100 years or more, to take all UK emissions for permanent storage.

The government is currently committed to supporting four CCS demonstration projects at coal-fired power stations, as well as supporting additional retrofit of those power stations, as required in the future. The first of these four projects is currently the subject of an ongoing competition, which was launched in 2007. There are two remaining entrants in the current competition, both post-combustion capture (a criterion of the competition): Scottish Power's project at Longannet and E.ON's project at Kingsnorth. It is expected that the winner of this competition will be announced in 2011, following further front end engineering and design (FEED) studies for both projects, which the government recently announced funding for.

A competition for the further three UK CCS demonstration projects is also expected to be launched in 2010, with the process to be completed in 2011, and the government aims to see all four projects built by 2018.

In terms of funding, an important milestone was recently reached, through the agreement of the Energy Act in the last days of the parliamentary 'wash-up' process in the run-up to the 2010 election. The Act contains the legislation to introduce the CCS Incentive – a levy on electricity suppliers to fund CCS demonstration projects – and was amended to allow support for CCS demonstrations on plants other than coal-fired power stations. This therefore opens up the possibility for a demonstration programme beyond the first four projects, which could also include CCS on gas-fired power stations.

The government has also recently published *Clean Coal: An industrial strategy for the development of carbon capture and storage across the UK*, setting out how the UK is working to deliver CCS, as well as looking beyond the demonstration programme to deliver a sustained CCS industry in the UK.[1] The strategy estimates that by 2030 the CCS industry in the UK could be worth up to £6.5 billion and sustain up to 100,000 jobs. A new Office of CCS has also been launched to take forward proposals in the strategy.

Looking beyond the UK, there have also been important announcements in Europe, including €1.05 billion to support six CCS projects across Europe from the Economic Package for Recovery (the Powerfuel Hatfield project in the UK is one of the six projects), as well as an agreement to allocate 300 million allowances from the New Entrant Reserve of the EU Emissions Trading Scheme phase 3 to CCS and innovative renewables.

In addition to activities aimed at developing suitable regulation and financing for CCS, there are also ongoing smaller-scale research projects that either are in operation or have just been announced. These include the Doosan Power Systems 40 MW OxyCoal pilot and the Scottish Power Longannet post combustion capture test unit, both in Scotland, as well as a recent UK government announcement to award funding to the Scottish and Southern Energy 5 MW Ferrybridge CCS project. Work is also being undertaken to improve estimates and understanding of storage capacity, particularly in deep saline formations.

Conclusion

CCS is a vital technology option in the fight against climate change, and the UK has made significant progress in developing a framework that will enable CCS demonstration projects to be built. However, the International Energy Agency has estimated that, to meet global 2050 climate change goals, 100 CCS projects will be needed by 2020, and more than 3,000 by 2050. This will require a significant step change in global ambition on CCS, and the UK will need to play its part. A sense of urgency is needed across the globe, to ensure that CCS can fulfil its role in reducing emissions, thereby ensuring that ambitious targets are met, whilst developing an exciting new industry.

Note

[1] HM Government (2010) *Clean Coal: An industrial strategy for the development of carbon capture and storage across the UK*, Department of Energy and Climate Change, London.

Judith Shapiro is the Policy Officer at the Carbon Capture and Storage Association (CCSA). The CCSA brings together a wide range of specialist companies across the spectrum of carbon capture and storage (CCS) technologies, as well as a variety of support services to the energy sector. The Association exists to represent the interests of its members in promoting the business of CCS and raising awareness of the benefits of CCS and to assist policy developments in the UK, the EU and internationally towards a long-term regulatory framework for CCS, as a means of abating carbon dioxide emissions. Contact Judith Shapiro at CCSA (tel: 020 7821 0528; e-mail: Judith@ccsassociation.org; website: www.ccsassociation.org).

8.3

Low carbon purchasing

Priorities around carbon and energy are helping to bring supply chains together, argue ERM consultants ***Nick Cottam*** *and* ***James Cadman****.*

If you happen to supply healthcare equipment to the NHS you may well be taking a fresh look at its carbon emission reduction efforts. The same could be true if you're a supplier to the supermarket chain Tesco or to numerous other customer groups, from the automotive sector to tool hire companies. Whatever the politicians failed to achieve in Copenhagen, there appears to be a renewed zeal for less carbon-intensive and more energy-efficient supply chains.

Of course, there's nothing like an economic downturn to make us all feel a bit stingier about the way we use resources. Doing more with less is not only a useful mantra for thrifty recovery, but it really can help to concentrate minds when it comes to energy and climate change.

The NHS is a sizeable case in point. Europe's largest employer currently spends around £400 million a year on energy and, according to the Department of Health's latest National Innovation Procurement Plan, has a carbon footprint of 18 million tonnes of CO_2 a year. That's a huge amount of carbon and energy, 60 per cent of which comes from procured goods and services. Add to this the fact that the UK Climate Change Act requires the NHS to achieve a 26 per cent reduction in emissions by 2020 and it's perhaps no surprise that NHS Procurement and Defra have been responsible for the development of an energy efficiency assessment tool that can be used by hospitals to assess the energy efficiency and related carbon emissions of new equipment.

The tool, which ERM helped to develop, should, at the very least, be a catalyst for another type of conversation along the supply chain. Assuming the equipment does the job, meets appropriate health and safety criteria and is sensibly priced, there is now a renewed focus on life-cycle running costs – and carbon. In this respect the tool takes the user through a five-step process as part of procurement. You would expect a viable piece of equipment to match up to the competition – if not beat its rivals hands down.

Whatever the shortcomings of politicians, it's not difficult to see why the stakes are getting higher. Rising energy costs and indeed energy security have become important issues for business. Carbon reduction and the wider climate change issue link neatly with energy use and, as we have noted above, both carbon and energy are becoming differentiators – certainly as part of the sales process, but also among investors and other stakeholders, who are starting to see the long-term value of more energy-efficient operations.

As a market leader Tesco has been determined to forge ahead in this as in other areas. Tesco has been working closely with suppliers – as well as ERM – to carbon-footprint a significant number of its own-brand products, the message being that here is an issue that simply isn't going to go away. In addition to suppliers, Tesco has also been engaging with customers on this issue, with a growing number of them understanding the meaning of the term 'carbon footprint' according to latest Tesco consumer research in this area.

From a supplier perspective, energy and carbon are not only becoming useful product differentiators, but they are also new ways to get close to the customer – and stay there. Shortly before Christmas 2009, the UK's largest tool hire company, Speedy Hire, launched a Green Options (GO) initiative designed to provide its construction industry and other customers with a number of lower carbon, more energy-efficient options for tool hire. Again, we have a two-way engagement, with customers being offered a greener option and suppliers being actively encouraged by Speedy to 'join the club' in order to ensure that their products remain attractive options, both for Speedy and for the end user.

Whether you are supplying the NHS or Speedy Hire, there is therefore both a pressure and an incentive to take the energy or carbon issue on board. Customers are asking questions, and there is an incentive to deliver real improvements in energy efficiency in order to win and keep their business. In Speedy's case, the company's CEO, Steve Corcoran, used the launch to invite new suppliers with innovative products to join the initiative. When that invitation comes from a company with the buying power of Speedy, there's got to be a very good reason to ignore it.

The backdrop to all of this – certainly in the UK and elsewhere in the EU – is part business and part political. Rising energy costs amount to a powerful incentive to be more efficient, wherever you happen to be along the supply chain. The carbon issue will either directly affect you as a business through such developments as the Carbon Reduction Commitment or affect you through the pressures and inducements now rippling their way along the supply chain. In the background of course are the politicians, gingerly setting targets and expecting business, not to mention the public sector, to meet them.

Add to all of this the less tangible but equally important issue of reputation. Riding on the back of GO, Speedy has just announced its own Product Innovation Awards scheme for green products. Now before you start sighing about yet another environmental award you have to remember that this is now becoming mainstream business for suppliers and for their customers. Build a reputation for innovative low energy, low carbon products and you get a chance to join the club. Ignore the issue and you might just find the business in need of some NHS-style resuscitation.

Nick Cottam and James Cadman are consultants with the international environmental and social consulting firm ERM, which operates in more than 40 countries and provides services to a wide range of public sector and Fortune 500 clients. Contact ERM (tel: 07834 978139; e-mail: Nick.cottam@erm.com; website: www.erm.com).

Part 9

Creating solutions

9.1

Shifting to a smart, sustainable age

***Molly Webb** at The Climate Group discusses the framework in which clean innovations are going to emerge.*

A congestion charging system built by IBM in Stockholm reduces carbon dioxide (CO_2) emissions by 40 per cent in the inner city. Wipro's building complex in greater New Delhi includes an integrated building management system as part of a retrofit, saving 2,267,844 KWh of power each year. Shiply.com saves carbon emissions equivalent to over 6,000 long-haul flights in just two years by helping keep delivery lorries full on otherwise empty return journeys.

What do these examples have in common? First, they all employ information and communications technologies (ICTs), an existing and fairly mature set of technologies, to a newly recognized challenge – climate change. Second, they allow both people and machines to act differently when they have better access to better information. These innovative approaches to energy efficiency can deliver 32 per cent of the required emissions reductions by 2020 at relatively low cost, and ICT applications specifically could save 15 per cent of global emissions across all sectors by 2020, according to a report by The Climate Group and the Global e-Sustainability Initiative (GeSI).

But there is something else these examples have in common. The existence of the technological capability alone will not achieve our sustainability objectives.

That technology deployment and behaviour change are needed to achieve sustainability goals is well understood. But *how* these are achieved is less clear. When a 'new' technology is being implemented, the attention (and excitement) is reserved for the LED light bulb, the solar thermal system, the building management system or the electric vehicle (EV). But the challenge is: who will pay for those or the infrastructure they require, and how will the benefits be shared?

The low carbon or 'clean' revolution is under way because of the implementation – not only the invention – of solutions. As with past 'revolutions' – the industrial and information revolutions for instance – we are living through a 'paradigm shift'. As in other shifts, the 'common sense' of past stable systems is gradually replaced such that a set of investors, policy makers, business leaders and the public understand how to benefit from the new set of technologies.

This is what Carlotta Perez, an expert on technology and socio-economic development, would call a 'techno-economic paradigm', not a technological revolution. It is never the technology alone that is important, but an ecosystem of technological, financial, policy and organizational changes that occur in a dizzying and often disruptive series of stages.

Why then do we often succumb to the allure of the technological 'silver bullet'? We believe in silver bullets because there is often a technological breakthrough that comes to define the paradigm – what Carlotta Perez calls the 'attractor' or 'big bang' of technological revolutions. The manufacture of Intel's first microprocessor in 1971 defines the information revolution, for example. But the real change happens when clusters of technologies and the associated innovations in policy incentives, business practices and infrastructure make it cheaper and more attractive to choose the new technologies than the norm.

The signs of shifting common sense may be recognized in what Clayton Christensen, author of *The Innovator's Dilemma*, has termed 'disruptive innovation'. A disruptive innovation is one that 1) finds new consumers and 2) creates a simpler offering that 3) is rolled out through a new business model. A classic example is found in computing, where functionality was centralized in mainframe computers until the introduction of personal computers (PCs), which were simpler and less expensive, tapping into a new set of consumers who bought lots of small machines rather than a few large ones.

But what does this mean in practice for sustainable and low carbon solutions? What does it mean for business, and what does it mean for government and their partners working toward societal outcomes? Will decentralized power systems with solar panels on every roof be the norm? Or will infrastructure continue to look pretty much the same but we will do everything we do today much more efficiently?

For an example of a disruptive innovator, meet Robert Matthams. He had his 'aha' moment when a delivery truck arrived at his university in Manchester to deliver a pool table from London, and was going to return empty. Aware of the environmental damage this was sure to cause, Robert saw a business opportunity. Researching further, he recognized that 25 per cent of lorries on Britain's roads run empty, resulting in an unnecessary 36 million tonnes of CO_2 emissions every year – that's 7.2 per cent of the UK's carbon footprint. Allowing more trucks to run fully loaded means fewer trucks need to be used to deliver the same amount of goods. He set up Shiply.com, an online transport marketplace that replaces the traditional subscription-based business model of the freight exchange. It is aimed at end consumers, and hauliers bid in a reverse auction to keep their vehicles full and offer the consumer a low price. Now, your eBay delivery in the UK can be sent on a lorry that might otherwise have been driving home empty. What Matthams did was find a way to use the excess capacity of lorries driving empty and fill it in a cost-effective way. He found new customers with a simpler, cheaper service.

Better Place, the software company turned electric vehicle company, has chosen to provide an end-to-end solution that will require a great deal of upfront investment by private and public funders, and the roll-out of a battery-switching infrastructure. While the high costs seem daunting, the business model is tantalizing: Better Place will treat miles driven by a car like minutes used on a mobile phone, only charging consumers for what they use. This approach will mean that customers optimize their use of vehicles, and Better Place can worry about the cost of the battery and sourcing the power from the greenest sources.

Disruptive business models are perhaps an obvious place to see the evidence of paradigm shifts, but they are not the only route to solutions. Partnerships and policies will need to be in place to move technologies from obscurity to mainstream, through a process that starts with awareness of new solutions through to affordability and acceptance.

An example of a successful partnership can be found in the Empire State Building retrofit. Consulting, design and construction partners Clinton Climate Initiative (CCI), Johnson Controls Inc (JCI), Jones Lang LaSalle (JLL) and Rocky Mountain Institute (RMI) participated in an eight-month modelling and analysis project that will save up to 38 per cent of the building's energy and $4.4 million annually, with a three-year payback. Developing robust solutions requires the coordination of several key stakeholders, and in this case engineers, energy modellers, architects, building management and tenants all participated early on. The group took a whole-building approach where the technically optimal solution was developed first, in order to avoid the usual piecemeal approach where individual systems in the building would be replaced or upgraded without optimal benefit.

What can government policy do to support innovation? Is a 'Better Place' all we need to accelerate the uptake of electric vehicles, which have been shown to be more efficient (and lower carbon) than the internal combustion engine?

Awareness of electric vehicles is high, with leaders such as Mayor Boris Johnson calling for 100,000 of them soon to be driving on London's streets. But they are currently the more expensive option because of the high cost of batteries. And they are less practical because of the lack of charging stations.

The vehicle industry, utility companies, IT companies and consumers will all be involved in rolling out vehicles and charging infrastructure to match expected vehicle purchases. Their common aim is to achieve cost equivalence between EVs and similar internal combustion engine (ICE) vehicles, building sufficient confidence from consumers. This will be possible only if a comprehensive policy and incentive framework is established through to 2020 in order to give stakeholders a clear view of the road ahead and reduce investment risks.

Governments will need to lead these efforts and employ a number of tools. Public–private partnerships can support education and demonstration to increase consumer awareness. Industry coalitions could be developed to accelerate fleet procurement.

Labelling programmes, public trials and accurate in-use information (eg range, recharging times, recharging grid location information and expansion plans) can raise confidence in the benefits of low carbon transport. Governments can also require standardized charging infrastructure and promote research and development, especially for advanced battery systems, smart grid use and energy storage.

If we aim for 'clean and green' to become the new 'normal', action is required that touches environmental, innovation, industrial, energy and information policies. What is certain is that the road ahead is bumpy and may not be paved with vehicle charging stations unless we can find ways to make it cheaper, easier and more attractive to do so.

Molly Webb leads The Climate Group's SMART 2020 work, which aims to roll out ICT-enabled solutions in the urban environment. For further information see www.theclimategroup.org.

9.2

Building on experience

*The renewables sector is beginning to capitalize on 40 years of oil and gas expertise, says **Gerwyn Williams** at J P Kenny.*

Offshore renewable developments have progressed over the past 15 years from near-shore demonstration projects into large-scale commercial operations. This development has been prompted by the increasing awareness of global warming and international treaties such as the Kyoto Protocol. Worldwide, countries are realizing the potential for renewable energy production as a sustainable source that will reduce greenhouse gases and secure energy supply. Throughout Europe renewable energy production targets have been agreed, which will see the UK produce approximately 30 GW of its electricity from renewables. The majority of this will be associated with offshore wind farms, and so we are likely to be home to more installed capacity than any other country. To achieve these targets, an investment of up to £100 billion is expected over the next 10 years. Significant sums are also expected to be invested in schemes to capture wave and tidal power in countries with ocean-facing coastlines such as Ireland, Portugal and the UK. Marine renewables represent a fantastic opportunity for UK industry to establish a world-leading industry and to create jobs and wealth.

UK companies begin with an advantage

The UK does start with a significant advantage in the race to lead marine renewables by virtue of its world-leading industries in oil and gas, its natural resource potential and its skilled workforce. In particular, many of the technologies that are used to develop the oil and gas found underwater have been originated in the UK, and many UK firms are firmly established as the best in the world. For example, much of the valving, control systems and piping components that are used to extract underwater oil and gas and that represent an investment of £10 billion per annum worldwide is provided by service companies and equipment manufacturers with UK headquarters. The trade association Subsea UK, which represents this sector, boasts around 200 members, ranging from multibillion construction companies such as Acergy and Wood Group to many niche suppliers of specialist materials, underwater robotic systems and professional services.

But the renewables and oil and gas sectors should work together

Many offshore renewable projects developed so far have not fully capitalized on the experience that's available within the oil and gas sector. Some offshore wind farms have been engineered by firms with predominantly onshore experience. Already some of these are exhibiting problems during operation with severe corrosion, structural fatigue and poor turbine availability reported. There have also been incidents of dramatic failures during installation of a kind that are now extremely rare in oil and gas.

Happily, the best resources are now coming into the sector. Excited by the size of the renewables opportunity, many oil and gas companies are developing business units that are focused on renewables and offer a blend of existing skills combined with those that are specific to new energy projects. And the renewables industry is also working to attract and make better use of suitable oil and gas skills. The development programmes run by the Carbon Trust, which seek to define improvement strategies and plans for future renewable projects, are particularly welcome.

Case study: Oil and gas expertise reduces operating costs of offshore wind farms

One of the Carbon Trust accelerator programmes, which was undertaken by J P Kenny, was conceived because the first batch of offshore wind farm sites achieve, on average, an availability of 90 per cent, compared with 97 per cent availability onshore. Whilst this difference can be explained by offshore conditions restricting either scheduled or unscheduled maintenance operations, the consequence for project economics is significant. The Carbon Trust initiated a research programme, funded by five leading utilities, aimed at improving the availability of future wind farms to at least 92 per cent, and to do this without significant increases to capital and operating costs.

The oil and gas industry has over the past 30 years pioneered systems and strategies in personnel and equipment transfers to offshore installations at far-shore sites in deepwater environments. Transfers are often restricted owing to the adverse marine and weather conditions. Currently, transfers from shore to in-field installations are routinely undertaken using helicopters, with inter-facility support provided through supply and support vessels. A range of bespoke inter-field vessels have been designed to enable launch and recovery to facilitate small-scale inter-field operations. These strategies, developed by the oil and gas industry, recognize that a combination of systems and an established base of operations in-field are commercially beneficial over 'day trips' or short-term deployments from shore. The commercial success of these strategies has resulted in the industry adopting them worldwide. The offshore renewables sector is also now recognizing the benefits of these strategies, which are being adopted.

Case study: Oil and gas expertise supports wave energy

Wave Hub is a novel system, located 10 nautical miles offshore from the north coast of Cornwall, which provides the electrical infrastructure to deliver electricity from wave energy converter devices (WECs) to the UK grid. Due to be operational at the end of 2010, it will allow WEC developers to test their equipment over several years in a fully monitored marine environment. Once running at full capacity, the system will be capable of providing sufficient wave energy to power 11,000 homes.

The Wave Hub will be installed in approximately 50 metres of water and will be connected to an onshore substation by a 25-kilometre-long subsea cable. The cable will be laid on the seabed, under the beach and through a directionally drilled duct under the dunes. The substation includes a transformer and electrical equipment.

An array of standard offshore oil and gas engineering techniques were employed in the design and construction of the Wave Hub project. The initial conceptual design was performed using a risk-based approach, which included multidiscipline workshops to consider the potential designs and rank them according to risk. Reliability analysis was then performed on each of the major components and the system as a whole.

The highly dynamic offshore environment presented numerous challenges for the proposed offshore infrastructure, including the cables and subsea hub apparatus. Owing to the lower capital investment associated with many renewable projects compared with oil and gas projects, careful consideration was required during the overall design approach to provide an economical solution.

We have started but more can be done

The improvements that we are beginning to see within the renewables sector represent the first steps. Unquestionably, there is much more to be gained. UK companies can become world leaders in the sector if they are first to recognize and implement the improvement opportunities. But for that to happen we must not just rely on the natural advantage of having the business in our backyard. Additionally, we must capitalize on the deep skills that have been created during 40 years of oil and gas.

J P Kenny is part of the Wood Group Kenny group of companies and is the world's largest independent underwater specialist engineering and management consultancy, with approximately 1,600 staff worldwide. J P Kenny provides a diverse range of services in the areas of marine renewables, subsea engineering, offshore and onshore pipelines, project management, development studies and asset management. Gerwyn Williams is the Group Managing Director of J P Kenny. He is a civil engineer with almost 30 years' experience in the energy and railway sectors. He has worked in a variety of managerial and engineering roles in Europe, the Middle East and the United States. Contact Gerwyn Williams at gerwyn.williams@jpkenny.com.

9.3

Finding energy solutions

***Chris Harrison** of the Low Carbon Innovation Centre at the University of East Anglia reviews the scope for developing solutions in clean energy.*

Political and legislative pressure, increased social awareness, rapid technological change and economic challenges: a list of typical external factors affecting any business? Certainly yes, but also the drivers of low carbon innovation and specifically innovation in energy supply.

The precise nature and extent of human influence on climate change will continue to be debated, but the necessity to innovate in order to guarantee against irreversible environmental change, ensure security of energy supply and protect against the extremes of market volatility is indisputable. The development of technology to generate and conserve electricity continues at a rapid pace alongside moves towards sustainability in public and personal transport and the reduction of energy and materials waste. Government incentives and genuine market opportunity are helping to drive this advance.

Clean technology clearly has a big role to play. Novel fuels from non-fossil sources offer potential in terms of long-term supply and price differentiation over their oil-based counterparts. Clean electricity generation at the large and small scales can provide security against price instability, independence from large suppliers and for some businesses an additional revenue source. Recent government initiatives provide direct financial incentives.

The following discusses the significance of some of these technologies for today's companies and how they may feature in corporate strategies.

Biomass

Anaerobic digestion (AD)

This technology uses micro-organisms to digest organic matter, for example food and farm waste, to produce methane gas. The gas can then be combusted to generate heat and power. Much of the attractiveness of AD comes from the fact that the feedstocks are waste materials. The technology lends itself well to users that generate significant quantities of these waste materials on their own site. Examples include food processing companies and farmers.

Systems such as those developed by Add Energy (www.addenergy.co.uk) can generate between 100 kilowatts and 1 megawatt of electricity and pay back the initial investment in the equipment in a few years.

As with all biomass-based technologies, questions have been raised about future availability of feedstock, which will be increasingly in demand as the technology becomes more popular. Investment in larger-scale plants is only likely to be achievable where long-term contracts guaranteeing the supply of feedstocks can be negotiated or where the control over feedstock lies within the hands of the biomass energy plant developer.

Gasification

This process takes organic material (for example wood chips) and converts it into synthesis gas ('syngas') inside a gasifier at high temperatures. The gas can then be cleaned up and passed into a combustion engine in order to generate electricity (and heat).

In 2006, the University of East Anglia (UEA) identified woodchip gasification as the optimum solution to fuel a new CHP plant on its campus, with an electricity output of 1.4 MW and 2.0 MW of heat. This heat is wasted in conventional power stations, but at UEA it part-energizes the district heating system, giving an efficiency of 84 per cent.

The UEA biomass CHP plant cost around £9 million to build. Payback time may fluctuate owing to outside factors, not least energy prices, but is predicted to be about six years. When it opens, the plant will reduce the University's headline emissions by 34 per cent. Two lorry loads of fuel are needed each day to operate the gasifier. The impact of transporting woodchip fuel to the University is estimated to be less than 100 tonnes of CO_2 per annum (based upon supply from an average radius of 50 kilometres).

With any proposed biomass gasification project, the availability of the feedstock must again be of key concern. Whilst in principle any organic matter can be gasified, in reality licences may be difficult to obtain for the use of waste material. Many parts of the UK have a potentially plentiful supply of woodchip from sawmills, etc, but again this is likely to change if more plants are built and demand significantly increases.

Small-scale wind turbines

Wind turbines may offer an efficient and cost-effective way of providing electricity for domestic or commercial use. One supplier, API Engineering (http://www.

api-engineering.com), supplies small-scale wind turbines with rated output powers ranging from 5 kW to 10 kW. The blade diameter varies from 5 metres for a 5-kW turbine to 7.5 metres for a 10-kW turbine, with tower options from 9 to 15 metres.

With the new government feed-in tariff (FiT), any business that wishes to reduce its electricity bills and carbon footprint will find a wind turbine an attractive investment. Wind turbines of these sizes are eligible for a FiT payment of 26.7p/kWh, greatly reducing the payback time of small turbines. The average annual electricity demand of an SME is around 25,000 kWh/year; a 10-kW small-scale wind turbine could generate this much at a site with good wind speeds.

A different business model, but one also assisted by the implementation of the feed-in tariff, is being promoted by a new venture: Windcrop (http://www.windcrop.co.uk). This business offers farmers and rural businesses on-site renewable generation by installing and operating small wind turbines. In exchange for the use of their land, the landowners receive discounted electricity. This approach is made possible by the 20-year committed support that the feed-in tariff provides and the ability for the tariff rights to be separately owned from the site. Windcrop obtains the feed-in tariff from the electricity supplier, and with the electricity payments from the site owner this provides the revenue stream to cover the ongoing maintenance costs of the turbine and a return on investment for the initial installation. Through economies of scale, Windcrop is driving down the level of initial investment so that the revenue provides an attractive rate of return.

Domestic energy

A recent report by the Open University and the Energy Saving Trust gives an insight into consumer attitudes and behaviours in response to the availability of grant-funded microgeneration systems for heat.[1] From a business perspective the survey identifies the early adopters of low carbon energy technologies and the most popular technologies.

Domestic energy use accounts for just over a quarter of all UK emissions, of which 75 per cent is for water and space heating. Microgeneration has a role to play, as there are significant gains to be made in this area.

The most common method of microgeneration is solar hot water. It has a wide appeal, with a third of adopters living in smaller, urban properties, reflecting the lower cost and smaller size of the technology. Solar hot water is also seen as less risky and more affordable (with a faster payback) than other technologies, for example heat pumps and biomass boilers. In the UK, 4.8 million homes (20 per cent of the total) could benefit, and one must not underestimate the importance of the visual impact of panels: 34 per cent of the 900 houses surveyed said that being able to visibly demonstrate their commitment to environmental concerns was a factor in the decision to purchase microgeneration technologies.

Those surveyed by the Open University also cited the low levels (typically 10–15 per cent of price) of grant funding as an important reason for not installing but identified reduced council tax after installation as a good lever for adoption. Low-cost loans were not viewed favourably as a funding mechanism.

In 2005/06 there were only 1,000 UK ground source heat pump installations. The technology is widespread in the United States, Germany and Austria, but many in the UK are put off by what is considered to be high cost (usually a maximum cost of £11,000) and longer payback times. Biomass heaters and stoves are still extremely rare in the UK.

We can see therefore that there are real opportunities both for distributors and for consumers of domestic renewable energy generation technologies. We hope to see central government continuing its support through funding initiatives to boost business as well as domestic demand to create the right conditions to emerge from the recession into the low carbon economy.

Note

[1] R Roy, S Caird and J Abelman (2008) *YIMBY Generation; Yes in my back yard! UK householders pioneering microgeneration heat*, June, Energy Saving Trust, London.

Dr Chris Harrison is the Chief Executive Officer of the Low Carbon Innovation Centre (LCIC), which was formed in 2008. Chris is also the Director of Carbon Connections, an HEFCE- and OSI-funded initiative to develop low carbon technologies and innovations, with a particular emphasis on transferring knowledge from the university research sector. Carbon Connections has successfully set up 26 ground-breaking projects, all on an investment basis, with a view to developing an evergreen Carbon Connections innovation fund. Some returns on investment have already been achieved, in less than three years. Chris has a background in technology and knowledge transfer and has been a founding director and board member of a number of university spin-out companies, including Syrinix Limited, which won the Timer Higher Education Business Initiative of the Year in 2006, and Im-Sense Limited, which raised one of the biggest private seed-investment rounds of any UK university spin-out. Contact Chris Harrison at LCIC (tel: 01603 591366; e-mail: chris.harrison@uea.ac.uk; website: www.lcic.com).

A new radioactive waste regime for the United Kingdom

In March 2007, the UK government and devolved administrations (for Scotland, Wales and Northern Ireland) published a policy for the long-term management of solid low level radioactive waste in the United Kingdom. The policy recognizes that radioactive wastes are generated by a myriad of industrial activities dealing with electrical power generation, university research, medical use of radioactive materials and the decommissioning of facilities where this work has taken place. Under this new policy, the nation has set out the objectives of building an environmentally sustainable scheme to safely treat, store and dispose of radioactive materials such that their impacts are controlled and moderated for existing and future generations.

A new UK Nuclear Industry Solid Low Level Waste (LLW) Strategy has been developed within the framework of the following principles set out in the policy:

- use of a risk-informed approach to ensure safety and protection of the environment;
- minimization of waste arisings (both activity and volume);
- forecasting of future waste arisings, based upon fit-for-purpose characterization of wastes and materials that may become wastes;
- consideration of all practicable options for the management of LLW;
- a presumption towards early solutions to waste management;
- appropriate consideration of the proximity principle and waste transport issues.

The UK Nuclear Industry LLW Strategy was submitted by the Nuclear Decommissioning Authority (NDA) to government for approval in January 2009. This comprehensive strategy stresses the principles of the 'waste management hierarchy', namely to avoid the generation of waste, maximize reuse and recycling of radioactive material, pursue waste treatment and volume reduction wherever possible and, as a last resort only, properly dispose of any remaining wastes. Safety and environmental responsibility are fundamental to any decisions for the management of nuclear wastes.

Much of the lower activity waste generated in the UK has historically been disposed of at the LLW Repository (LLWR) in Cumbria. As part of its charter, the Nuclear Decommissioning Authority was assigned ownership of the repository and charged with developing a national waste strategy to implement the new policy. As part of that effort, the NDA ran a comprehensive procurement competition to manage this work. Three international consortia vied for the work and, in April 2008, UK Nuclear Waste Management Ltd (UKNWM) was awarded the contract.

The LLWR contract included both the operation of the site repository for the safe handling and disposal of LLW and a key partnership role with NDA in the development and implementation of a national waste strategy. As the 'UK Integrator' for LLW management, UKNWM is taking a programmatic approach for a truly integrated national LLW programme in the UK.

Under UKNWM's international sponsorship, the repository has completely revamped the way low level radioactive waste is now managed. Drawing on international best practices, the repository is now poised to safely manage radioactive waste in a manner that efficiently and effectively segregates the materials into various waste management 'routes' that are designed to optimize expenditures borne by British taxpayers. These routes provide for treatments such as metal melting that can recycle 90–95 per cent of the material back into the supply chain (just as happens with aluminium can collections at council tips). Incineration of combustible materials, coupled with very efficient radioactive gas filters, can similarly reduce the waste volumes by more than a factor of 20. Use of fit-for-purpose landfills for the lowest concentrations of contaminated material, which account for approximately half of the volume of expected decommissioning rubble and soil, further reduces and optimizes the UK's future disposal of radioactive waste.

Governmental policy recognizes the opportunities for appropriate reuse of materials before they become waste. Opportunities for reuse exist well before a material becomes a waste, for example plant, equipment and buildings that have reached the end of their original intended purpose but may continue to have value elsewhere. Other materials may provide opportunity for reuse, including soil and rubble. With all of these opportunities, the key to realizing them is making potential users aware of these materials. LLWR recognizes that these opportunities exist largely within the nuclear industry for radioactively contaminated materials and that there is a general preference for this over reuse outside the nuclear estate. LLWR strives to actively promote reuse of materials throughout the nuclear industry.

Recycling is the preferred way forward for the treatment of metallic LLW. Recycling materials for a second (or further) use presents a significant opportunity to the nuclear industry. Specifically, the LLW Strategy recognizes metal treatment and recycling as the main opportunity in this area, although it should be noted that there are other opportunities, such as recycling of concrete and rubble for alternative use. Metallic waste accounts for approximately a third of LLW in the UK. Metal decontamination and metal melting have been demonstrated as an effective way to manage these wastes and can achieve recycling rates of up to 95 per cent of incoming material. In practice, this process broadly involves the removal of surface contamination, often by conventional metal cleaning processes such as dry grit blasting, followed by a clearance process to release the clean material to the recycling market.

Decontamination of metal wastes already takes place at a number of NDA and non-NDA sites. In addition, there are also a number of contractors in the supply chain that provide services in this area. Whilst current levels of recycling are encouraging, there is scope for increasing the treatment of metallic waste. It is LLWR's intent to increase the application of metal treatment in a way that demonstrates best value for money. LLWR believes that, at the current time, use of the supply chain will provide the capacity required for this increase and should be a primary consideration over development of and investment in new metal treatment facilities at waste-producing sites.

All of these initiatives are now being actively worked by LLW Repository Limited. In cooperation with the various licensed nuclear sites across the UK and in close consultation with the Environment Agency, Nuclear Installation Inspectorate and numerous other regulatory bodies, LLWR expects to deliver to the public a much improved radioactive waste regime. Proper execution of these new strategies should greatly extend the life of the existing repository – well into the second half of this century and perhaps beyond. This would preclude, or at least significantly delay, the need for the identification, siting, planning, construction and licensing of a replacement repository. The taxpayer would benefit from hundreds of millions of pounds if only a portion of this scenario plays out. The stakes are big and the effort intense.

The UK has taken a bold step to completely scrap the old business-as-usual schemes that worked for the first 50 years of the nuclear industry. Today LLWR seeks to bring 'enlightened' use of space and monetary resources to the nuclear industry. It is doing it in a way that benefits its employees and its host communities, and minimizes the impact on future generations. The future is bright and limited only by the imagination of LLWR's workforce.

Dick Raaz, Managing Director, LLW Repository Limited. For additional information, please visit www.llwrsite.com.

MATRIX

The Northern Ireland Science Industry Panel – facilitating business leadership to exploit technology and R&D for economic growth

Introduction: Northern Ireland and the global knowledge economy

The ongoing transformation of the global knowledge economy and the consequent increase in high-end competition present significant challenges for Northern Ireland's economy. Northern Ireland's business sector needs to enhance its competitiveness and productivity in key areas. As a result of many years of political instability and turbulence, while Northern Ireland's private sector has many clear examples of business excellence, the region's dependence on public sector investment remains a significant problem.

The lower levels of competitiveness and productivity compared to similar regions are further exacerbated because of the region's preponderance of small and micro-businesses. It has been a sustained mantra in recent years that Northern Ireland is at a disadvantage because it has so few large indigenous businesses.

But, as a result of the work of MATRIX: The Northern Ireland Science Industry Panel, a new economic model is being fostered in which having a large volume of smaller-scale firms in the high-technology business base can be turned into a serious competitive advantage.

MATRIX vision: industry leadership

As the greatest investment in the delivery to market of innovative products comes from industry, MATRIX believes it imperative that industry is required to show the lead in a market-driven approach to innovation. Northern Ireland's business demographics indicate that, while its lack of large firms is a major factor in determining the level of business investment in R&D, SMEs can be amongst the greatest innovators. Modern, outward-looking smaller firms also provide flexible supply chains that can attract larger firms.

MATRIX focused on this dynamic when presenting its first advisory report to the Northern Ireland Executive in October 2008. The report identified the potential to create global leadership positions through the agglomeration of industry capabilities in a new kind of collaborative cluster model. MATRIX proposed that by developing business-driven communities – facilitated by government, inspired by academia and enabled by the region's exemplary further education colleges – Northern Ireland could transform its economy in as little as a decade.

MATRIX believes that these clusters – styled Industry-led Innovation Communities (IICs) – can restore to the high-technology business base the ambition, confidence and drive that the political turmoil and macroeconomic environment of the past 30-plus years have helped to stifle. But it also recognizes that this new model requires courage from businesses to provide leadership, and also courage from government to step aside and adopt a new role in facilitating the process.

Structuring an Industry-led Innovation Community

The IIC approach also places a new onus on the private sector in terms of:

- social responsibility to bring smaller businesses forward into new global markets;
- developing the skills, particularly vocational skills, of the workforce;
- attracting the venture capital that will translate innovative ideas into new products and processes; and
- capturing and directing the intellectual inspiration of academia.

Industry and wider private sector players should identify the real-time market opportunities for the Community, and would also have a continued horizon-scanning function. Importantly, the Community should seek private sources of funding, through venture capital, industry investment and bank loans.

Industry also has the responsibility of providing the social functions of: developing participating SMEs, particularly new, high-technology spin-outs from universities and businesses; the development of industry placements through strong linkages with further education; and the development of strong vocational skills aligned with Northern Ireland's future key markets.

IICs will contain not only high-technology firms but also the full range of supply chain organizations needed to sustain the Community's ambitions. This would include, among others, legal services, financial services, specific skills providers – both further and higher education – and a range of sub-supply firms from diverse backgrounds and sectors, including many SMEs supplying basic goods and non-high-tech components. IICs will also draw in third sector and voluntary organizations where they have a role to play. In short, IICs present new opportunities across the whole economy.

The principles of the Communities will be based on:

- engaging the collaborative industrial and intellectual talent in Northern Ireland with a view to meeting growing global market needs;
- unifying research programmes across sectors, including the interfaces between the various disciplines within each sector;
- partnerships that facilitate knowledge and technology transfer between industry and academia to work on challenging problems;
- levering private sector support and investment through new funding mechanisms and venture capital;
- new relationships between key players in Northern Ireland to develop R&D in Northern Ireland's indigenous industry, while also attracting international industries to the region;
- exploiting the opportunities in the multidisciplinary nature of science and technology as applied to Northern Ireland's sectors where the complexity of the research requires scope, scale and synergy of equipment, facilities and human resources; and
- creating excellence in research and education as measured by international merit reviews.

Government support – the Innovation Gateway

Government's primary role is to facilitate the creation of the IICs, assisting with the definition of the 'rules of engagement', and through initial facilitation of the Community. This facilitation would include the development of each Community's leadership structure and operating model, and provision of legislative and intellectual property advice to provide protection and reassurance or comfort for all players, but in particular small business, to work in partnership.

The planned Innovation Gateway to support IICs will be a first-stop shop to government support. It will draw together the miscellaneous strands of public advice, guidance, financial interventions and other support available into a single, easily navigable point of contact. This has the potential to make a significant contribution to reducing the barriers to support that collaborative business ventures are perceived to face, as well as potentially reducing the layers of bureaucracy across public sector support programmes by drawing together existing support in a more efficient and manageable way.

MATRIX – thought leadership

MATRIX will continue to provide thought leadership in steering the development of IICs and supporting industry as such communities evolve. Already a number of nascent Industry-led Innovation Communities have emerged, and they show a range of models and progress at various rates of development. Market opportunities have been identified in areas such as renewable energy, connected health, composite materials, smart grid technologies and many others. Over 100 companies are now fully engaged in collaborative activities, along with universities, colleges and public institutions.

But, despite this diversity, early work undertaken by MATRIX has identified that there are a number of common steps that must be addressed in building vibrant IICs:

- establishing *industry leadership* within a Community;
- articulating the *market trading* requirements to make a Community a success;
- developing a clear *IP focus*, both in creation and in exploitation;
- understanding the current *Northern Ireland capability* and seeking to grow this;
- establishing a stable *Community formation*, representing a wide group of participants;
- sourcing *funding* using various sources and models, private as well as public;
- working with government to influence *policy alignment* with a Community;
- developing a *portfolio management* approach that will sustain short-, medium- and long-term opportunities; and
- working with government to develop *human capital* for a Community's future.

Without seeking to be prescriptive, Table P9.1 is indicative of expected deliverables associated with maturing Industry-led Innovation Communities.

Table P9.1 Expected deliverables of maturing Industry-led Innovation Communities

Maturity	*Deliverables and Outputs*
Year 1	Defined leadership and governance structure.
	Defined market scope, including key themes.
	Agreed vision, aims and objectives.
	Identified funding and resources.
	Opportunity analysis.
	Development of a technology advisory group.
	IP strategy.
	Outreach and communications strategy.
	Agreed work programme.
Year 2	Established policy workgroup to work with government to address issues and barriers to growth.
	Agreed technology transfer programme with academia.
	Community skills strategy to address the skills gap.
	Technology and market roadmaps developed.
	Agreed apprenticeship model with further education.
	Venture capital links established.
	Established work and research programme, including an established proof of concept mechanism.
Year 5	Established work and research portfolio over a one-, three- and five-year horizon.
	Published technology roadmaps.
	Established Community apprenticeship and KTP schemes.
	Established Community/government/education skills workgroup.
	Established UK and EU research programme.
	Two to three licence and patent agreements.
	Eight to 10 academic research papers published.
	One to two spin-out companies.
	Strong venture capital investment.
	Associated competence centre established.
	Evidence of growing leadership in UK and EU markets.
	Ongoing horizon-scanning mechanism in place.
Year 10	Recognition of leadership at EU and global market level.
	Four to five licence and patent agreements.
	Two to three spin-out companies created.
	One to two spin-ins attracted.
	Twenty to 25 internationally accredited academic papers published.
	Full Community/skills alignment.
	Two to three associated competence centres.

Conclusion

Northern Ireland already has many of the component parts for a successful knowledge- and technology-driven economy. The challenge of pulling these together to compete more effectively in the global marketplace requires industry leadership supported by sound and informed guidance.

MATRIX's role as thought leader to the roll-out of the IICs model ensures both. In this way Northern Ireland will be better placed to capitalize on global market opportunities and again establish the region as a world leader in exploiting key areas of technology and R&D.

Bernard McKeown, Head of MATRIX Secretariat, Department of Enterprise, Trade and Investment, Northern Ireland. For more information please visit www.matrix-ni.org.

Part 10

Clean commercialization

10.1

The business model

From clean technology to clean business, have you got the right model, asks ***Julian Wheatland*** *at Hatton International.*

Many businesses with brilliant technology fail, some survive and fewer still thrive. Why is it that so many new enterprises, with extremely clever technology and clearly identifiable markets, can fail to profitably connect with their customers? There are many issues such as management team, marketing strategy and competitor reaction that will have a major impact, but the biggest single question that a company faces, and the most significant decision it will ever take, comes before all of these: *what business model shall we adopt?*

The golden rule

There is one golden rule, above all others, that new technology companies can apply to help them avoid the mistakes made by hundreds of failed businesses every year: *challenge the business model.* The most common mistake made by management teams with an innovative technology, in large corporations and small start-ups alike, is that they pursue the first business model that occurs to them.

Whether your new technology (clean or otherwise) is a clever component within a large assembly, a unique piece of software or perhaps an entire machine, how will you decide what to do yourself and what you leave to others? Will you manufacture or design, outsource or license, distribute or partner, service or maintain, sell or lease?

There are an infinite number of business models that can be followed and, most importantly, an enormous variation in strategic power and profitability associated with each one. This is not a decision to be left on default. It is well known that Gillette makes most of its profit from razorblades, not razors, and GE makes most of its profit from finance, not aircraft engines or wind turbines.

The process of designing the right business model is essentially one of selecting which combination of product and service offerings (revenue opportunities) you will offer. The first step, therefore, is to *identify all of the potential different lines of revenue that could be generated.*

Approaching the business

Sometimes it can be easy for entrepreneurs and inventors to get sidetracked by the vast social impact that their technology could have, or the step-increase in value that it will bring. In some respects, with the future of the planet potentially at stake, this diversion is an even bigger risk in the clean tech sector than across the broader technology industry.

So, in order to make a start on challenging the business model assumptions, it is important to be clear about two things: 1) The aim is to build a sustainable growing business and, therefore, the principle issue is *how do we make money from this technology?* 2) *The largest value opportunity in the supply chain may not be in the technology.* If necessary, we may even give the technology away in order to capture the big value elements.

The most successful new market entrants, in all segments of industry, enter the market by challenging the status quo. A new technology is often little more than an enabler.

The clearest recent example of this is the Apple iPod: it was based on known and established technology, but Apple disrupted the entire music industry using business model innovation rather than just technology innovation. Having achieved moderate success on the launch of its stylishly designed new range of MP3 equivalent players, it then achieved *transformational* and *disruptive* success when it combined the new range with easy, legal access to downloaded music, through an innovative online retail experience.

Clean technology is a relatively new industry sector, but many of the markets that clean tech companies are entering are dominated by large incumbent players (eg oil companies, energy utilities, building materials suppliers, etc). Therefore, in order to achieve disruptive success, serious attention should be paid to the existing industry structure and how it can be turned on its head.

Five steps to identifying a winning business model

1. *Challenge industry assumptions* – how can you turn the existing industry structure on its head?
2. *Identify multiple lines of revenue* – get paid for many things, not just one.
3. *Identify other products and services* – what else can you bundle with the core product to maximize margins?
4. *Model different combinations* – there isn't just one single right answer; play with the options to see where most value exists.

5. *Choose what you are going to do* – decide this only after you've considered all of the things you could possibly do.

Guide to the four business model elements

Let us assume that you have a smart technology, with a unique capability, that addresses an identified market need; the question, therefore, is to work out how to get it most successfully to market. In challenging both the pre-existing industry assumptions and the opportunities for maximizing revenue, there are four main elements of the business model that should be considered in detail:

- *Customer identification* – who are your customers?
- *Product sourcing* – should you manufacture, outsource or sell the IP?
- *Service offerings* – can you offer maintenance, repair or finance services?
- *Distribution channels* – can you re-engineer the supply chain?

Customer identification

An identified market need is not the same as an identified customer. An identified customer is a specific someone who will pay for the product or service combination that you are offering. Your potential customers will be determined by where you sit in the supply chain and what you offer.

Given what you have and what you know:

- Can you concentrate on design and sell or license your intellectual property?
- Can you focus on the high-value components and supply these to OEMs?
- Can you bypass traditional retailers and wholesalers and supply directly to end users?

In general, it is a good idea to think about who specifies your product or service and where the power lies in the supply chain. For example, many photovoltaic film manufacturers are now concentrating on silicon manufacture and pulling away from module assembly – an activity that is fast becoming commoditized and has low strategic power.

Product sourcing

If the ultimate application of your technology is to produce a product, then you need to decide if you are going to manufacture it yourself or leave that activity to others. The simplest business model to envisage is in-house manufacture, but it's also the most difficult to master. Efficient manufacturing requires the acquisition of a whole set of additional skills and capabilities.

- Is manufacturing the place where you can capture most value?
- Do you require specialist manufacturing equipment that would be difficult to outsource?

- Do you wish to build a core competence in efficient manufacturing?
- Can you produce the product in-house as efficiently as a third party could?
- Are there unprotectable know-how secrets that would be at risk by outsourcing?
- Could you gain strategic or cost advantage from outsourced production close to market?

Another consideration might be to avoid handling the finished goods at all. If the intellectual property (IP) is in a form that could be readily licensed, then why not leave the manufacturing and marketing issues up to specialists in this field? This 'design to licence' model is a low risk, low capital expenditure option that has been successfully adopted by companies such as ARM Holdings, the leading designer of mobile chipsets.

- Where do your key strengths and capabilities lie?
- Is your technology unambiguously protectable and patentable?
- Could you achieve a higher market share by supplying technology to several manufacturers rather than competing with them?
- Can you develop new products faster by channelling investment into R&D rather than operational infrastructure?

Service offerings

Many new businesses take too long to realize that their core offering is not their only line of revenue. More significantly, many successful businesses make more profit from what appear to be, at first glance, incidental activities.

After-sales services (maintenance, spares and repair) are the high margin items for aircraft manufacturers, making the difference between profit and loss. Could this be the same for wind or hydro turbine manufacturers?

Providing finance packages to fund the acquisition of new high cost capital equipment is the basis on which many aircraft and motor companies survive. Not only does the financing drive demand for the core product, but it is handsomely profitable in its own right. This is a model that could easily be applied to renewable power plants (particularly as the output renewable energy is often at a fixed regulated price with utility grade risk). But also think for example of domestic CHP boilers or other energy-saving equipment – could this be financed and funded from the customer's energy bill savings?

- Are there after-sales products or services that could extend the relationship between you and your customers?
- Can you lock customers in with genuine spare parts?
- Can you make customers' buying decisions easier with an integrated finance package?
- Can you build a deeper relationship with your customer through a long-term lease?
- Could you partner with a bank and share its revenue?

Think about what your customers really want. They may be buying solar panels, but what they really want is a flow of electricity; they may be buying building management software, but what they really want is lower energy bills. Many businesses are now contracting to provide the entire business process rather than just the equipment.

- Can you create a higher value comprehensive service by combining the product, finance, service and maintenance with operational management?
- Can you access an economy of scale by providing a service to multiple customers?
- Is this a non-core business process for your customers?

Distribution channels

Most industries are characterized by a rigid and fixed approach to the supply chain, often with substantial historic investment in infrastructure and little innovation. Successful entrepreneurs often achieve success from the way they shake up their industry rather than just the products they create; therefore re-engineering the supply chain can be a major source of value creation.

- Can you disintermediate parts of the value chain that aren't adding much value?
- Do you need to partner with others (eg installers) in order to deploy your products in the market?
- Can you go directly to your end customers and cut out intermediaries?
- Are there new channels or intermediaries that have never been used before?
- Can your product be distributed over the internet, thereby never having to take physical form (eg software)?

Conclusion

There are a vast number of different permutations, combinations and strategies that can be adopted in developing a clean technology business. There is no single right answer as to which should be pursued, but there is a significant impact on value creation (and likelihood of success) if the choice is not made carefully.

The golden rule is to challenge every element of the business model and ask yourself 'Why is it that way?' and 'How could it be different?' Challenge yourself and challenge the industry assumptions. Success and value creation are derived as much from business model innovation as technology innovation.

Julian Wheatland is Chief Executive of Hatton International, a specialist in technology commercialization and international technology transfer. Hatton assists young start-ups and large corporations to structure, finance, develop and market technology-related ventures. Prior to founding Hatton International, Julian built the international investment arm of the Consensus Business Group, the $800 million technology investment fund specializing in renewable energy and clean tech projects and technologies. Contact Julian Wheatland (tel: +44 05602 143975; e-mail: jwheatland@hattoninternational.com).

10.2

Proof of market

*Proving your markets matters just as much as proving your concept, says **Peter White** at YTKO.*

In the clean tech sector, there's no shortage of innovation, whether it's driven by legislation or by invention. So undertaking a proof of concept study – to discover and document whether the IP actually delivers – is almost a reflex action for innovators. There's often public money, too, such as R&D grants to soften the financial blow. But the attrition rate for clean tech innovation is unacceptably high in the UK. There are many good – and bad – reasons why a new idea might fail, but only a few opportunities for success. Relying on the proven technology concept alone to pull through customers, industry acceptance and general awareness is an approach that is resource inefficient and statistically doomed to failure. This 'innovation-dependency' attitude is still the business planning method commonly adopted in the UK.

It's also an approach that might just produce results in other sectors than clean tech. In other industries, such as automotive, there are defined and accessible supply chains that carry new ideas through SMEs, to the Tier 2 or 3 contractors, to distributors, up to the Tier 1 integrators, and to the major OEMs, and consequently into the market. They may be difficult chains to link into, or resistant to change, but they exist, and they offer hooks to grapple on to even for the company that's got pure technology on offer.

The environmental sector, despite – or because of – its size, is diverse, diffuse and difficult to define and isolate. The supply chains are absent, dysfunctional or 'under construction', even though many would claim the sector is maturing fast. So any proof of concept struggles to find a connection to a needy customer, or even a champion.

It's innovation, yes, but is it needed?

In fact, successful innovation arises when a company offers a product or service that's both technically viable and commercially marketable. Proving the technology, through proof of concept, demonstrates technical viability. Proving the marketability, through proof of market, shows commercial potential.

Many, particularly government-funded, attempts to stimulate and manage innovation in the low energy or green sector collect a load of ideas and inventions and then attempt to find a market for them. It can work, but it demands considerable, highly skilled resources to champion the idea, demonstrate the concept and the approach, and persuade the market that this is the answer to some previously unarticulated – and probably undefined – needs.

Today, many new ventures are launched without adequate understanding of the demands of the market into which they will be sold. Overestimation of the market size and the eagerness of the customers to buy and implement and underestimation of the speed of the competition are common causes of business failure.

Shouting about innovation still doesn't get sales

Even in the most ready-to-buy market, a company has to prove the inherent value to the customer integral to its offering. If that value is not obvious, or not specific, or not sufficient to make the customer buy, then the solution is to prove that value by working together with customers to find where the value lies. That's proof of market: a document with validated market size, competition, opportunity and – most importantly – the cost that the market is ready and able to pay to gain the value that the product proposes.

Getting market data is relatively simple. Engaging with market players is a little more difficult: why should they agree to meet and discuss their needs, especially if the supply chains are unclear or fragile?

All customers want to do their job better. These are people who are looking for an outcome. It may be doing a job that they haven't previously been able to do, or simply performing that job better, or removing obstacles in their way. They are focused on efficiency, quality and performance and want to discover solutions – potentially from innovative new products and services. They will take your call, they will meet and they will help to develop your products.

Proof of market and value propositions

The time to do a value proposition is always at the earliest possible stage in development. It not only defines what the real worth of your innovation is, but also indicates how – and to whom – the concept should be marketed, and customers' eagerness to buy and implement, and all before those expensive start-up funds have been spent on moving to production.

A value proposition attempts to demonstrate quantified benefits to prospective users, benefits they will receive through the implementation of the offering. Kick-starting the whole, essential business development process by working with the customers to meet – or better exceed – their needs and wants proves that your offering has value in their situation.

A value proposition isn't simply a sum showing how many times faster, or cheaper, your offering is. It takes into account how much your solution costs to buy, implement and maintain, and then details what the savings or advantages are. Value propositions work best when you're selling business to business. If you're in the consumer marketplace, then you'll need good market research to give you a clear idea of what value your customers will put on intangibles such as status and fashion – even on innovation itself.

Let's be specific: the four steps here should be enough for any company, large or small, to determine whether its newest concept will sell or sit on the shelf:

1. Start off by describing: what the prospect could improve, such as productivity, efficiency, revenues, safety and time to market; what they can reduce, such as costs and staff turnover; and what they might create, such as satisfaction, position and new services, by buying the innovative new idea.
2. Then project how much this improvement would be worth in terms of cash, reduced timescales, lower carbon or upcoming legislation, or against any other drivers. The customer will provide typical costs of people, energy, waste, materials and machinery.
3. Now prospective users can receive this 'proof' about what they'll be able to do differently. It should be produced as a scenario of a wonderful, innovative future – as a report, brochure, PowerPoint, mini-website or video, but with facts and figures. And, at this time, any interested customer will ask straight out: what will it cost me? But this is pre-production. Who knows? Best guess? Panic?
4. Don't tell them. Mutually agree on what the saving – in money, time, CO_2, whatever – really could be, or the extra productivity, or conformity. Be specific, but keep it experimental and informal. And ask them what proportion of that likely saving they'd be prepared to pay. Sticking to talking value sets the agenda, enables joint agreement on the value, and sets the price.

All of this is common sense

Like much of marketing, it's obvious and sensible, and essential and overlooked. It sits neatly alongside early-stage innovation, and informs those concepts and creativity. It ensures there's no ivory tower of invention, and provides a reality – and profitability – check, so there's a business model to back your innovation. And it adds new resources to your innovation team: customers. They're the people who daily struggle with environmental and carbon problems, and who know exactly the value of what the innovation will solve. They'll do that for nothing, and then pay you money when you can prove your concept, your market and your value to them. Get engaged.

And, remember, in the clean tech sector there is the possibility of developing triple-bottom-line proofs of market that can generate environmental (conservation), economic (sustainable use) and social (benefit-sharing) returns.

Real-world experience

Viridian Solar in Cambridge achieved a British Board of Agrément (BBA) certification for its Clearline range of solar water heating panels, not only a first for solar, but the first for any renewable energy technology. From starting with just two people in 2003, it moved to a purpose-built 25,000-square-foot facility in 2009. From the outset of its product development, Viridian created a consortium of potential customers and worked with them to define the product specifications and the product outputs. By engaging with its potential customers throughout the process, it ensured that these customers would help to define the value offered by its innovation, thus reducing the possibility that the benefits of its novel product would go unrecognized, or be too costly.

Peter White is the founder of YTKO, the European economic and enterprise development organization. He describes his company's work as 'creating customers for science and technology', and works closely with scientists and technologists to create sustainable market-driven enterprises. He is a leading practitioner of proof of commercial concept, using innovative processes to develop and accelerate market engagement and revenues for early-stage science. His innovation and enterprise expertise spans life sciences, where he is Director of the Yorkshire Enterprise Fellowships, the largest pre-incubation project in Europe, healthcare, clean tech and ICT. He sits on the European Commission's Sector Innovation Panel for biotechnology, and is a non-executive director of three technology companies, including one developing a high performance optical processor, for which he holds three patents. He is an honorary alumnus of the Theseus Management Institute, France, an editorial board member of the International Journal of Innovation and Regional Development, *and board member of the Yorkshire Concept Fund.*

10.3

Clean tech start-ups

*Early-stage specialist **Lesley Anne Rubenstein** at LAR Consultancy reports on the dos and don'ts for clean tech ventures.*

Starting up a business is rarely easy, especially in a recession. It therefore helps to learn as much as one can, as fast as one can, about the sector. This includes current trends, what to avoid, the needs and demands, etc, in order to figure out where the opportunity lies so that your business will make the most of a particular opportunity. This chapter looks at the typical commercial questions that start-ups and spin-outs face in the clean tech arena. What do such pre-revenue ventures have to get right if they are going to successfully get off the ground and stay off the ground? What mistakes do they typically make?

Questions to ask yourself

1. What are the market opportunities?
2. How does our innovation compete?
3. What are the direct or obvious benefits? What are the derived benefits? What are the perceptions?
4. Who are our main clients and/or partners? What do we have or can we create what they need?
5. Who are the decision makers and how do we get to them?
6. Where will our product end up? First tier? Second tier? Will it be a component of an existing product? Will it be a stand-alone?
7. Will the end client agree to test it?
8. What are the product regulations? How do we get certified? What will that cost?
9. Where can we source the raw materials? Are our suppliers green?

10. What IP can we create? How can we protect it? What will it cost? Which patent attorney should we use?
11. What skills do we have? What do we lack? Who do we need to recruit? Where will we find such skills?
12. What engineering, modelling and product development work needs to be implemented? Who can do that for us?
13. Does our business plan make sense? Who can help us with it?
14. How much finance should we raise and when? From where (VCs, banks)? If from VCs, who has invested lately, in what area, at what stage? Who can help us to get investment-ready?

Carbon Trust incubators

The above questions are no different to those that any start-up would need to ask and resolve, although in the UK there is specific help for start-ups in the clean tech sector, in the form of Carbon Trust incubators.[1] There are six such incubators, staffed by experts in the clean tech sector, who can help to find answers to these questions, develop a sound business plan, help your company to become investment-ready and even help to raise the required finance. Eligible applicants can receive up to £70,000 worth of free business, technical and fund-raising support from them. An eligible applicant can be a small business, a spin-out business from a company or research institute, or an overseas organization willing to relocate to the UK.

To qualify for the free business incubation services, you must be a UK business that can demonstrate the following:

- *Carbon reduction.* You must show the potential to make major carbon savings, through either energy saving or low carbon energy generation.
- *Business proposition.* You must have a realistic plan to grow your business to deliver your goals.
- *Management team.* You must have the nucleus of an impressive team dedicated to the success of your business.
- *Technology or service.* You must have a unique technology or service proposition.

TTP Group, one of Europe's most successful innovation companies, operates a Carbon Trust incubator and provides an excellent example of how such services can turn an idea put forward by an early-stage company into a multimillion-pound venture. The Carbon Trust incubation support service is delivered by TTP and is free to the supported company; and the incubator does not take equity or require matched funding.

Many start-ups do not realize that they are eligible for paid-for support and mentoring, because they do not see that they are de facto carbon-reducing businesses. For example, any business that is developing a product that will lead to energy savings compared with existing products or behaviours, uses less material or energy in its manufacture, or has a higher energy output for similar energy input (including fossil fuel energy) is a carbon-reducing business and hence may suit the criteria for zero-cost assistance.

Start-up and early-stage companies can be helped in many ways, including:

- provision of detailed technical marketing and advice on sales strategy;
- provision of support with intellectual property and patent strategy, including help from technical specialists in the drafting of patents;
- help with obtaining investment to support growth, including assistance from TTP's own venture capital fund managers, one of whom, in the fog of venture funds, is likely to be interested in your business plan;
- TTP carrying out independent technology assessments of the technology, which can be provided to potential investors;
- advice sourcing raw materials and finding subcontractors in, say, India or China;
- introductions to first-, second- or third-tier companies and corporates to help ensure that the product under development can be integrated into the end product; and
- advice on design for cost and regulatory issues. Regulatory engagement is frequently very important in the clean tech sector. For example, one company TTP worked with found its product was close to being banned because of a clumsily drafted safety directive aimed at a completely different product. Only rapid and active intervention prevented the misunderstanding being written into law.

For an early-stage company, trying to do all this alone does not make sense. Its chances of success are greatly enhanced by obtaining Carbon Trust incubator support.

More generally, the clean tech sector is defined by resource efficiency, but as with any other business sector it has to have an economic driver; it cannot be driven by ideology. There have been applicants where the inventors believed that, because their product would provide a significant reduction in carbon, it would succeed on the market. This is not so and is a common mistake. People will not buy an energy-saving device, say solar panels, unless the return on investment makes sense. This sector is no different from other sectors in that respect. Often, without tax breaks, grants and/or subsidies, it does not make sense to purchase a particular product, and that is why legislation in this sector is so important.

Examples of long-established 'clean' legislation (often directive legislation such as pollution control) can prove useful in predicting market responses, particularly timing, to new low carbon legislation. If a company pollutes it is fined, or vehicles are taken off the road if SOx and/or NOx emissions are higher than a legislated limit; this creates clear commercial drivers to conform, but commercial demand for compliant products frequently appears only shortly before the legislation takes effect. Companies relying on this form of commercial driver must allow for a late and sudden demand spike in their cash flow and resourcing forecasts.

Some markets can be stimulated by perception, and therefore companies in these markets should be spending some of their budget on PR. Some key demographics will pay extra if they believe that the product they are purchasing is also reducing carbon (eg washing machines that are energy 'A' listed), and others will buy from companies they believe enforce a green policy, such as Tesco and Marks & Spencer. These are typically concerns for large consumer-facing companies, but the implications can ripple back through the supply chain to the low carbon start-ups that supply them.

TTP's dos and don'ts

TTP offers some dos and don'ts for early-stage clean tech companies.

Dos

- Find USPs and derived advantages and focus on them in your marketing.
- When looking for venture capital investors, check what they have recently invested in and determine their criteria for investment; court several at the same time.
- Talk to investors *before* you need investment – what are they looking for?
- Talk to your end clients (who *are* your end clients?) to ensure correct product definition in the early development stages and avoid redesign issues. Solicit endorsements of your approach or product from them and show this to potential investors.
- Look for market outlets for the company's capabilities; find several niches.
- Manage your IP – it is as important as the IP itself. When licensing, segment your IP by market, timing, geography and application.
- Get an independent technology company to evaluate the advantages, disadvantages and risks of your proposed product, and make sure you add the results to your marketing material.
- Design for manufacture such that costs are minimal.
- Determine what your core business is for the long term.
- Realize how legislation affects your market penetration; talk to your MP, local council, etc.

Don'ts

- Don't focus on a single niche if others are possible too.
- Don't work in a bubble; make sure you know what your competition is working on.
- Don't court one investor but, rather, meet with several; make it known that you have other funding options (but don't say with whom).
- Don't start to raise funds too late: it can take a year to raise the amount needed. Don't wait till you have a working prototype before you start to look for funding.
- Don't think your prototype is the finished product.
- Don't try to do everything yourself when the Carbon Trust and other schemes may be able to provide support and mentors who can increase the range of skills and awareness of markets, competitors and a host of other issues many times over – at no cost to your business.

ISIS Carbon Trust incubator

Dr Chris Moody, Managing Consultant at the ISIS Carbon Trust incubator in Oxford, had this to add:

> *The main issue for clean tech start-ups is indeed the government incentives such as subsidies, grants and tax credits, especially in renewable energy, where countries or states guarantee a higher-than-normal buying rate from*

renewable sources due to subsidies in place. These will differ from state to state, country to country.

The other problem is that, within a particular country, the guaranteed rate can change over time – a rate that may have made a particular renewable energy source economic can suddenly become uneconomic, and the high capital expense invested becomes a liability.

Do: If you are looking for funding in the UK, make sure you understand the rules for foreign ownership. Having the manufacturing and R&D in the UK may not be enough for certain grant sources.

Don't: Overstate the size of the market or the value of what you are doing, as you will lose credibility and add to the problem of credibility for the sector itself.

At the 'coalface'

Graham Cooley, CEO of ITM Power Plc, formerly CEO of Sensortec, Metalysis and Antenova, says:

First off, I'd like to point out that I don't agree with the way 'clean tech' is used as a buzzword to imply that it is a separate industrial sector. Any technology that saves energy, is efficient in its use of resources, raw materials, etc is a 'clean tech' company! You have to ask yourself when you are starting up, what do I have that is different, unique? What do I have to offer the market? What does the market actually need? How am I going to position my product/service such that it meets the need in a 'market pull' manner? If that cannot be articulated, you have a problem. Many start-ups make the mistake of offering too much, instead of narrowing their proposition down to a 'killer' proposition that no one else can offer, being the best at fulfilling a particular need – this, in fact, is the company's unique selling point.

With technology companies, the market moves quickly. However, the technology takes a while to develop, with a constant need to raise capital. By the time the prototype is ready, the money has often run out and the market has almost certainly shifted. If the funding runs out before the prototype is ready, more needs to be raised at a risk of share value dilution. So not only must the selling proposition be right, one needs to realize that the company is aiming at a moving target, namely the market.

The successful marketing of clean tech products is reliant on government environment legislation. The legislation could potentially 'kill' the market opportunity for your product, if not in place in time. Normally the technology precedes the legislation, and the product will not get to market if the demand is not there, because the end user does not have to comply with, for example, a particular carbon reduction demand, or energy reduction requirement, etc. So, for clean tech companies, start-ups have to keep a close eye not only on the market, but also on the legislation, ie the company has two moving targets to watch intensely.

You may even need to lobby the government to ensure that legislation is in place by showing how your technology can solve current environmental targets. Ensuring that you have a non-exec director on your board who can access the stratum of politicians who are involved with environment legislation is crucial. Californians understand this very well – the Bloom Box 'energy server' company has the former US Secretary of State Colin Powell on its board of directors, and the heads of Google and Walmart and the governor of California, Arnold Schwarzenegger, were all at the product launch. Their boxes are affordable because 20 per cent of the cost is subsidized by the state and 30 per cent of the cost is a federal tax break due to the box being 'green'. These incentives are helping to create the market demand, and their clients include Walmart, Google and eBay.

Graham concluded that if he were to offer one piece of advice it would be this:

'In any early-stage company, there must be a sense of urgency, which every employee must feel, because there is far less time than one would think (or hope). Everything must happen quickly or, due to the moving targets, the company could easily miss the opportunity.'

Thoughts from overseas

Aviv Recycling Industries, located in Israel, operates a country-wide collection and recycling system for post-consumer plastic bottles. Their recycled material is sold to the packaging, textile and other industries in Israel, North America and Europe. Aviv's Manager, Uzi Kelberman, remarks:

I agree that the main difference from other sectors is due to the close relationship with new legislation, subsidies and short-term trends. Most clean tech initiatives are driven by new legislation and/or trends, which are not necessarily fully established. A start-up needs to look at bringing real USPs for the long run, rather than short-term solutions. There are many cases where companies start up because of advantages created by short-term subsidies or other governmental support, but as soon as these disappear the initiative loses its advantage. The same is true for new trends which do not hold any real economic advantage. I believe that long-term success lies in creating true USPs with a clear economic advantage, whatever the industry.

Arie Brish, founder of cxo360, a clean tech consulting business located in Austin, Texas, and previously the CEO of a high-tech telecommunications company, shared the following thoughts:

The clean tech sector reminds me of the dotcom era in the early 1990s in that it is a new industry. Many technologists that have moved from the regular hi-tech industry over to clean tech do not appreciate that oftentimes the key advantage does not necessarily lie in the technology itself. The sector can be very conservative and not as willing to try something completely new; they *prefer to follow rather than to lead and will try it when a reputable company has tried it successfully. This is often because of the huge capital expense involved – if the start-up has developed a component that will save energy and want to add it on to a $2–3 million wind turbine, firms are reluctant to be the first to try it. Alpha- and beta-testing sites are hard to engage.*

Another difference is that the funding for clean tech operations can be quite different. For the hi-tech industry proper, one can turn to a VC. Clean tech companies may need to purchase half an acre of land, in which case the project will probably be financed via a bank, where the considerations are quite different from those of a VC.

Due to the clean tech industry being heavily government legislated and subsidies, grants and tax breaks making the economic 'make or break' decisions, the economical decision needs to be made per country – what is economical in the United States may not make economic sense in the UK or Germany.

In short

It is clear from all the experts interviewed for this chapter that a clean tech business in some ways is no different to other technology businesses, namely there has to be a clear technological advantage, well-defined USPs, and a business model that makes sense. It is also clear that, in this sector, economic drivers may change from country to country, or state to state, as well as over time, so not only is the marketplace changing, but in order to survive long-term you have to keep an eye on the legislature in your target markets. Obviously, the better your business case, regardless of tax incentives, grants and subsidies, the more you will be able to reduce the inherent risks to this particular sector. As a start-up, you would be well advised to get as much free or subsidized business and technological advice and assistance from sources such as the Carbon Trust incubators in the UK. Don't 'go it alone' if you don't have to.

Note

[1] Contact details for the Carbon Trust incubators may be found at http://www.carbontrust.co.uk/emerging-technologies/help-develop-my-company/pages/default.aspx.

Lesley Anne Rubenstein founded LAR Consultancy to work with early-stage technology- and innovation-led companies, helping them get their products into the UK, European and US commercial markets. She also helps them to get investment-ready for VC funds and grants. In addition, she writes business guide books and frequently lectures on business-related topics. Previously, Lesley established and managed the first technological incubator in Israel, which was initially set up as a charity and later on privatized. Shortly after she left, it was the first incubator to be floated on the Tel-Aviv Stock Exchange. In all, she has led three business and technology incubators and innovation centres in Israel and the UK. She has a Master's degree in management and a Master's degree in medical sciences, as well as electronics technician training in the military. For further details see www.larconsultancy.co.uk.

IP
EIP
GREEN

10.4

Value in green technology patents

*The next 20 years will be decisive in setting the technological course for tackling climate change, says **Neil Forsyth** at EIP Green.*

A patent creates a 20-year monopoly during which the patent proprietor can prevent third parties from working the patented invention in a given territory. The next 20 years will be a decisive period in the global push to tackle climate change, and investment in the green technology sector is destined to grow enormously during this period. Investing now in patent protection within the green technology sector therefore represents a prodigious opportunity.

According to the United Nations Environment Programme,[1] global investment in green technology grew from an annual $7.1 billion in 2002 to $112.6 billion in 2007, representing over a 1,500 per cent increase – a huge increase by any standard. The upward trend in the green technology sector looks set to continue. It may be interesting to reflect on the proposition that, if a patented invention were to capture just a 1 per cent share of a $100 billion market, it would represent a potential annual revenue of $1 billion. The incentive for individuals and companies to patent innovations in the green technology sector is readily apparent.

The green technology sector is moving fast, and that pace of change is being mirrored in the intellectual property sector. The European Patent Office (EPO) has recently carried out a study on global patenting trends in green energy technologies, and initial data released by the EPO indicate a marked increase in patenting of green technology over the past few years.[2] The Clean Energy Patent Growth (CEPG) index,[3] which measures the number of granted US patents relating to green renewable energy, indicates a 23 per cent increase in the number of granted US patents from 2002 to 2008, and the results from 2009 show this trend accelerating. Further indications of the growing trend in patenting of green technology can be seen in results collated by Miller, Peterson and Tsang,[4] which show an increase of around 55 per cent from 2002 to 2007 for international PCT patent filings relating to green technology.

Of course, some companies in the green technology sector are already benefiting from patent protection. The proven value of patents in three significant green technology areas, wind power, hybrid vehicles and solar power, is demonstrated by the case studies below.

Wind power patents help secure settlement with industry giant

Aloys Wobben ranks 21st in the Global Green Rich List[5] compiled by the *Sunday Times*, with an estimated fortune of £2.2 billion. Aloys Wobben founded Enercon in 1984 and invented the first gearless wind turbine back in 1992; since then, Enercon has grown to become one of the world's largest wind turbine manufacturers.

Aloys Wobben has been a prolific filer of patent applications and since 1994 has built up a patent portfolio containing over 1,000 patent filings across a wide variety of jurisdictions around the globe for inventions relating to wind turbines and wind energy generation.

In the mid-1990s, Enercon had a patent dispute with a wind power subsidiary of US-based firm Kenetech over alleged intellectual property theft; Kenetech filed for bankruptcy in 1996 and, after several other owners in between, its patent rights were bought out by the industrial giant General Electric (GE Wind Power). In 2004, Enercon and GE settled their ongoing patent disputes with a worldwide, long-term cross-licence arrangement.

Pioneer takes on market leader with hybrid vehicle patents

Paice Corporation is a US company that has developed drive-train technology for hybrid cars, ie cars that combine a conventional combustion engine with an electric propulsion system. Paice filed its first US patent application on hybrid car technology in 1992, with patent filings to date numbering a relatively modest few dozen.

Paice's business model contrasts greatly with that of Toyota, which since 1994 has pursued an extensive patent filing strategy, with patent filings based on its hybrid car technology numbering several thousand. Research shows that Toyota accounts for around 43 per cent of total hybrid car patent families filed by car companies globally.[6]

Owing to Toyota's dominance of the hybrid car market, many competitors have been forced to take out patent licences with Toyota, or develop in areas not covered by Toyota's extensive hybrid car patent portfolio. However, according to a citation analysis, Paice has four of the top 10 dominant hybrid car patents, including the top two, compared to only a single patent in the top 10 for Toyota.

Despite the mismatch in size of their hybrid car technology patent portfolios, it seems that a few key patents have put Paice in a strong position, and it has accordingly taken a more aggressive stance with Toyota than other of its competitors; indeed, Paice has enjoyed success to date, with the US courts finding in its favour and awarding past damages for patent infringement. Whilst seeking a permanent injunction (no longer automatically awarded in the United States upon a finding of patent infringement[7]), Paice was awarded a set royalty for each infringing hybrid car imported by Toyota into the United States.

Unable to prevent Toyota from importing its hybrid cars into the United States via the courts, Paice resorted to a different forum in September 2009, and requested that the US International Trade Commission (ITC) investigate Toyota's hybrid car imports in view of several of its US patents. An ITC trial is currently underway considering the Paice/Toyota dispute and could result in award of an exclusion order preventing importation of Toyota's hybrid cars into the United States. However, Toyota may move to avoid such a damaging scenario by agreeing a (potentially very significant) financial settlement with Paice before conclusion of the trial.

Solar power patents help attract huge investment

eSolar Inc, a US-based solar technology company founded in 2007, has developed concentrated solar power (CSP) systems that use heliostat mirrors to reflect and concentrate solar rays on to water heater tanks, the steam from which is then used to drive turbines.

eSolar has filed over half a dozen patent applications covering various aspects of its CSP technology, including heliostat calibration and tracking, heliostat array layouts, and solar thermal receiver configurations.

Despite the small size and young nature of its patent portfolio (none of its patent applications had yet been granted), eSolar completed deals with several companies in different countries, including a $10 million equity deal with NRG Energy Inc in the United States, a $30 million patent master licensing deal with ACME Group in India, and a patent master licensing deal with Penglai Electric in China, which could reach a total investment of $5 billion.

Patent office encouragement of green technology

Patentees in the green technology sector have been given a boost through introduction by patent offices of expedited processing schemes for patent applications relating to green technology. Since 2009, such schemes have been launched by several major patent offices around the world, including those of the UK and the United States. Take-up of the schemes has been brisk thus far, with over 1,000 requests for entry into the US scheme[8] since its launch in December 2009, and around 100 requests accepted for entry into the UK scheme[9] since its launch in May 2009.

Obtaining rapid grant of a patent may be desirable for a number of reasons, for example:

- *Warding off competition*: competitors are less likely to move into a market if there is a granted patent protecting it.
- *Infringement*: litigation can be initiated only once a patent is granted, so action against an infringer can be taken earlier with a granted patent. Having a granted patent allows swift remedy in the form of an interim injunction against a competitor.
- *Investment*: investors may prefer a granted patent before they will invest in an invention.
- *Marketing*: a patented product is more marketable than one having only patent pending status.
- *Licensing*: income from licensing can be significantly increased once a patent is granted.

What does the future hold?

The value of patents for green technology innovations is burgeoning.

It seems that opportunities will continue to present themselves to innovators in the green technology sector, if they file patent applications now, for some considerable time to come.

Notes

[1] United Nations Environment Programme and New Energy Finance (2009) *Global Trends in Sustainable Energy Investment 2009*, http://www.unep.org/pdf/Global_trends_report_2009.pdf.

[2] http://www.epo.org/topics/news/2009/20091229.html.

[3] http://cepgi.typepad.com/.

[4] TR Miller, JW Peterson and TC Tsang (2008) Patent trends in the cleantech industry, *Intellectual Property and Technology Law Journal*, **20** (7), July.

[5] http://business.timesonline.co.uk/tol/business/specials/article5816774.ece.

[6] Justin Blows and Mike Lloyd, *Who Holds the Power? Lessons from hybrid car innovation for clean technologies*, Griffith Hack, Melbourne.

[7] eBay Inc *v* MercExchange L.L.C., 547 U.S. 388 (2006).

[8] http://www.uspto.gov/news/pr/2009/09_33.jsp.

[9] http://www.ipo.gov.uk/about/press/press-release/press-release-2009/press-release-20090512.htm.

Neil Forsyth is head of EIP Green, the green tech arm of EIP, a unique firm of patent and trademark attorneys with offices in London, Bath and Cardiff. EIP Green specializes in providing a full range of intellectual property services to innovators within the green technology sector. Contact Neil Forsyth at EIP (tel: 020 7440 9510; e-mail: nforsyth@e-ip.com; website: www.eipgreen.com).

Index

NB: page numbers in *italic* indicate figures or tables

Acergy 189
ACME Group 228
'Act on CO2' 142
Add Energy 193
Agência Nacional de Energia Elétrica (ANEEL) 53
Air New Zealand 153
Airtricity 41
Alert Me 36
Amatitlán project 70–71, 72
Anglo African Farm 154
Antenova 222
API Engineering 193
Apple 210
Aquamarine Power 40, 89
AquaSpy 31
ARM Holdings 212
Ashford Borough Council 128
Atlantis Resources Corporation 90
Automotive Council 25
aviation fuel 152–55
- biomass fuels 153–54
- carbon capture 154
- and local communities 154–55
- synthetic paraffinic kerosene (bio-SPK) 153

Aviv Recycling Industries 223

Babcock & Wilcox 99
Bain & Company 84
Bali roadmap 69
BASIC countries and clean energy 51–54
- companies 51–52
- future developments 54
- reasons for investment 52–53
- role of policy 53–54

Beijing Deqingyuan Agricultural Science and Technology Company 52, 53
Better Place 185
Bio Partners Ltd 154
biomass 21, 110–14
- anaerobic digestion (AD) 193
- biofuels 21, 144–45, *see also* aviation fuel
- choosing a processing system 113–14
- feedstock variability 112–13
- gasification 193
- handling problems 111–12
- processing of *111*
- solutions 112

BioRegional Quintain 128
Bisignani, Giovanni 155
Bloom Box 223
Bloomberg New Energy Finance 34
Bluemotion 142
Brish, Arie 223
British Board of Agrément (BBA) 217
British Gas 6, 95
Buffett, Warren 34
buildings, low carbon 124–28
 commercial buildings 126–27
  CRC Energy Efficiency scheme 127
  energy performance certificates 127
 definition of zero-carbon 124–25
 existing residential buildings 125, 126
 new residential buildings 5, 23–25, 125–26
  and Building Regulations 125
  Code for Sustainable Homes 126
  and development planning 125
business models, successful 209–213
 customer identification 211
 distribution channels 213
 golden rule 209
 identifying a winning model 211–12
 product sourcing 211–12
 service offerings 212–13

Cameron, James 54
carbon capital 69–72
carbon capture and storage (CCS) 30, 57, 170, 173–76, *174*
 capture processes *174*
 challenges of 174–76
 definition 174
 Office of CCS 175
 skills 58
Carbon Disclosure Project (CDP) 52
Carbon Reduction Commitment 178
Carbon Trust 5, 40, 41, 117, 136, 189, 220
 Carbon Trust incubators 219, 224
Cazenove Capital Management 65
Centre for Alternative Technology 11
Ceres Power 6
certified emission reduction (CER) credits 70
CETO Wave Power 90
Chernobyl 99
Cheviot Asset Management 67
Cheviot Climate Assets fund 67
China Merchants Bank 53–54
China Vanke Company 52, 53
Christensen, Clayton 184
Churchill, Winston 135
Cisco 35, 36
Clean Coal: An industrial strategy for the development of carbon capture and storage across the UK 175
Clean Development Mechanism (CDM) 69, 70
 Amatitlán project 70–71, 72
 and the future 72
 success of 71–72
Clean Energy Patent Growth (CEPG) index 226–27
Clean Power Technology 143
Clearline 217
ClearlySo 66
Climate Change Act 2008 129, 173
 and the NHS 177
Climate Change Capital 54
Climate Change Levy (CCL) 19
Climate Group 183
climate security 7–8
Clinton Climate Initiative (CCI) 185
Code for Sustainable Homes 126
Committee on Climate Change (CCC) 4, 129, 143, 173
Community Energy Programme 136, 137, 138
construction, resource management in 121–23
 government policy 122
 improving efficiency 122–23
 measurement of waste 123
Continental Airlines 153

Cooley, Graham 222, 223
Cooling the Planet programme 170
COP15 (UN Climate Change Conference 2009) 18, 51, 53, 142, 169, 177
  Copenhagen Accord 13–14, 53, 69
  Copenhagen Communiqué 72
Corcoran, Steve 178
CRC Energy Efficiency Scheme 127
Crest Nicholson 128
Crown Estate 43, 84, 90
cxo360 223

Darrieus turbine 89
Darwin, Charles 135
Department for Business, Innovation and Skills (BIS) 94
Department for Communities and Local Government (CLG) 24
Department for Environment, Food and Rural Affairs (Defra) 104, 177
Department for Transport (DfT) 21, 62
Department of Health (DH) 177
'disruptive innovation' 184–85
DNV (Det Norske Veritas) 42
Domestic Energy Assessors 130
Doosan Power Systems 176
Drax Power 22

E.ON 175
East London Sustainable Energy Facility (ELSEF) 106
eBay 184, 223
Ecoconnect 66
Ecole Polytechnique Fédérale de Lausanne (EPFL) 153
Econetic 142
Economic Package for Recovery 175
economic security 9–10
EcoSecurities 70
Electric Power Research Institute (EPRI) 41
electric vehicles 4–5, 21, 143–44, 147–50, 185
Electricity Network Strategy Group 85
Emissions Trading Scheme (EU-ETS) 19, 70, 153, 175
Empire State Building 185
End of Life Vehicle Directive (2000/53/EC) 31
Enercon 227
Energy Act 2004 115, 175
Energy Action Plan 43
energy performance certificates 126, 127, 129
Energy Saving Trust 131, 136, 194
  Sustainable Refurbishment (CE 309) 131
energy security 8–9
energy service companies 11
Energy Star 35
Energy Technologies Institute 5
EnerNOC 36
Environment Agency 65, 199
eSolar Inc 228
Estates and Buildings 135, 138
EU Climate and Energy Package 107
European law
  End of Life Vehicle Directive (2000/53/EC) 31
  Landfill Directive (99/31/EC) 20, 34, 104, 107
  Renewable Energy Directive (2009/28/EC) 19
  Waste Electrical and Electronic Equipment Directive (2002/96/EC) 31
  Waste Incineration Directive (2000/76/EC) 107
European Marine Energy Centre (EMEC) 20
European Nuclear Energy Leadership Academy (Enela) 101
European Patent Office (EPO) 226
European Sustainable Investment Forum (Eurosif) 65
exchange traded funds (ETFs) 67
existing buildings, retrofitting of 5, 24, 50, 126, 129–32
  barriers to 130

business opportunities 130–32
Empire State Building 185
Exosect 29, 30–31

Federal Aviation Administration (FAA) 155
Federation of Master Builders (FMB) 132
feed-in tariffs (FITs) 19, 30, 42, 48, 50, 85, 90, 93, 94, 95, 194
Five Fund Forum 67
fluXXion 31
Ford 142
Foresight Group 67
FTSE Environmental Markets Classification System 65, *66*

General Electric 31, 210, 227
Generation Investment Management 67
Genzyme 35
geo-engineering 169–72
algae-coated buildings 171
artificial trees 170
recommendations 171–72
technologies 170
Gillette 209–10
Global e-Sustainability Initiative (GeSI) 183
Global Green Rich List 227
Google 35, 223
Gore, Al 67
Gorlov turbine 89
Graham, Lindsey 13
Gree Electric Appliances 52
'green economy', the 13–15
business opportunities 13, 15
climate change policies 13–14
growth in clean tech industry 14
and the UK 13, 15
Green Energy Awards 137
Green Funds 67
Green Options (GO) initiative 178
Greenbank Investments 65
Greenwich Millennium Village 122

Hadley Centre 171
Hammerfest Strom 90
Home Energy Advisors 130
Homes and Communities Agency National Affordable Housing Programme 126
housing *see* buildings, low carbon
hybrid cars 4, 5, 227–28
Hyde Housing Association 128
Hydraulic and Maritime Research Centre (HMRC) 41, 43

IBM 183
Impax Asset Management 65
Industry-led Innovation Communities (IICs) 202
'innovation dependency' 214
Innovator's Dilemma, the 184
Institution of Mechanical Engineers (IMechE) 170, 171
Intel 184
intellectual property (IP) 74–79
as a business asset 75–76
and innovation 74–75
Intellectual Property Office 78
management of 77
patents 76
recycling 78
respecting other peoples' 77
strategies for IP protection 76–77
Intergovernmental Panel on Climate Change (IPCC) 70
International Air Transport Association (IATA) 152, 154, 155
International Atomic Energy Agency 99
International Energy Agency 39, 173, 176
investment, in clean tech 14, 15, 18, 29–37
the '3Rs' 37
clean industrial processes 30–31
the clean tech sector 34–35
corporate attitude 32
energy efficiency 30

energy generation technologies 30
exit possibilities 32
investing successfully 33
investment appetite 32
opportunity subsectors 36
regulation 35
waste 31
water 31–32
Invicta Biomass Fund 67
Invicta Capital 67
IPCC 72
ITM Power Plc 222

Japan Airlines 153
Johnson Controls Inc (JCI) 185
Johnson, Boris 185
Jones Lang LaSalle (JLL) 185
Jupiter Ecology Fund 64–65

Kelberman, Uzi 223
Kenetech 227
Knauf Eco Door Jamb 122
Kyoto Protocol 18, 52, 69, 70, 188

La Rance 88
Lagarde, Christine 15
Landfill Directive (99/31/EC) 20, 34, 104, 107
landfill gas 20–21
Landis+Gyr 36
Libralato 143
Lloyds 42
LLW Repository (LLWR) 198, 199
LLW Strategy *see* UK Nuclear Industry Low Level Waste (LLW) Strategy
Lockheed Martin 90
Low Carbon Vehicle Partnership (LowCVP) 142, 143, 144
Low Carbon Vehicle Procurement Programme (LCVPP) 62
Lycos 35

Marine Current Turbines (MCT) 40, 90
Marine Renewable Industry Association 42
Marine Renewables Development Fund 43
Marine Renewables Proving Fund 43
markets, role of 4–6
and electric vehicles 4–5
in energy generation and supply 5–6
in housing 5
and hybrid vehicles 4, 5
Marks & Spencer 220
Materials Handling Engineers Association 114
MATRIX: The Northern Ireland Science Industry Panel 201–06
Matthams, Robert 184–85
Mercedes-Benz 148
Mercer 65
'Merton Rule' 48
Metalysis 222
microgeneration 46–50, 115–18, 194–95
barriers to 116
and companies 49
cost of development 46
definition 115
driver, timeline of *47*
heat pumps 117
and individuals 49
and investors 49–50
micro-CHP systems 117–18
fuel cells 118
Stirling engine 117
technologies 116
see also solar power
Microgeneration Certification Scheme (MCS) 49

Näsholm, Professor Torgny 165
National Climate Change Plan 53
National Energy Efficiency Award 135
National Health Service (NHS) 177, 178, 179
National Health Service (NHS)
NHS Procurement 177

National Innovation Procurement
Plan 177
National Nuclear Centre of
Excellence 99
National Nuclear Laboratory 99, 101
National Skills Academy for Nuclear
(NSAN) 101
New and Renewable Energy Centre
(NaREC) 20
Nissan 143
Northern Ireland Executive 201
NRG Energy Inc 228
Nuclear Decommissioning Authority
(NDA) 197, 198
Nuclear Installation Inspectorate 199
nuclear power 97–102
benefits of 98
European Nuclear Energy Leadership
Academy (Enela) 101
Generation III reactors 98–99
Generation IV reactors 99
National Skills Academy for Nuclear
(NSAN) 101
nuclear waste, disposal of 197–99
safety of 99, *100*, *101*, 101
skills base 101

ocean energy 20, 39–43, 88–91
advantages of 40
challenges of 40–41
developers and companies 89–90
development of 41–42
economics of 90–91
as an industry 42–43
market size 90
ocean thermal energy conversion
(OTEC) 88
resources 88–89
technologies 89
Wave Hub 20, 190
Ocean Energy Development Unit 42
Ocean Engineering & Energy Systems
(OCEES) 90
Ocean Power Technologies (OPT) 40,
89

Oceanlinx 40, 90
Office for Low Emission Vehicles
(OLEV) 25
Open University 194
OpenHydro 40, 90
Organization for Economic Co-operation
and Development (OECD) 31, 59,
61
Ortitlan Limitada 70
Osmosis Climate Solutions 67
OXIS Energy 149–50
Oxy-Gen 143

Paice Corporation 227–28
patents, for green technology 226–30
advantages of 229
for hybrid vehicles 227–28
patent processing for green
technology 229
for solar power 228
for wind power 227
Pelamis Wave Power 40, 88, 89
Penglai Electric 228
Perez, Carlotta 184
Philips 31
Planning Act 2008 62
Powell, Colin 223
Powerfuel Hatfield project 175
PowerPoint 216
PPS1 125
procurement 176–78
Product Innovation Awards 178
Project Better Place 144

Rathbone 65
refuse-derived fuel (RDF) *see* waste,
energy from
RegEnBoost 143
renewable energy 18–22
and business opportunities 18–19
Government regulations /
incentives 19
renewable technologies *20*
biofuel 21
biomass energy 21

landfill gas 20–21
other technologies 21
wave and tidal energy 20
wind power 19, 20
Renewable Energy and Energy Efficiency Partnership 51
Renewable Energy Directive (2009/28/EC) 19
Renewable Heat Incentive (RHI) 19, 21, 48, 50, 95
Renewable Transport Fuels Obligation (RTFO) 19, 21
Renewables Obligation system 85
Renewables Obligation Certificates (ROCs) 20, 42, 107
Renewables Obligation Order (RO) 19, 107
RenewableUK 84, 85
Rocky Mountain Institute (RMI) 185
Rolls-Royce 90
Roundtable on Sustainable Biofuels (RSB) 153
Royal Institute of Technology (KTH) 166
Royal Institution of Chartered Surveyors (RICS) 128

Salter's Duck 88
Schwarzenegger, Arnold 223
Scott, Sir Walter 135
Scottish and Southern Energy (SSE) 41, 176
Scottish Environment Protection Agency 135
Scottish Power 175, 176
Scottish Renewable Obligation Certificate (SROC) 90
Scottish Renewables 135
Seagen turbine 88, 89, 90
Sensortec 222
Shiply.com 183, 184
Sleipner project 174
Small Business Research Initiative (SBRI) 24
SmartForTwo Electric Drive 148
SMARTWaste system 123
Society of British Gas Industries (SBGI) 117
solar power 93–95
patents for 228
solar heating 94–95
solar photovoltaic systems 93–94
Soros, George 34
Speedy Hire 178
start-ups, clean tech 218–24
Carbon Trust incubator support 219–21, 221–22
overseas 223–24
questions to ask before starting 218–19
Statoil 174
Stirling, Robert 117
Subsea UK 189
Sustainability and Environmental Advisory Group (SEAG) 134, 135
Sustainable Energy Authority of Ireland 42
sustainable investing 64–68
Sustainable World Capital 67
SweTree Technologies 165
synthetic paraffinic kerosene (bio-SPK) 153

Technology Strategy Board 5, 6, 24, 25
technology transfer 69–72
Amatitlán project 70–71, 72
and the Clean Development Mechanism (CDM) 70–72
definition 70
Tesco 177, 178, 220
Three Mile Island 99
Tidal Generation 90
tidal power *see* ocean energy
Toyota 227–28
Prius 143
Trident Energy 90
Triodos 67
Trucost 29
TTP 219, 220, 221
Tyndall Centre 171

T-Zero model 130

UK clean tech industry, development of 57–63
  industrial development 60–61
  innovation 61
  planning 62
  procurement 62
  skills, manufacturing 58–59
  tax 59–60
UK law
  Climate Change Act 2008 129, 173
  Energy Act 2004 115, 175
  Planning Act 2008 62
UK Low Carbon Industrial Strategy, The 61, 130
UK Nuclear Industry Low Level Waste (LLW) Strategy 197–99
UK Nuclear Waste Management Ltd (UKNWM) 198
UK Sustainable Fund 67
Umeå Plant Science Centre (UPSC) 165
UN Climate Change Conference 2009 *see* COP15 (UN Climate Change Conference 2009)
United Nations Environment Programme (UNEP) 71, 226
United Nations Food and Agriculture Organization 31
United Nations Framework Convention on Climate Change (UNFCCC) 69, 70
  Analysis of Technology Transfer in CDM Projects 71–72
Universities Superannuation Scheme (USS) 65
University of East Anglia (UEA) 193
University of Edinburgh 134–38
US International Trade Commission (ITC) 228

value propositions 215–16
VB/Research 67
vehicles 25–26, 141–45
  alternative fuels 144–45
  challenges of 145
  and customer preferences 142
  electric vehicles 4–5, 21, 143–44, 147–50, 185
    lithium-ion batteries 147–48
    new battery technology 148–50
  hybrid vehicles 4, 5, 227–28
  increase in numbers of 3
  petrol and diesel cars 143
  and regulation 142
Vestas 62
Viridian Solar 217
Volkswagen 142

Wallenberg Wood Science Centre 166
Walmart 223
Waste Electrical and Electronic Equipment Directive (2002/96/EC) 31
Waste Incineration Directive (2000/76/EC) 107
Waste Strategy for England 104
waste, energy from 104–07, 110
  combustion 105
  Fischer-Tropsch process 106
  gasification 105–06
  investment in 107
  pyrolysis 106
Water Supply and Sanitation Technology Platform (WssTP) 159
water technology 159–63
  clean water technologies 161, *162–63*, 164
  integrated water resources management (IWRM) 160
  and investment 161
  water consumption 160
  water industry 160
Watson Brown 31
Wave Dragon 90
Wave Hub 20, 190
wave power *see* ocean energy
wind power 19, 20, 83–86
  challenges of 84

finance 84–85
and the grid 85
planning 85
potential of 83–84
small-scale turbines 193–94
Windcrop 194
Wipro 183
Wobben, Aloys 227
Wood Group 189
wood technology 164–66
cellulose fibre 165, 166
Wood, Peter 128
Worcester Bosch 95
World Energy Council 40
World Summit on Sustainable Development 2002 51

Zed Homes 128
Zero Carbon Britain 2030 strategy 7, 8, 11

Index of advertisers

Bio Partners 151	www.bio-partners.co.uk
British Gas 92	www.solartechnologies.co.uk
Cleantechcom Ltd 87	www.jwgconsulting.com
Earthenergy Ltd 45	www.earthenergy.co.uk
EIP Green 225	www.eipgreen.com
Hydraulics & Maritime Research Centre 38	http://hmrc.ucc.ie
J P Kenny Ltd 187	www.jpkenny.com
LLW Repository Ltd 196	www.llwrsite.com
M&W UK 103	www.mwgroup.net
Matrix 200	www.matrix-ni.org
McLellan & Partners Ltd 17	www.mclean.co.uk
Mewburn Ellis Llp 73	www.mewburn.com
National Nuclear Laboratory 96	www.nnl.co.uk
Nottingham University Business School *xiv*	www.nottingham.ac.uk/business
Oxis Energy Ltd 146	www.oxisenergy.com
RenewableUK 82	www.renewable-uk.com
SweTree Technologies 164	http://swetree.com/
Technology Strategy Board *xi*	www.innovateuk.org
University of Edinburgh 133	www.ed.ac.uk
University of Greenwich 109	www.bulksolids.com